Acclaim

MW01089960

"Far Away in the Sky: A Me. and compelling portrayal of the human catastrophe caused by the ..... is also an adventure story about the exploits of the aid workers, air crews, and all those involved with the airlift. It was a very dark time and Koren skillfully puts the reader right in the middle of it. A book well worth reading."

-Don Schlenger, Returned Peace Corps Volunteer

"While in Nigeria serving in the Peace Corp during the mid-1960s, David L. Koren first learned the Igbo people's saying: '*Uwa di egwu,*' or, the world is deep. Yet, the phrase acquired deeper meaning once he volunteered to help the Biafran airlift, an NGO-orchestrated endeavor to fly relief aid in to those starving in the southeastern region of Nigeria during the country's civil war. *Far Away in the Sky* is a detailed memoir of Koren's experience and a human look at the dynamics of humanitarian aid."

-*PITT*, University of Pittsburgh magazine

"It is such a fascinating read that the journalist in me feels obliged to share this with the present generations of Nigerians whose struggle with everyday life leaves them little or no time to reflect on the living past. My personal mission is to give the generation of millennials eyewitness information about their parents' and grandparents' experiences that will ground them. I think your book contributes greatly to that."

-Ladi Olorunyomi, Nigerian Journalist

"I first met Dave Koren shortly after his presentation of *Far Away in the Sky* had left me speechless. As I shook his hand, I introduced myself and said, "You're crazy!" But I knew his adventures were a worthy addition to his (or any) lifetime. Even more compelling than his story, told in wonderfully accessible prose, are his musings about the bravery of some people in extreme situations…and the perfidy of others, often those whose calling demanded more.

-Tony Palermo

"Your memoir is invaluable, and I am deeply grateful for it."

-Charles Ahlgren, Returned Peace Corps Volunteer

"The heroic role you played in the airlift of some of the children from the Biafran genocide saved lives for which humanity will remain eternally grateful."

-Eze Eluchie

"It is now a lot of years later, but *Far Away in the Sky* keeps its protagonist's youthful enthusiasms and frustrations with the airlift story, while incorporating a lifetime of reflection in its organization and conclusions. It is a rewarding book and a pleasure to read. Koren can write, and his writing entertains mightily."

-David Strain, Friends of Nigeria

"Unlike so many memoirs of humanitarian missions, Koren never glorifies his role or hides his shortcomings as one individual with limited capacity to influence events beyond his control or capacity. He fully understood the limits of his idealism."

-Dick Hughes, Returned Peace Corps Volunteer

"Thank you for your labor of kindness and love. I am grateful for what you did, and many return your love many fold!!!"

- Chike Nzerue

"My people say '*mkpulu onye ko k'oga wolu*'. The seed that one sows one will reap. David L. Koren, you have sowed into the hearts and souls of Biafrans; I can categorically tell you that you and your seed will not hear the last of a grateful people whose friends heard their cry and came to their help."

- Uzodinma Atuanya

FAR AWAY
IN THE
SKY

A Memoir of the Biafran Airlift

David L. Koren

A PEACE CORPS WRITERS BOOK

FAR AWAY IN THE SKY: A MEMOIR OF THE BIAFRAN AIRLIFT
A Peace Corps Writers Book
An Imprint of Peace Corps Worldwide

Printed in the United States of America
by Peace Corps Writers of Oakland, California.

For more information, contact peacecorpsworldwide@gmail.com.
Peace Corps Writers and the Peace Corps Writers colophon
are trademarks of PeaceCorpsWorldwide.org.

ISBN-13: 978-1-935925-62-0
Library of Congress Control Number: 2016941795

First Peace Corps Writers Edition, June 2016

Book design by Kimberly Norris

Edited by Julie Stockman

Photos edited by Carolyn Schultz

This book is dedicated to my parents,

Leo and Marion Koren

who endured my adventures,

and to

Reverend William McCrae Aitken

of the World Council of Churches.

May he not be lost in history.

CONTENTS

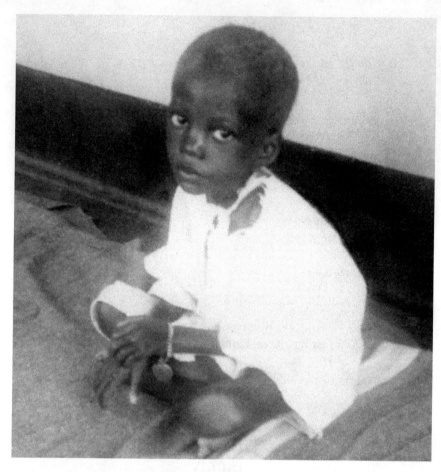

"Don't you know me?"

INTRODUCTION
PEACE CORPS WRITERS EDITION

As a report from a war that occurred in the 1960s, the kernel of *Far Away in the Sky* remains intact, but this edition presents two consequences that unfolded later: one is a result of the war itself realized in our time, and the second follows from the publication of the first edition. The war had a distant outcome; the book had a more immediate impact.

During the Nigeria-Biafra War (1967 to 1970) I worked as a volunteer on the Biafran Airlift bringing food to starving Biafrans. We flew at night to avoid the Nigerian MiGs. In 18 months of operation, the Airlift delivered hundreds of thousands of tons of food and saved an enormous number of children from starvation. Because we flew at night, landing on a road in the rainforest to avoid falling bombs, and then roaring out of Biafra before daylight, those of us who delivered the food never met any of those who received it. After the war I never knew what happered to all those people that we fed. Now, after I published *Far Away in the Sky*, I know.

Sometimes after unloading our planes in the dark, we evacuated children in the final stages of starvation. One boy, lying limp on a mat near the plane, looked up at me in the gloom and said, "My father, why don't you speak to me? Don't you know me?" As he was about to pass into eternity he felt that no one — not his father, not God, no one — knew who he was. He survived. He grew up to be a successful adult. He has a name. Nearly a half a century later, because I wrote *Far Away in the Sky*, I learned his name. Now I want *you* to know his name.

Three people whose life trajectories brought them into the time and space of Biafra gave me their narratives, and I will weave their stories into mine. Two of them, Larry Kurtz and Tom Hebert, were Peace Corps Volunteers who served in Nigeria before the war. Like me, they were recruited by UNICEF to work on the Biafran Airlift. Unlike the rest of us, Johnny Correa was an American veteran of the Korean War working for Biafra as a mercenary. Shortly after the war he handed me his narrative. I wondered why he gave it to *me*, specifically, until I wrote this edition and laid out his story side by side with mine. Then I knew. All of our experiences, and the meaning we derived from them, both intersect and diverge. They are the different trajectories of a filigree, a weave that defines the concept space of Biafra. Where their views differ from my views, they add to the fullness of the tapestry.

But this is not a war story. The book is an account of a civilian church-operated relief effort in wartime. It involves two groups of people: those who delivered the relief aid and those who received it. In such stories, the recipients are usually incidental to the brave and virtuous humanitarians. Not here. Each group is essential to the meaning of this episode in human history. The chapter titles in this book are given in the Igbo language with English subtitles. The major ethnic group among the Biafrans spoke Igbo, a language that expresses their wit, intelligence, and deep understanding of the human condition, and therefore I choose their insights to organize the chapters.

My credentials to tell this story derive from my experience as a Peace Corps Volunteer among the Igbo people of Eastern Nigeria from 1964 to 1966 and as a UNICEF Volunteer on the Biafran Airlift in 1968-69.

January 2016

Ohuhu Community Grammar School Library

FOREWORD

FAR AWAY IN THE SKY

The publishers of *Half of a Yellow Sun* by Chimamanda Ngozi Adichie, a novel set during the Biafran war, offered a free book to former Nigeria Peace Corps Volunteers who promised to tell their Biafra stories. I promised. I got the book. It so powerfully evoked my memories of that time, forty years in the past, that I was afraid I had promised something too big. I could say a lot, and there was a deadline.

Until I read that book, those memories were tucked snugly away in my past. Somewhere in a box at the back of a closet laid a pile of inert Biafra memorabilia. I had no desire to access it. Some of it was best left forgotten, but mainly I didn't want to overwhelm my promise. It would take long enough to write the vivid memories provoked by Adichie's book.

But I had another reason to write about my involvement in the Biafran Airlift. I wanted to understand it. Why was I there? What strange attractor pulled so many diverse people into its loopy orbit around Biafra? Was the Biafran Airlift the greatest private humanitarian effort of all time, or was it something much more complex? Or more banal?

I wrote the piece off the top of my memory, assisted by a few old photographs. If my memories were not historically accurate in all details, the distillation of those memories into a residual core of meaning guided my writing. The *Friends of Nigeria*, an organization of returned Peace Corps Volunteers, published it on its website under the title, "The World Is Deep." The title is a translation from the Igbo language of Nigeria.

Comments about the article arrived from around the world. Ndaeyo Uko, a journalist who was writing a history of the Biafran Airlift, flew from Australia to interview me at my home in Pennsylvania. Mr. Uko asked me detailed questions that required deeper information. Other people encouraged me to expand "The World Is Deep" to a full book. I searched out the old box of memorabilia and found a cache of audio cassette tapes. Elsewhere I found a cassette player that still worked when I inserted a fresh set of batteries. More than forty years old, the glue holding some of the tapes to the spindles had decayed, and the tapes no longer turned. A friend of mine, Bob Kalan, helped with the delicate job of dismantling the cassettes and reconnecting the tape.

The tapes were a shock — a sudden, bright window into my past. Events, people, sounds leapt out in clarity and detail long eroded from my memory. I reported events out of history that may be recorded nowhere else. There were many things on the tapes that I had not remembered. But writing the book was not a matter of just transcribing the tapes. The tapes had detail, but they were rambling. I was very poor at reporting dates. I would say things like, "On last Wednesday's Boeing..." To find out the date of that Wednesday and others, I had to transcribe all the tapes word for word on paper and comb through them to establish an exact timeline of things. I checked and cross-checked, finding things on one tape that made sense of something I said elsewhere.

Over the course of a year, I pieced it all together. It was like doing an archeological dig on my own life. It felt weird. I wanted to verify what I said whenever possible, knowing that I am claiming historical accuracy and that future scholarship may be based on what I wrote. For instance, when I referred to a moonlit night at the Uli airstrip, I checked astronomical tables to determine the phase of the moon on that night. The spellings of some names, like Captain McCombie, are guesses based on my pronunciation on the tapes.

In 1968 and 1969 the story of mass starvation in Biafra played out in the world's media, but reporters tended to interview heads of state, directors of relief organizations, colonels, and the big actors on the scene. My story flows around the lower echelons: the flight crews, the mechanics, the laborers, the quiet missionaries in the middle of the action, and the children.

As the fuller story emerged it was gratifying to realize that its meaning to me remains intact. Memory fades; meaning abides.

The tapes, widened points of memory, revealed a lot, but hinted at much more that is not recorded, that is lost. They represent no more than flickers in the overall darkness of history.

I offer this peek into the past.

October 2011

C-46 N69346

AUTHOR'S NOTE

Maps fascinate me. They contain boundless information about geology, geography, history, and political relationships. I've provided a basic map in this book so that you have a sense of where the action takes place. But I encourage you to go further. Use the map programs on the Internet – or use your globe. Zoom in to explore the details of a place, such as the magically beautiful island of São Tomé. Zoom out to catch the relationships between places. Fly along the coast of West Africa from Libreville to Liberia. Check out the course of the Niger River from where it rises in Guinea and flows through Timbuktu, down through Nigeria to the vast Niger Delta. See where the River once defined the Western shore of Biafra near the towns of Ihiala, Uli, Mgbidi, and Awomama along the Trunk "A" Road. Feel the sense of history where it intersects with geography.

West Africa 1968

18

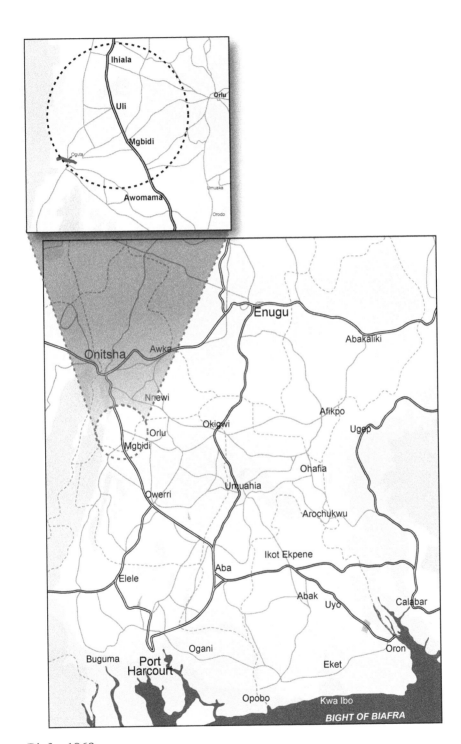

Biafra 1968

A story that must be told never forgives silence.

-- Okey Ndibe

PART I

David Koren at Amaogwugwu

CHAPTER 1

Onye Ma Echi?

Who Knows Tomorrow?

Maybe the flight rules were more relaxed in African airspace, but I had never before experienced such an extreme turn, looking straight down the left wing at the treetops as our Pan Am Boeing 707 banked steeply on approach to Lagos, Nigeria. The sun rose over an endless canopy of palm trees on the first day of January, 1964, and I was committed to living under that canopy for two years. It was my first trip to Africa.

On my second trip to Africa, January 15, 1966, I arrived during a military coup. The captain of the green- and white-painted Nigeria Airways/Pan Am 707 announced that we were denied permission to land at Lagos. "Nobody knows who's in charge down there. Nobody will make a decision about what to do with us. We may have to divert to another country."

A coup? In Nigeria? That happened all the time in South America. But not Nigeria. Newly emerged from colonial rule, Nigeria was the bright hope for democracy in Africa. As an American Peace Corps Volunteer, I had witnessed a lot of raucous politics in the last two years, but I never anticipated a military coup, or, worse, what was yet to happen to Nigeria. We circled far above the coast of Africa, waiting.

We maintained a holding pattern for about 45 minutes before we were cleared to land. A little surprised that we would actually land in the middle of a coup, I wondered if there was still fighting down there. Maybe they had to bring this plane in because it was a Nigeria Airways flight. I had a window seat – I always have a window seat – so I watched intently as we landed and taxied. Soldiers occupied the airport. A line of them with their guns angled to the ground watched us walk down the ramp and across the tarmac to the terminal. I was supposed to make a connecting flight to Enugu, capital of the Eastern Region. I had been stationed in the village of Amaogwugwu in Eastern Nigeria for the last two years, and I was just returning from home leave. After completing my two-year tour of service, I re-upped for another year, because I was having the time of my life. There were no connecting flights that day.

Other than our pilot nobody had said a word to us about a coup. In Customs, the workers and baggage handlers appeared relaxed and the inspectors acted as stiff and officious as usual, in spite of the soldiers posted by the doors. One man tried to elicit a bribe from me. In its own way, that was reassuring. Arriving passengers were escorted to the Catering Rest House, where we were given rooms and meals for the time being. While we were in the dining room, all the lights went out. When the lights came on again, we had all stopped eating. Nobody was speaking. We looked around the room at each other, listening for gunfire. There was none.

Later a steward escorted me to my room, small and clean, with a crisply made bed, a dresser and a chair, plain walls without decoration. Normally, we have some idea of what we will be doing tomorrow: we will go to school or to work; at ten o'clock we will have a meeting or a calculus exam; in the evening we will watch a favorite TV show or do the laundry. Now, when I looked ahead, I could see nothing. I didn't know if there would be a counter attack on the airport tonight or even if I would wake up tomorrow. I slipped off to sleep, in a small windowless room, in a distant land, unable to adumbrate any sense of future.

The future took form without help from my imagination. The next day, a flight was arranged to the Eastern Region. Nigeria Airways found a pilot who would fly a DC-3 to Port Harcourt, but no one would risk going to Enugu. As for news of the coup, there were only rumors. One rumor had it that pilots landing in the regional capitals were being hauled off the planes and shot. Passengers from our international flight were given the option of remaining in Lagos until things stabilized or risking the flight to Port Harcourt. I chose to get out of the capital and try to reach the village where I was stationed, near Umuahia, which was between Port Harcourt and Enugu.

When the passengers crowded into the plane and the doors closed, an official came running out of the terminal waving a handful of papers. The pilot, a beefy Englishman, yelled to him out of the cockpit window. "No! I'm not signing the bloody manifest! This plane is way overloaded, and I'm not taking responsibility for it!" A DC-3 was a venerable old plane widely used in World War II on risky missions in the jungles of Asia, across the Himalayas, and far North to Alaska. The military version of this plane, a C-47, made thousands of flights into Tempelhof Airport in Berlin in 1948 to break the Soviet blockade of that city, an enclave in East Germany. It was a twin-engine propeller plane painted green and white with Nigeria Airways colors, much smaller than the big Boeing jet that had carried us across the ocean yesterday. When parked, it sat on its tail wheel with its nose poked up in the air.

If it was overloaded, the old plane didn't seem to mind, and we took off smoothly. It was a sunny day in the dry season. We flew along the coast, over the rainforest canopy, over the Mid-Western Region and the towns of Okitipupa and Warri, over the Niger delta and the great River Niger itself, and over the Rivers Province towns of Buguma and Degama and on to Port Harcourt.

This was my second flight from Lagos to the Eastern Region. On my first trip to Nigeria, two years before, I had flown from Lagos directly to Enugu in a DC-4, a four-engine propeller plane, a type of aircraft also used in the Berlin Airlift under its military designation as a C-54. As a new country, Nigeria was building up its air transportation infrastructure using inexpensive, obsolete aircraft. Nevertheless, the plane was well-maintained and the flight was smooth. A stewardess, fresh from her flight attendant training, asked me if I wanted coffee or tea.

"Coffee, please," I said.

"Sorry, sir, we don't have coffee."

"Oh, well, I'll have tea then."

"Sorry, sir, we don't have tea. Would you like juice?"

"Yes, please." The fresh orange juice tasted very good.

As a Peace Corps teacher, I would find out that rote learning was common in Nigeria. The stewardess was trained to memorize the sentence: "Would you like coffee or tea?" So she said it. My challenge would be to encourage a more rational way of learning, which would be both fun and frustrating for my students and for me.

Two years later on my second trip to Nigeria, after the DC-3 landed in Port Harcourt, Nigeria Airways provided a small bus, painted in the airline colors, to transport the passengers to Enugu. The bus met us at the terminal, and with no delays we headed out to the Aba road, a two-lane paved road with wide laterite shoulders carved out of thick bush, its tall trees towering over the roadway.

Comfortable and air conditioned, our bus was an anomaly among the other vehicles on the road — bicycles carrying large bundles or jugs of freshly tapped palm wine, ubiquitous black Morris Minor taxis, and Mammy Wagons. While Nigerian men tended their yam farms, drove lorries or locomotives, worked in the market as carpenters or butchers or mechanics, or served in government, women were the traders. They traded in local markets and traded over long distances, hauling goods, people, goats, and chickens in their Mammy Wagons. Men drove them; women owned them.

Mammy Wagons consisted of a truck chassis and cab, usually built by Mercedes, with a wooden structure erected on it, essentially a long box with bench seats, a roof, side doors behind the cab, and a door at the rear. Open slats served as windows, and tarps could be lowered to keep the rain out. They were painted bright colors, usually yellow, and every one had a slogan on it in large letters, written on the sides and up front over the windshield. The slogans were in English, Pidgin English or the Igbo language. They represented local wisdom or humor, and as Peace Corps Volunteers, we checked out each Mammy Wagon to read its slogan.

"Ije Oma," Safe Journey, I liked, and "No Condition Is Permanent." Others were: "Will Is Way," *"Leave am for God,"* and "No Telephone to Heaven." Passing each other going north and south, one said, "God Is Love," and the other said, "Love Is Blind."

"God dey, Man dey," in Pidgin, was offered in answer to the question, "Why does God permit suffering in the world?"

"Odi na aka Chukwu" meant, "It's in the Hands of God."

"Chinyerem aka." God gave me hands. In Igbo culture it signifies that God will give us a helping hand when we are in need. Over three years, as I blended my own culture and sensibilities with the African culture around me, the amalgam took on a fuller meaning for me, just as Chinua Achebe blended his Western education with his own Igbo culture and derived a deeper wisdom of the human condition. I came to adopt "Chinyerem aka" as my own personal slogan. With my hands I can shape my world and my destiny.

Port Harcourt was a large city, the second larger of Nigeria's two main ports, about 90 miles south of Umuahia. On school breaks, PCVs (Peace Corps Volunteers) would often travel to Port Harcourt, by taxi or Mammy Wagon, for the city life and Kingsway, a huge department store that was as well equipped as Macy's. It was air-conditioned, which felt very cold if you were used to living in the heat. The first time I traveled to Port Harcourt was in 1964, my rookie year. About four months after I arrived in Nigeria as a new PCV, I went with another Volunteer for a weekend excursion into the Rivers Province, an area composed mostly of islands surrounded by water and mangrove swamp.

On that first trip, in May of 1964, at 8:30 a.m. we boarded a government motor launch, which was normally used to patrol the inland waterways. The few towns scattered throughout the Delta could be reached only by water, and some were as far as 80 to 100 miles inland. We chugged along through mangrove swamps broken only by an occasional side passage. We took a side passage and rounded a bend, where we came upon a town, Buguma. It was situated on an island about three miles across, and it was like no other town I had seen or imagined, like a lost and forgotten city. In colonial days, large buildings, stone cathedrals, and schools had been built on it. It had been a thriving place. Now it had a vague look of ruin about it. Half-erected buildings stood long uncompleted, overgrown with vegetation. The people who lived there were poor, but cheerful, making a basic living by fishing, farming, or trading. Two PCVs were stationed there, but they had gone to Port Harcourt for the day.

Back on the launch and out in the mangrove waterways, we saw an occasional canoe loaded with people or produce or a fisherman casting his net. Twenty miles farther on we came to Degama, larger than Buguma, with large old buildings better maintained and still in active use. There were fine large homes with plenty of gardens and walks, occupied by government officials and some expatriates. We learned about the fascinating history of this region, and the trading empire built by King Jaja and his huge war canoe. King Jaja opened an alternate sea port at Opobo, to the east of Port Harcourt, accessible to deep water trading ships.

Fifty years later, that scene has transformed into tar and black muck from five decades of massive oil spills on the scale of the Deepwater Horizon disaster in the Gulf of Mexico in 2010. In Nigeria, no one cleaned it up. The fish are dead, and the few remaining people are poor and sick. But as I described in a letter home to my parents about that weekend jaunt in 1964, the sunset colors in our wake were stunningly beautiful and the waterway was clear and full of life.

On January 16, 1966, the day after the coup, riding to Umuahia on the Nigeria Airways bus, we came to Aba, the first major town along the road. The bush gave way to inhabited spaces. Shops built from bamboo and woven palm fronds lined the laterite shoulders. Tightly woven palm fronds could keep the rain out in the rainy season and block the sun in the dry season. Larger buildings constructed of concrete block, some two stories tall, were roofed with corrugated galvanized metal. These roofs were called *gbam-gbam* for the drumming sound of the rain on them. Modern gas (petrol) stations adjoined the palm-thatched market stalls: Mobil, Texaco, Shell, and Phillips. Overhead, utility poles carried power lines all over town. Billboards advertised Pepsi, Ovaltine, and Galleon cigarettes.

If there were signs of upheaval, fear, nervousness, or commotion among the people because their country had just experienced a military coup, I did not see it. I saw people going about their daily business.

Morris Minor taxis crowded with people went back and forth, and people walked along the roadsides, stopping to buy oranges, fresh bread, tins of tomato paste, clothes, kerosene, or most anything. Women in brightly colored wrappers and head ties, with lots of yellows and reds, tended small charcoal tins on which they cooked yam chips in palm oil. Some sold small paper wrappers full of peanuts – *groundnuts*. Others sat behind mats on which they had made small piles of kola nuts. One woman, on her way to her market stall, balanced a large enamel pan on her head carefully packed with enamel trays and smaller pots and jugs — evidently her trade goods for the day. Her purse rested on the very top of the whole pile.

Since Aba was a regional hub, roads led out from there to other major towns in Eastern Nigeria – Owerri to the west, Ikot Ekpene to the east and Umuahia to the north. Owerri was an administrative and business center, and the road continuing out of Owerri led to Onitsha on the Niger River, the largest market town in Eastern Nigeria. Halfway between Owerri and Onitsha were the smaller towns of Mgbidi and Uli.

Ikot Ekpene to the east was famous for its raffia market. PCVs spent their slim savings buying local crafts like baskets, mats, musical instruments, and wooden carvings, especially large masks. Two of my Peace Corps friends lived there. Bill Rogers taught secondary school math and Elner McCraty taught biology at the local high school.

When we reached Umuahia, the Nigeria Airways bus dropped me off in one of the motor parks, which were the central transportation hubs of any town. At the motor park, you could find local bush taxis – Morris Minors – going to nearby villages, or you could find long distance taxis – Peugeot 403s – headed for Port Harcourt or Enugu. You might even hop on a Mammy Wagon with a slogan announcing an uncertain future, like *"Onye Ma Echi?"* I gathered my luggage – or *collected my loads* – and bargained for a bush taxi heading my way. We waited until the taxi was *complete*, that is, crammed with passengers going the same route, and everyone's loads were jammed into the boot or secured on the roof. The chickens were tied and placed on the floor at our feet.

So one day – a long day – after the coup, I arrived at my school, Ohuhu Community Grammar School in the village of Amaogwugwu. I had come home, finally home, to a place where I had lived and thrived for two years. I felt good. It is a useful ability to feel comfortable in an uncertain universe.

Onye ma echi? Who knows tomorrow? No one. But tomorrow comes. Let it.

Barbecuing a Chicken and a Goat

CHAPTER 2

Anyi Gburu Okuko na Ewu

We Killed a Chicken and a Goat

From 1961 to the present, more than 220,000 Americans have served as Peace Corps Volunteers around the world, from Eastern Europe to Africa to remote Pacific Islands. They have lived in mountain villages and deserts and mud houses in rainforests for two years or more. They learned the local languages and cultures. Thousands of PCVs worked in Nigeria from 1961 – among the first groups to serve anywhere – until all were evacuated when war broke out in 1967. Nigeria encompassed the greatest diversity of cultures of any African country, speaking 256 different languages. Nigeria PCVs were immersed in many of those cultures. I taught school among the Igbo people of Eastern Nigeria. Some PCVs struggled with the experience; I thrived; all of us changed in profound ways, bringing the benefits of that experience home.

1

Ohuhu Community Grammar School was a proprietary school started in 1962 by Dr. Michael I. Okpara, leader of the Ohuhu clan of 37,000 Igbo people in the Bende Division. Okpara was also the Premier of the Eastern Region of Nigeria. Although everyone knew there had been a coup, there were few details on the radio or in local newspapers. No police or government officials showed up urging people to be calm and go about their business. But people did remain calm and went about their business anyway. Change in government was happening in capital cities far away with no local impact. January 15, 2016 was the 50th anniversary of an event that most Nigerians consider a disastrous pivotal point in their history. Because I was there and wrote about it in the first edition of this book, a Nigerian journalist, Ladi Olorunyomi, contacted me for an interview a day before the anniversary. Among other questions, she asked, "Were the villagers aware of the monumental change in the country's political leadership/direction and was there a corresponding change in everyday life at school and in the village?" Curiously, no. That scope, that long look down the future path of the country, was not envisioned at that time.

Gradually, news began to unfold of what happened with the coup. A group of junior Army officers had taken over the government with the goal of ending corruption. They killed a number of government officials, including the Prime Minister of Nigeria, Alhaji Sir Abubakar Tafawa Belewa, and also the Sarduana of Sokoto, Amadu Bello, the religious leader of the Muslims of Northern Nigeria. The coup soon took shape along regional and religious lines. Many of the coup leaders were Igbos from the Eastern Region, while the ousted leaders were Hausas from the North. Northerners were mostly Muslims while Southerners (Eastern and Western Regions) were predominantly Christians.

Major General Aguiyi-Ironsi, Supreme Commander of the Army, and also an Igbo, opposed the coup and halted it. He brushed aside the coup leaders and formed a military government, but pledged to uphold the anti-corruption goal of the coup. Former political leaders who weren't killed were thrown in jail, including Dr. Okpara. Ironsi was a Sandhurst educated soldier who had commanded the United Nations forces in the Congo. It was said that once, while in the Congo, and in true British fashion, he walked out in front of a raging, rioting Congolese mob armed only with his swagger stick and told all the bloody fools to go home. They didn't understand a word of English, but nevertheless they got the message and took off.

A week after the coup, I wrote home to my family telling them not to worry: the country was calm and Nigerians seemed to be quite happy that the army had thrown out all those corrupt politicians. In fact, it was much safer, because all the political rioting and killing had stopped. Before the coup, lorries full of political thugs, high on Indian hemp (powerful cannabis) would tear through the streets causing havoc and intimidating voters.

Like most schools in Nigeria, Ohuhu Community Grammar School was a boarding school. Students stayed in dormitories on the school compound during the three semesters of each year, with breaks of three or more weeks in between, when the students would go home. Home was usually in the Igbo community, but students from all over the Eastern Region were recruited, including Efiks, Ibibios, and Ijaws from the Rivers Province. Classes were held in the mornings, followed by lunch, which was prepared by the school cook and served in the student cafeteria across the compound. The services of the kitchen staff and the cost of the food came out of the students' school fees. Education was not universal and was not supported with public funds. It was a big deal for families or villages to raise the tuition money; some students started school but couldn't afford to finish.

After lunch came siesta time, strictly enforced, when everyone took a nap. At first, I thought this was a waste of time, and I wanted to keep teaching. It wasn't long before I acculturated to relish naps. It was during the hottest part of the day and best to remain inactive. Afterwards, students studied or worked on the compound, which often meant cutting the five acres of grass. There were no lawn mowers, so the students chopped the grass with long-handled sickles called *cutlasses*. I worked in my garden. Sometimes I sat on my stoop in the heat and watched the puffy white clouds float above the tops of the palm trees, or I studied the columns of army ants marching by.

Once, when the students were chopping grass, I saw a sudden eruption of screaming and running. Someone had spotted a snake. A little too casually, I walked over and killed it with my garden shovel.

"Meesta Koren, you no de fear am?" My students asked if I was unafraid, as they cautiously returned to see if the snake was really dead. I was teaching them English, but when we spoke informally or in high stress situations, it was okay to speak Pidgin English, and I was having fun learning Pidgin.

"Not really," I said. Our roles reversed, and I became the student. They carefully explained to me how deadly the snakes around there could be.

"Na gaboon viper bite you, si'down, say bye-bye. One minute you be dead." True, a gaboon viper was a very large snake and could inject a massive amount of venom, but smaller, neurotoxic snakes could be deadly, too. Later, I had a high adrenaline fight with a green mamba in my house, with a meter stick in one hand and a baseball bat in the other. I never went out at night to close my shutters or to go to the outhouse without a flashlight, and one night I killed an adder with my trusty bat.

They made me bury the snake carefully, the head in one place and the body in another, because even the venom from a dead snake could still be deadly.

During the dry season, the students carried buckets of water on their heads from the stream a half-mile away to fill the rain barrels on the compound, including mine. To drink it, I had to boil it and pour it through a porcelain filter. Actually, my cooksteward did that. Then, he put the water bottles in my kerosene-operated refrigerator.

In the evenings, the students studied in the classrooms or in their dormitories. They read by candle light or by kerosene lantern with the wick turned down way low to conserve fuel. To prepare lessons or correct papers, I used a mantle-type kerosene lantern, which I could turn up very brightly.

I taught three classes of English grammar and three of English literature, with about thirty students in each. (The names of all my students are listed in the appendix. I still have my grade book.) One of the books

I taught was *Animal Farm* by George Orwell. I developed a routine. I memorized Squealer's speech to the animals in which he justified keeping all the milk and windfall apples for the pigs. When we came to that part of the book, I leaped up onto my desk and delivered the speech, passionately. I concluded, "Surely, Comrades, surely there is no one among you who wants to see Jones come back?" The students were stunned. They loved it. Then I taught them to sing "Beasts of England."

> *Beasts of England, beasts of Ireland,*
> *Beasts of every land and clime,*
> *Hearken to my joyful tidings*
> *Of the golden future time.*

They learned the whole song and they belted it out, loudly, rocking the classroom building, massively disrupting all the other classes. It was wonderful.

In my third and final year, I also taught general science. It was part of the curriculum, but because it was in the lower grade levels, I had some latitude about what to teach. Many subjects were taught and learned by rote. The teacher copied class notes on the board, notes that he had copied down when he was a student, including spelling errors. So a body of words got dumped from bucket to bucket, like water into a barrel, on down the line. I wanted to teach the core concepts of science: measurement, observation, drawing your own conclusions rather than accepting received wisdom. I created my magic water experiment.

From our new chemistry lab, I selected a number of differently shaped glass containers, like an Erlenmeyer flask, a round bottom flask, a graduated cylinder, and a beaker, all of 1000 milliliters capacity. In the prep room before class I prepared another container with exactly 1000 milliliters in it, laced with red food coloring.

It may not have been obvious to the students that the containers, all with very different shapes, held the same volume of liquid. I lined them all up on the desk. Then I brought out my red liquid.

"If I pour this into the flask, will it fill it? Will it not be enough? Or will it spill over?" Hesitantly, there were a few murmured answers. Ideally, the teacher was supposed to tell them what was right. I asked the same question regarding the other containers, with the same result.

"I have prepared this solution of magic water," I told them. "I will prove to you that it is magic. No matter what container I pour this into, it will exactly fill it up. It will not spill over, and it will not be too low."

They watched me. I waved my hand over the red water and mumbled something mysterious. I poured it into the graduated cylinder. It came out right at the fill line, 1000 ml. I called them up to the desk to check it. From the cylinder I poured the water into the Erlenmeyer flask, then the beaker, then the round bottom flask. Each time, it exactly filled the container.

"You see. It is magic water. No matter what I pour it into, the water will always fill it." Then I waited, a few minutes of uncomfortable silence, while I looked at them.

"*Meesta Koren! No sah!*" said a boy in the back of the group. "*No magic. Dey are all de same.*"

Yes! Yes! He had thought it out. He had to visualize the same quantity of fluid in very different shapes, some he may have never seen before. They all tried pouring, and I called their attention to the volume lines scribed on each container. I got out a series of 100 ml containers, and they all experimented with those. They touched them with their own hands. They saw with their own eyes. They thought with their own minds.

Better than a bucket of words.

2

The new chemistry lab had once been the school library. Other than teaching, building up that library had been my main project since I arrived at the school in January 1964. It was so successful by 1966 that the Ohuhu College Council had agreed to allocate more money to construct a new building for the library and buy more books. My Peace Corps predecessor at O.C.G.S., John Levy, had 320 books sent from the States. In the two weeks between my arrival and the beginning of classes, I jumped into the task of cataloging the books. Because I had worked in the Cornell University Library system as a student for four years, I was familiar with the Library of Congress classification system. But Cornell had over a million books. This small library would do well to acquire 1000 volumes, so I selected the simpler Dewey Decimal System.

John Levy had left the school to marry another PCV. They married on January 8, 1964, and John moved to his wife's school in the village of Isingwu. On January 9, John and Kaye invited me over to their house for dinner: meat loaf, mashed potatoes, baked beans, and apple spice cake with white icing. That same week, I went to another PCV's house for a taco party, including cold beer. Perhaps two years down here under that boundless rain forest canopy might not be so strange.

My first day at the school was very strange. Someone came to my back door and clapped his hands. Clapping hands served the same function as knocking on a door. Standing there was a short, wrinkled old African man in a faded khaki safari suit. He opened a bag to show me what he had in it. He was very proud of it and grinned hugely, revealing two or three teeth. Some hideous thing grinned up at me out of the bag, a gaping mouth full of sharp teeth, shrunken brownish skin stretched over its skull, dead eyes gazing at me.

For a moment, I lost my place in the universe. I lost any sense of where I was or who I was. The man said something. I didn't understand him. He said more. Eventually I made out the word, "fish." He pulled the whole creature out of the bag. It was about two feet long, and it was indeed a dried fish. It was called a stockfish. The Norwegian fishing industry caught and dried millions of these cod, shipping them to West Africa and Mediterranean countries as a source of protein, vitamins, iron, and calcium. They were as hard and stiff as boards. I think you could drive nails with them. People boiled them in soups like vegetable soup, *egusi* soup, okra soup, or bitter leaf soup. Even so, the pieces of boiled dried fish were very hard to chew.

The man's name was Simon, and he had been John's cook steward. John had loaned him to me until I could hire my own. Hiring a personal servant felt way out of place for a Peace Corps Volunteer, something comfortable only to wealthy Americans. But it was expected of us. It provided employment for people. Besides, Europeans, and any educated people, were not expected to do anything with their hands. In George Orwell's essay, "Shooting an Elephant," he describes the dilemma of a British officer in colonial India. Although the British ruled, the subject people nevertheless imposed an imperative of behavior on the rulers. The British officer did not want to shoot the rogue elephant. The elephant had returned to its placid ways, and the officer felt that killing it was unnecessary. But the people expected that of him; he was a British officer and British officers shot elephants, so he shot the elephant out of cultural necessity. A subject people can exert some subtle controls over their masters.

I hired a steward, named Silas, but there was a practical side that made it more acceptable. Teaching turned out to be a very demanding job, especially at the end of each term, with grading exams and making out report sheets and attendance records. I worked from morning until night. I didn't have time to go to the stream to fetch my own water, wash my own clothes by hand, go to the market, cook, and clean house.

Cultural imperative or not, however, I was not going to give up doing things with my own hands, nor would most American PCVs. I was going to build things for myself and dig in my own garden. In the Umuahia market, I bought a set of carpentry tools: a hammer, a saw, a square, a plane, nails, and sandpaper. I made shelves and furniture. I made a bamboo bar for another Volunteer, Joanne McNeece, to use in her living room. I befriended an extension worker from the Ministry of Agriculture, who got me some seeds: corn, beans, onion, carrots, tomatoes, and watermelons (*egusi*). He showed me how to lay out the plots and plant the seeds according to the best methods for that area. When some of the students saw this, they wanted me to teach them a course in agriculture. I couldn't do that, but I told them I would supervise a school garden based on extension bulletins from the Ministry.

People got used to this behavior from hundreds of young Americans in their country. Part of the Peace Corps mission was to knock down cultural barriers. We made an impression. When I first arrived in the country, kids would wave at us and yell, "Englishman!" By the time I left, English people were getting annoyed when kids yelled at them, "*Piss Cups!*" That's how they pronounced "Peace Corps."

Unlike the British officer in India, we were not in a position of power. We were respected for our education and our status as helpers, but because we had no political power over people, there was little back pressure to behave in certain ways. Where we didn't conform, we were excused as eccentric foreigners. However, departure from common, universal decency was not excused or excusable.

Culture is deep, complex. Cultural assimilation follows labyrinthine paths. For me, the transformation began with an overwhelming sense of freedom. I had a motorcycle. I was riding down the paved road to Ikot Ekpene with the throttle wide open. At that moment there were no other cars or cycles on the road, no people, no buildings. I was racing down a road in a West African rainforest, far from home, far from anyone telling me what to do, on my own, far from the unseen constraints of my own culture. It was the greatest sense of freedom I had ever felt.

At the school, far from the Peace Corps Director's office in Enugu, I had to depend on myself. Without the unseen constraints of my own culture, I was also without the unperceived supports as well. I had to reach down deep in myself to pull out resources I never knew I had — to find out who I really was at my core, and to act on that. That too was a powerful sense of freedom.

Too much freedom, perhaps. When letters came from the Peace Corps office, I would get impatient with any directives, as if they impinged on my freedom or diminished my sense of self-sufficiency. Once, I threw away a letter from the Peace Corps Office without opening it. Later, I found out that it contained an offer of school supplies that would have been a substantial benefit to my school. I missed the opportunity, and I felt miserable about it. It put the brakes on my notion of cultural independence, and led to sincere humility. Over the course of three years I absorbed elements of the Nigerian culture in which I was immersed, learned to appreciate the best of my own culture, and melded the two within myself.

Culture derives from the beliefs and behaviors of a people and is embodied in the language. During my three months of Peace Corps training at UCLA at the end of 1963, we had excellent language instruction in basic Igbo. We used an instruction manual prepared by the Foreign Service Institute of the Department of State together with Igbo speakers who were students at UCLA. Our teachers were UCLA language professors. Igbo is a tone language. *Akwa, akwa, akwa,* and *akwa* are four different words — cry, cloth, egg, or bed — their meanings dependent on the order of high and low tones on the two syllables. We spent hours in the language lab each day. Through headphones we listened to an Igbo speaker say a word or phrase, then we repeated it on tape. We listened to the speaker's voice and our own, and we kept repeating until the two versions matched.

It has been more than forty years since I have heard the Igbo language spoken, but I still remember some of it.

Ndeewo or *Kedu.* Hello, how is it?

O di mma. It is good.

Ndo. Sorry — sympathy, not apology.

O di egwu! Wonderful! Full of wonder, amazing.

One day at O.C.G.S., while I was talking to one of the other teachers, Mr. Ezeronye, we heard news of a tragic accident involving a Mammy Wagon. Many were killed or badly injured.

"Uwa di egwu!" said Mr. Ezeronye, snapping his fingers as an expletive gesture.

"What does that mean?" I asked. "I understand, *o di egwu,* but what is *uwa di egwu?*"

"The world is deep," he said. "Deep" carries complex connotations of the unfathomable, the enigmatic, the sublime, great sorrow or wonder.

Ulo akwukwo meant school, library, or house of books. Library work was one of my greatest endeavors in Nigeria.

Some expressions were fun to say because of the musicality of the words and the tone patterns.

Anyi gburu okuko na ewu. We killed a chicken and a goat. For important occasions or celebrations, going to the trouble and expense of killing and cooking a chicken and a goat was a great honor to the guests.

For a cultural experience, one of my students, Jonathon Onyema, took me to his village of Umukabia every Saturday night for about a month for a session of drumming and dancing. He guided me along bush roads as I carried him on my Honda. In the village, drummers sat in the center of a large circle walled by woven palm fronds. Dim lanterns barely outlined the moving figures within. Men beat on drums, *ekwe*, large hollowed out logs called slit gongs, and *ekpete*, bongo-like drums with goatskin stretched over one end. There were large drums and small drums. One very old man sat at the center in front of a log, a slit gong, very much larger than himself. He pounded on it with his fists as he sang out. Depending on where he struck it, it gave out different tones, all deep sounds because of the size of the cavity, sounds that carried a long way in the night. It was a "talking drum." Because Igbo was a tone language, a given sentence carried a specific tone pattern. When people far away in the bush heard the tones of the drum, they understood the sentence. In my bed at night I could hear the drums from the village of Amaogwugwu announcing the birth of a child or the death of an elder.

Eight men beat drums of different sizes. A master drummer set a different rhythm for each drum, and all rhythms blended into one complex, perfect rhythm. It was loud. It was thundering. As a guest I sat with a few others right next to the drummers. The sound reverberated in my chest cavity. Once again, I dropped out of space and time, encapsulated by sound.

Women danced in a circle around the drummers, out near the wall of the "corral." One woman who was directing the others blew on a whistle, one, two, or three blasts to signal a maneuver to the others. As they danced they wore strings of shells, called *chaka-chaka*, around their ankles, shaking them in time with the drums. The drummers and dancers sweated with the exertion.

Jonathon told me that this dancing was not a common thing in his village. The people were rehearsing for a new yam festival and they wanted to preserve these dances, because they were part of a tradition that was slipping away in the modern world of the 1960s. One of the dances was from the Rivers people. The content of the song expressed what good fighters the Japanese were in World War II. Many Nigerians had fought for the British Empire in that war.

On another occasion, an Easter Sunday, I drove 12 miles north to Uzuakoli to visit the leper colony. The choir from Methodist College Uzuakoli sang the service. All the lepers sat behind the choir on one side of the large stone church. The rest of us sat on the other side. The whole service was in Igbo, including the songs, which the choir sang beautifully. I sang the Igbo hymns right along with everybody else. Near the end of the service a group of Igbo women with gourd rattles and a drum sang a lively indigenous piece. One woman made an amazingly cool sound by beating on a clay jug with two holes in it, one at the top and one on the side.

It was a combination of an Easter service and a discharge service. Following the church ritual, everyone went out into the lawn and garden area where 21 ex-lepers were given their certificates stating that they were completely cured of leprosy – or, risen from the dead in a very real sense. They were discharged from the colony. It resembled a graduation ceremony. They stood in line on the edge of the grass, and as their names were called, they went up and received their certificate, and shook hands.

"*Unu kuoro ha aka!*" said the minister. Clap for them. As they came off the field their friends and relatives applauded and cheered. Some of the men were carried away on the shoulders of their buddies, while hunters shot off their guns in the air. Some of the women broke down and cried like babies. After all, many had been there as long as ten years with no hope, expecting to live as "unclean" outcasts until they rotted away and died. They surely felt that they had risen from the dead. Until only two years before, these discharge services were solemn and sad, because even though the lepers were wholly cured, nobody else believed it, and they were not welcomed back. But now it was understood and accepted that they were cured, and the discharge ceremonies were highly emotional.

The world is deep. *Uwa di egwu.*

In my first month at Ohuhu Community Grammar School one of the teachers, Mr. Ihukwumere took me to his village. I enjoyed talking to him. He was very well spoken in English and aware of the outside world. I believe he taught history. He did not remain at our bush school very long; perhaps he found a better position. He taught me a lot about local culture.

Mr. Ihukwumere was a tall, bearded, heavyset man with light brown skin. While the other teachers wore European-style slacks, shirts and shoes, he wore a native wrapper and walked in sandals with a slow, easy gait. Another teacher who had a normally black African complexion accompanied us to Ihukwumere's village. Along the path we passed two men going the other way. They made some comment.

"Did you hear what they were saying?" Mr. Ihukwumere asked me.

"No, I didn't understand," I said.

"There goes a white man, a black man, and a yellow man," he translated. It was meant as an amusing observation. The comment did not carry the taint of racism it may have had back in America. There were no nuances of privilege associated with black, yellow (light brown), or white, and all the while I was in Nigeria, I never felt the sting of prejudice.

In the center of the village was a large mud-walled structure with a peaked roof of woven palm fronds. I was led inside. It was unlit and very dark as I stepped inside out of the sunlight. My eyes twitched from the sting of wood smoke. As my eyes adjusted to the dark, I saw a large circle of men, some young, many old, seated in silence around the wall of the building. All were dressed in customary wrappers like Mr. Ihukwumere. Opposite the door sat the chief, or headman of the village.

Igbo enwe eze. The Igbo have no king, as the saying goes. The headman of a village or clan holds his position by merit, not heredity. I was seated to the left of the chief, about 120 degrees from the door, next to Ihukwumere. When I sat down, the circle was complete, and a man approached the chief with a plate containing several kola nuts and a knife. Using the knife, the chief separated the nuts into their lobes. The plate was passed around and everyone took a lobe. I chewed mine as the others did. It was very bitter, but I ate it, knowing that this was a very important ceremony in Igbo culture.

"*Onye wetara oji, wetara ndu,*" said the chief. He who brings kola, brings life.

Next, a man handed the chief a lump of chalk. The chief took it in his right hand and made two parallel marks across the inside of his left wrist. Then he passed the chalk around the circle. Each man made the same marks. So did I. Ihukwumere leaned toward me and whispered an explanation.

"In the days of the slave trade, if a stranger walked through the village, he might be snatched and sold to the slave traders. But if he had the chalk marks on his wrist, it meant that he was under the protection of the village and he could not be taken or harmed in any way. Other versions of the chalk mark are used throughout Igboland."

I felt the weight of this honor. The ceremony had been held for me. I was safe in their land.

3

In the first letter I sent home to my family from Ohuhu Community Grammar School, I talked about the possibility of them collecting books to send to our library. John Levy, Ann Morgan, another PCV in the Umuahia area, and many other PCVs, built excellent school libraries with a generous donation of books from home.

By June of 1964, I had finished organizing the books John had provided plus some the school had bought — 400 in all. Students were using the library, which consisted of one bookshelf at the rear of the science lab. I chose four students to be my assistants: Matthew Nwuba,

Patience Igweonu, Christian Okonkwo, and Godzeal Umezurike. Matthew and Patience, as senior students, were my main assistants for three years.

The school renovated another building adjacent to the science lab for a library. I designed reading tables, chairs, stools, bookshelves, and magazine racks, and I commissioned a carpenter in the Umuahia market to build them. I included several six-foot tall stands on which to put bright kerosene lanterns so the students wouldn't have to read in a wee spot of candlelight. The school authorized me to spend more than $300 on the furniture, a very large sum for a poor bush school, showing that they were backing me fully in my plan to make a first-rate library. The school was encouraged by the efforts of my family back in the States. My Grandparents, David and Vera Dickson, my aunt Lois Patrus and cousins Carol, Donna, and John in Butler County, Pennsylvania held book drives at Glade Run Presbyterian Church and Holy Sepulcher Catholic Church. My mother, Marion Koren, and my brother, Jim, in Ithaca, New York, gathered books at local schools.

My father, Leo Koren, helped with another project. He shipped some model airplane kits for the students to assemble and fly – balsa-wood gliders. Holding it with one hand, you slipped the wing and tail sections through slits in the fuselage and threw it. It was just for fun. If you slid the wing all the way forward in the slit, the plane did loops. If you placed the wing at the back of the slit, the plane glided straight for a long way. Many maneuvers were possible by dampening and warping the wings and tail surfaces. The kids loved them, as I had.

By October of 1964 the building renovation was complete. The students had a wonderful time helping me paint the interior. The furniture arrived. It was a great success. It looked like a first-rate library. People from the Ohuhu College Council, who had authorized the expenditure, were impressed. I got a letter from my former high school English teacher, Miss Elliot, saying that Ithaca High School would be glad to provide books, including two sets of encyclopedias, books on geology and chemistry, thirty books each of *Plane Geometry* and *Modern Biology*, many paperback copies of *High School Biology*, plus fiction and a *Reader's Digest* series, seven hundred books altogether.

The library project drew attention. People from Amaogwugwu village were impressed and wanted me to start a community library there. The Nsulu Community Library in Nbawsi, fifteen miles to the south, needed help. Somehow they had received 3000 books from the United States back in 1956, and the books were still sitting there in piles. I worked with two other PCVs, Bill Elliot and Jerry Durley, to catalogue the books and organize the library. Two hundred books were hopelessly worm-eaten and had to be thrown out. It would be a long-term project.

People valued books and prized education. A group of PCVs set out in a Volkswagen bus from Ikot Ekpene headed southeast to Uyo and then south to Eket to go swimming on a white sand beach in the Gulf of Guinea. Somewhere along a dirt road – muddy, actually – between Uyo and Eket we slid off the road and rolled over in a swamp. The water wasn't deep, so we were in no danger, but we were far from anywhere and hopelessly stuck. A group of men from a nearby village in Ibibio-Efik territory came to our rescue. We all shoved and heaved until the bus was back on the road. As PCVs, we didn't have much money between us to reward the men, but there was a box of books in the back of the van. We offered the books and they disappeared in seconds. Books were valuable.

I rate my biggest success in serving Ohuhu Community Grammar School as recruiting Ric Holt as a Peace Corps science teacher. Ric had been my best friend at Cornell, and we were intrigued by the possibility of Peace Corps service when it was proposed during the Kennedy-Nixon presidential campaign. He had been in a five-year engineering physics program, so he was still in school when I went to Nigeria. I suppose that my letters to him during that year had some influence on his decision to volunteer. Through some heavy campaigning with the Peace Corps, I managed to get him assigned to our school in January 1965. The school was delighted to have him. As I had worked on the library, Ric built up a terrific science lab. As I had done with the library, he designed all the lab furniture and ordered all the equipment. He even booted me out of my library (temporarily) for his Chemistry lab.

In April of 1965 the Eastern Region Government, headed by Dr. Michael I. Okpara, proprietor of my school, opened a big, beautiful modern library in Umuahia. In addition to loaning books, the library's function was to encourage and assist the growth of independent libraries in Umuahia Province. When I talked to the head Librarian there, he was delighted with my library work in the school and the community. He wanted me to work through the Main Library in developing community libraries, and he wanted me to extend my service for another year to work exclusively with the Library.

Five hundred books collected in Pennsylvania arrived in July of 1965, shipped by Catholic Relief Services of New York City. My mother, Marion Koren, served as the liaison with CRS for all the books. It caused a great amount of excitement as everybody crowded into the library while I opened the crates of books. My grandfather, David Dickson, did an excellent job of packing. The plywood he used for the crates would become shelves and cabinets in my kitchen.

The large lorry that brought the books also delivered 350 fifty-pound bags of powdered milk! Surprise! No one had ordered it; no one knew who sent it. The school had received notices that the books were to be delivered, but there was no mention of milk. A label on the bags said it was "Donated by the People of the United States of America." We were sure it was intended for someone else, but the driver insisted that the milk delivery was meant for O.C.G.S. Maybe Catholic Relief Services sent it to us as a bonus. I calculated that, with water added, it amounted to about 35,000 gallons of milk for two hundred students.

The books were a treasure and the milk a disaster. Milk is a suitable beverage for babies and Northern European adults, but not so much for adult Africans, and the students didn't like it. What to do with the milk caused a big palaver in staff meetings. First, we placed a sack of milk in each dormitory room, so the students could help themselves if they liked. That led to the Great Milk Riot. Students found it hilarious to throw handfuls of the powder at each other. We removed the milk from the dorms. School was suspended for a day for a major clean up. Next we put a bag in the student cafeteria where the cook could mix some milk for the students to use as creamer in their tea. That was a low-level success, but it left a large number of bags that we had to store somewhere. One was assigned to Ric and me. I've always enjoyed milk, so I kept a cold bottle of milk in my refrigerator. Our problem was to keep ants away from the dry stuff.

I wrote letters to Catholic Relief Services and the Peace Corps trying to find out why we got the milk and how to get rid of it. Months later a lorry arrived to haul away what was left, with no explanation.

Foreign aid can be a complicated, twisted endeavor with spurious intentions and unintended consequences. Since the labels on the milk sacks said the people of the United States donated them, some people thought that Americans were more crazy than kind. "The People of the United States" actually meant the U.S. Government. The government subsidizes American dairy farmers. A way to do that would be to buy whole milk from the farmers at inflated prices, dry the milk, and ship it off to distant lands as foreign aid. Fine. But milk or any other commodity should not be just dumped. It should be targeted to those who need it. The milk that came to our school could have been well used by impoverished families with small babies to feed. Let strong babies grow up healthy and contribute to the development of their countries.

All the books from home, including the seven hundred from Ithaca, had arrived by August 1965. I would definitely have to extend my Peace Corps service for another year to catalog all the books and to supervise the building of a new library. Big changes were coming to the school. In addition to the new library the school would be building new boys' dormitories and new staff quarters. The government was paving the laterite bush road leading past the school. A big Caterpillar tractor was cutting a wide path through the rain forest. Concrete pillars were being installed along the roadway to carry electric wires. Pipes were being laid for a public water supply. Civilization was enveloping us.

4

During school breaks we worked on Peace Corps sanctioned projects, but occasionally we got vacation time. In August of 1965, I spent a week at the Peace Corps Hostel in Enugu and hung out with other volunteers at the Hotel Presidential swimming pool. Elner McCraty was there relaxing and sunning with the rest of us. As a light-skinned African American, she got sunburned. We teased her about it. The Peace Corps doctor, Rob Chapman, reclining on a lounge chair, declared that she would suffer no permanent damage. Once we were comfortable teasing her about being black, someone wondered aloud what we should call her; in news from back home we learned that Malcolm Little was to be called Malcolm X, because "Little" was a slave name.

"We could call you Elner Zed," said Irwin Cohen, who taught at Government College, Umuahia. "Zed" was the British–African pronunciation of the letter "Z," which Americans pronounced "Zee."

Elner accepted the teasing with good humor. If she hadn't, she would have let us know it – she had been a leader of the Congress of Racial Equality (CORE) before joining the Peace Corps, leading the desegregation of Milwaukee, placing her small body in front of big sheriffs and going to prison for her stand.

From Enugu I caught a ride to Ibadan in Western Nigeria, north of Lagos, a large modern city with a beautiful new campus at the University of Ibadan. While hanging out in a bar one evening, six of us Volunteers concocted a mad plan for adventure. About ten o'clock at night we went to the motor park and arranged a ride by Mammy Wagon going east through the Mid-West. All night we bounced around in the back on sacks of food, snatching a little bit of jerky sleep. The driver dropped us at a deserted crossroads near the town of Ore sometime before dawn, assuring us that another lorry would be coming along to carry us south to the town of Okitipupa. We dozed by the road, feeling that there was some small chance that a ride would actually come along. After all, what's an adventure without uncertainty?

Occasionally, an adventure can be defined as a nightmare that you survive. Another Mammy Wagon came along and took us down to

Okitipupa. We rented a large dugout canoe with the intention of paddling it sixty miles south through creeks and inland waterways to the coast at Aiyetoro, then one hundred miles west by inland waterways to Lagos.

The canoe held the six of us, three men and three women, plus two guides, with paddles, fore and aft. We each bought our own ornately carved canoe paddles. By dusk of the first day we had been paddling for six hours. We were exhausted, our arms aching, looking for a place to stop for the night. There was nothing but mangrove swamp all around us. The guides kept paddling, so we did too. Around each bend, I expected to see a huge dinosaur raise its head up out of the water, munching on vegetation. In the fading light we rounded a bend and came upon the Empire Hotel, a bamboo building built on stilts out into the water, painted a vibrant blue and silver. The proprietor was a friendly, talkative guy named Mr. Broke-and-rich. He had comfortable beds to rent for seventy cents a night. He served native chop, whiskey, and cold beer.

On the water the next day, narrow passages through the mangroves opened up into lakes where we saw other canoes, small and large, carrying people and goods. Fishermen tended their nets. Two guys in a canoe pulled up alongside and started to pass. Without a word spoken, the six of us picked up our pace. We dug our paddles in the water and pulled hard. The other guys pulled hard. Soon we were zipping across the water, and other people on the lake turned to watch. By force of numbers we out-raced our more experienced competitors. As they fell back, we eased up, gushing sweat.

At Aiyetoro we found a big surprise. A whole village, called The Holy Apostles Community, was built on sturdy pilings out in the water. Heavy planking, newly cut and neatly planed, constituted the decking, walkways, and buildings. They had electricity and plumbing and a modern machine shop. Some of the people made a living as fishermen or shipbuilders, but the main source of income for the community was a fleet of large three deck motor launches carrying passengers and trade through the inland waterways and along the coast to Lagos. Think of Mississippi river boats with diesel engines instead of paddle wheels.

The people welcomed us as guests, giving us good food and comfortable rooms for the night at no charge. They were a religious community similar to ones that sprang up in the United States in the early 1900s. Their leader, who called himself Mr. Authority, promised them eternal life. They could not die and they didn't reproduce, he said, although we saw children among them. Many of the people were educated and skilled. They came from all over Nigeria and gave all their wealth and possessions to the community. I wonder if the community still exists. All those in the United

States disbanded when their immortal leaders inexplicably died.

They were gentle people and they gently persuaded us to abandon our notion of canoeing the one hundred miles to Lagos. Instead, we rode comfortably on the upper deck of one of their launches, witnessing the thriving trade of the inland waterways of Nigeria's coast. We stopped from time to time as canoes came out of the mangroves piled with sacks of produce, coconuts, or palm nuts. People loaded the sacks onto our lower deck for transport to Lagos. I watched from the port side, upper deck. I saw a young woman, possibly a teenager, standing in a canoe heaving sacks onto the deck. Her large breasts were covered tightly by a tee shirt with the words "Bronco Busters" stretched across the front. She caught me staring.

"White man, you like me?" she said. Embarrassed, I couldn't say a thing.

"How much you go pay?" Other people on deck were politely not looking at me, and I eased over to the starboard side of the boat to see what was going on there.

I stayed in Lagos for a couple of days, enjoying the beaches and city life before returning to Eastern Nigeria. From Lagos I wrote my mother a quick note. Just for fun, I wrote it in Pidgin English.

> Wait small time, and I write you good letta. I beg you no vex now. I de have fun too much dis holiday for Enugu, for Lagos, for every place. Small time now I go back for my place (Umuahia). Den I go write you good-good letta. Plenty-plenty good ting na happen dis time – oh!

By April of 1966 my new library room was ready on the top floor of a two-story classroom building with lots of windows and light and a good cross breeze. Incredibly, the school authorized me to spend over $1000 on more books and more furniture. In addition to Matthew and Patience, my student librarians, I appointed four more students to help with all the work. I spent my next vacation typing out a catalog, and I began training another teacher to help me and to take over after I left at the end of the year. Starting with the second term, each class in the school was scheduled for one library class a week, in which I taught them how to use a library for research and for fun. In my regular English classes, I gave assignments requiring the students to use the library. For instance: "Find all sources with information about the Nigerian election crisis." Ric gave library assignments from his science classes.

On May 20, 1966 a partial annular solar eclipse would be visible from our school. Ric and I prepared the students for it. In class, we discussed the celestial mechanics of eclipses and how to view them safely. Ric built a model of the earth-moon system from laboratory equipment: a retort stand, a clamp, a wire, a rubber ball, and a ping pong ball. He also built a pinhole camera. On the day of the eclipse, we all went outside on the compound and watched it unfold. Jonathon Onyema, a senior student at the time, explained to the younger ones what was happening.

The American space program was in full bloom then with regular two-man Gemini flights preparing for the Apollo moon shot. From the United States Information Service office in Enugu, I got literature and films of rocket launches. Using the films, I gave talks on the space program at our school and others, such as Government College, Umuahia, where Irwin Cohen taught. I had a small telescope, and some of the students would come over to my house in the evenings and look in astonishment at the moon.

Some evenings I sat on the veranda with Mr. Nsofor, the principal. We talked about many things, and he taught me some Igbo. The fireflies were called *umumuwarri*, a lovely sound that I practiced over and over. That bright star up there was called *Ada Onwa*, The Daughter of the Moon. It was Venus.

At the beginning of each term, I took my grade book over to Mr. Nsofor, and we went over all the student names as I learned how to pronounce them.

Peace Corps Volunteers got news from the local newspaper and from what we called *time-n-newsweek*. The international editions of *Time* and *Newsweek* were available in Umuahia, and we bought both of them from the newsboys, *onye akwukwo*. As we rode into town on our motorcycles, the boys came running after us, waving copies of the magazines. We gathered at someone's house on the day the magazines came out and we read them — devoured them — cover to cover, including the ads, in complete silence.

5

Six months after the January 15, 1966 coup, a counter coup ousted all the Igbos. Ironsi was shot, along with Igbo officers and soldiers. Gowon was installed as head of state. Igbo civilians in Northern Nigeria were slaughtered and their property confiscated or burned. One Peace Corps Volunteer in Kano in the North said she was sick of seeing dead bodies lying in the streets. A mass exodus began of refugees fleeing the *sabon garis* of the North and returning to the Eastern Region. Every day hundreds arrived at the train station in Umuahia with fresh tales of horror. One train brought a headless body. Larry Kurtz, another Peace Corps Volunteer stationed near Abakaliki in the Eastern Region, wrote:

> So Igbos came pouring back into the Eastern Region from all over the country. They brought their horror stories. Hatred and mistrust grew. Their president had been killed. Any Hausa who happened to be in the East had to get out.

All of these people were absorbed into their villages of origin, even where generations had passed between those who had left and their descendants who returned. New huts were constructed and donations of food and clothing were requested. PCVs contributed along with everybody else. Although this was a great burden on the local population, it was effective in caring for the refugees. Therefore, there were no refugee camps with deplorable conditions to catch the attention of the world media. Little changed in the lives of people in the Eastern Region after the first coup, but the second coup produced a thunderous impact.

From my home in Amaogwugwu, I felt all this unfolding around me, completely outside of any experience I had ever had.

Toward the end of 1966, there was increasing talk of secession and war. I discussed it with my students. I told them that war would be very bad. They were less concerned about it. They had no concept of the horrors of modern warfare. I was reading about Vietnam in *time-n-newsweek*; they were not. Isaac Mba, a short, tough, energetic student said, "We will fight them. If we win we will rule them. If they win they will rule us." A year later Isaac was killed, shot in the head during Biafra's hopeless defense of Nsukka.

Peace Corps Volunteers discussed the darkening situation among ourselves. What would we do if war broke out around us? We joked that if things got really bad, the United States Marines would come in and get us out. We joked, but from time to time we looked over our shoulders up at the forest canopy and listened for the helicopters.

My termination date of December 4, 1966 approached. I felt that it was time for me to go home. The pervading sense of menace was one thing, and then bugs were another. One evening I filled my dinner plate with a heap of my favorite West African food, groundnut chop. I plunked it down on the raffia place mat on my table, and thousands of ants ran out from under it. I couldn't eat. Sand flies – we called them foot-biters – delivered fiery stings on ankles and wrists every evening and morning.

Sausage flies — big, slow, lumbering bugs — would buzz around the room in the evening when we turned the lamps on. They would crash into the walls and fall stunned to the floor. Then they'd buzz up and do it again. And the snakes, of course. And the spiders. Small ones. Large ones. Very large ones.

And rain. I was so sick of rain. Every day it poured. When I had to go to Umuahia for something on my Honda, I got soaking wet and cold and covered with muck. When I went to put on some clean, dry clothes from my drawer, they were all damp and moldy. All this I tolerated placidly for three years, but as I thought more of home, my toleration grew thin.

In November, there was a whole round of send-off parties for us, one every weekend. Ric and I wanted to reciprocate and thank the school and the people of Ohuhu for the unmatchable experience we had had in Nigeria, and the sense of having a second home. So we killed a chicken and a goat and barbecued them. Dr. Okpara, recently released from prison, was the guest of honor. Now a private citizen as far as Nigeria was concerned, he still led the Ohuhu clan. We invited all the students, staff and management. We hired a band. We bought lots of beer and pop and Nigerian chop. We made a great vat of popcorn, known as *oji bekee*, white man's kola. When you visit an Igbo home you are offered kola. When you go to a white man's house you get popcorn.

Dr. Okpara conferred on us the honorary title of Bende Warrior Chieftain, along with the appropriate garments – a wrapper and jumper of fine Akwete cloth and a woven cap. Bende is a division of the Igbo people, which includes the Ohuhu clan.

I stood up in my new clothes to give thanks.

"*Bende kweno!*"

"*Ha!*" The response.

"*Bende kweno!*"

"*Ha!*"

"*Enyimba enyi!*" The elephant of the village (a mighty person) is our friend.

"*Ha!*"

"*Enyimba enyi!*"

"*Ha!*"

Dr. Okpara and the other dignitaries and guests seemed amused. The students put on a big show of drumming and dancing using some of the drums and other musical instruments that Ric and I had bought. With classroom chalk they wrote "*Bende di ike*" (Bende is strong) on my slit gong. We ate chicken and goat and *garri* and *fufu* with *egusi* soup and stockfish.

In December 1966 I took my loads to Enugu for my flight home.

Soldiers manned checkpoints on all the roads, looking for "contraband and spies." At one checkpoint, a lorry pulled out while a soldier was still inspecting the load, hauling him away unexpectedly. At the next checkpoint another soldier asked everyone if they had seen the missing *"soja man"* (soldier man).

The commercial planes were still flying between the Regions, and I left Nigeria with the memory of soldiers at airports.

UNICEF Volunteers Leo Anderson, Larry Kurtz, and Barry Bianchi

CHAPTER 3

Onye Nwe Uwa?

Who Owns the World?

On May 30, 1967 Lieutenant-Colonel Chukwuemeka Odumegwu Ojukwu, military governor of the Eastern Region, declared independence for the Republic of Biafra, citing the inability of Nigeria to protect its citizens in the East. "His secession speech," said Larry Kurtz, who was still in the region, "was the most eloquent speech I had or have heard. Igbos were exuberant and sure of their success. The civil war began. Peace Corps evacuated." The rest of the world largely ignored this event down in Africa — their conflict points of interest were Vietnam and the Middle East — until a year later, when stories of mass starvation began to trickle out.

1

After I left the Peace Corps, I went to graduate school for a master's degree in broadcast journalism, first for a semester at the University of Pennsylvania, and then for a year at Syracuse University. I was still not ready to settle into a long-term career. I followed the course of the Biafran War through the *New York Times*, wondering about the fate of my students and friends: Patience, Matthew, Isaac, Jonathon, Okon, Mr. Nsofor, Mr. Ibe, Doris — so many. During this period, I received a letter from the Committee for Nigeria/Biafra Relief inviting me to volunteer once again. That was an intriguing thought, but one with no sense of reality attached to it. Me, dashing off to war? No way. My original motivation for joining the Peace Corps had nothing to do with a gallant desire to save humanity, but to do something interesting while I put off stepping onto a career path that would lock me into a fixed future. So I flipped the letter on a pile of junk mail and forgot about it. Over time more junk mail accumulated on top of it, burying it, as the concept lay buried in my mind, down deep, incubating.

By September of 1968, I was almost finished with graduate school. Classes had ended in May, but I had one more paper to write to complete the requirement for a master's degree in broadcasting. If I did not write the paper I would get an incomplete for the course and not graduate. I struggled with the paper. It was assigned by a professor who was a self-described manic-depressive. During a manic phase he showed us an ugly little film titled, "Very Nice, Very Nice." We were to write a paper explaining why "Very Nice, Very Nice" was only seven minutes long. I could make no sense of that, and I didn't write the paper. Later, in a depressive phase, the professor shot himself. I never completed the degree.

So I thought about finding a job. There were few prospects. My state of mind resembled how I felt during my final months of undergraduate school at Cornell in 1963. Back then, as I approached graduation, I felt like I was in a room that was slowly filling up with water: when I graduated I wouldn't be able to breathe. There had to be a way out. While working at the University Library, I had met a fellow student named Bob Buckle. He had recently returned to Cornell after taking nine months off to teach at a new school in the village of Awomama in Eastern Nigeria. He wrote a book about it, a private publication called *Not For Ourselves Alone* printed in December, 1960. It looked homemade, home-typed, raw, and unedited. I bought a copy from him for $1.50. I still have it. It is a remarkable book, vivid with the people and places he found in his village and the impact the experience had on his own life. According to Amazon.com, a final edition was published in 1969, and on the list of best sellers, 9,423,931 books sold more copies than Bob's did. Definitely, it was an overlooked gem.

At Cornell, Bob had met a Nigerian student named Ben Nzeribe. When Nzeribe completed his doctorate, he returned to Nigeria in 1959 to develop his village, Awomama. Under the direction of Dr. Ben Nzeribe "a village post office and secretariat was built, wells were dug, roads constructed, markets improved, and the high school was planned and built," Bob Buckle wrote. Dr. Nzeribe recruited Bob to teach at the new school, Community Grammar School, whose motto was "*non nobis solum*," not for ourselves alone.

What a fascinating idea – that you could go off to Africa and teach for a while. Later, I passed a Peace Corps recruitment table in the lobby of Willard Straight Hall, the student union. I returned to the table and asked the recruiter, "If I sign up, will I get to choose where in the world I would go?"

"What's your major?" he asked.

"English."

"For English majors, the two programs starting in the Fall would be for the Philippines and Nigeria." I picked up an application, to think about it.

I applied to the Peace Corps, and I was accepted for the Nigeria training program at UCLA beginning October 4, 1963.

By September of 1968 I had completed a loop around the spiraling trajectory of my life – college, Peace Corps, college again, then…what? I didn't have a job; I wasn't married; I had no commitments. I was loose. This condition of being loose with no commitments is a dangerous vacuum. It can lead to actions outside the range of normal choices. In my passage through this vacuum, I got married and went off to war.

The concept of going to Biafra to help with the relief effort began to gain buoyancy in my mind, floating up from the depths. It would be a job, sort of. I dug out the letter from the Committee for Nigeria/Biafra Relief. They had found my name and address from a list of Returned Peace Corps Volunteers. It was vague — not enough to plan a career on. They listed a telephone number in New York and I called to get more information. This committee was acting only as a recruiting house for volunteers whose services they would offer to any of the relief agencies working in Nigeria and Biafra. The committee told me that as yet they had received no calls for volunteers, but were hopeful. It sounded very tenuous, but I sent in the application.

A week later I got a letter from the Committee saying that they had approved my application and were putting me on the active list. They would let me know if any of the relief agencies wanted a volunteer. This was getting a little closer, but nothing I could count on, so I continued thinking about my career prospects. Then — epiphany! The starvation story was by now very big in the news and all branches of the media were trying to get reporters into the blockaded enclave of Biafra. This was difficult. Suspicious Biafran officials were being very careful about whom they allowed to enter their country via blockade running night flights to their secret airstrip in the rain forest.

Broadcasting is a difficult business to break into, even with a graduate degree, and I thought I saw a way that might give me a chance. From Syracuse, I called up all the networks and told them that I had nearly completed a graduate degree in broadcasting and that I was going to Biafra. Could I help them get the story out? Network news people were interested but skeptical. Two weeks of telephone calls and letters went back and forth. The only result was an enormous phone bill. CBS asked me to send an audition tape with a couple of stories on it. I sent one. They were unimpressed.

It was an idea whose time had not come. I dropped it and continued to wait for word from the Committee. None came. Growing restless, and annoyed too, that I wasn't getting anywhere, I decided to go to Boston to visit my brother, Jim, for a while. He was four years younger than I, and he had finished his degree at Cornell. Like me, he hadn't found a satisfactory way to apply his education to a career. Jim and his friend,

Paul Olsen, who lived in Plymouth, New Hampshire, were talking about starting a Volkswagen repair business, a kind of Zen and the Art of VW maintenance. I notified the Committee where I could be reached, and I took off for Boston in my old 1960 Volkswagen bug. I had bought it used for $600 out of my Peace Corps readjustment allowance.

About fifty miles outside of Boston on the Massachusetts Turnpike my engine died, just after I had used most of my money to fill up with gas. This was bad. I felt like my life was going to hell in a rush. From an emergency call box, I called for a tow, and Sturbridge Auto Service Center sent a truck to haul me in. I called my brother. Jim came to pick me up from the garage. He had a complete set of VW tools, and between us we were mechanics enough to fix the car for about $40 worth of parts. But he was broke too, and together we didn't have $40. With a working engine the car was worth about $300. I was forced to sell it to Sturbridge Auto for the cost of the tow and $25. We used about $10 of that to buy beer on the way back to Boston. There was nothing to do but get drunk.

When we reached Jim's apartment, his roommate, Rob Chickering, told me that I had gotten a call from some committee in New York. They wanted me to go to Biafra in ten days.

What a jolt! I couldn't be ready in ten days. Feeling despondent about my prospects, I hadn't renewed my passport or gotten my shots. I called the Committee. They said that UNICEF wanted a couple of people to go to Calabar, a Biafran city that had been captured by the Nigerians. I didn't like the idea. I'd be working under Nigerian officials when my sympathies by then were decidedly with Biafra. I wanted to be in the enclave itself where I could meet my friends. It was where I had lived for three years. On the other hand, I couldn't be sure that an assignment in Biafra would come up, and at least I would be close to the action. It was a tough decision, but I told the Committee that I would wait for an assignment in Biafra.

I hitchhiked back to Syracuse and began getting ready. I got my passport and shots. I was in an optometrist's office getting a new pair of glasses, when, somehow, the Committee traced me there and called. They had something definite. I was to work at Biafra's airstrip helping to unload the relief planes as they came in at night. I would have to sign a contract with UNICEF for six months. It was perfect. That was where I wanted to be, and six months was the length of time I wanted to stay. About a week later, the Committee sent me a plane ticket for New York. I was on my way.

Funny how fast things could go from dismal to super.

It goes both ways.

2

On Monday morning at 9:00 a.m., October 7, 1968 I reported to the Committee office, prepared to leave for Amsterdam that evening, where I would catch a plane flying down to West Africa to join the relief airlift.

The office of the Committee for Nigeria/Biafra Relief was a tiny cluttered room containing three desks and some files. It was located within a large suite of offices that housed UNICEF. No one was there. I sat down and smoked a cigarette, feeling a little nervous. After fifteen minutes of fidgeting, I got up and found a UNICEF secretary in the next office.

"Do you know if anyone from the Nigeria/Biafra committee is around?" I said.

"There's no one in the office? Um, well, they don't usually keep regular hours. Sometimes they come in late and work late. But I'm sure someone will be along soon. Would you like some coffee?"

"Thanks. Black." Back at the Committee office, I waited. After two years of living back in the States, I had to relearn the African art of waiting. Things occurred on African time. No hurry. No frantic urgency. Relax. Wait. *"Chere,"* as they say in Igbo. Or, *"Wait small,"* as it is said in Pidgin English. The people in the committee were former volunteers, so I supposed they were relaxed about keeping appointments. After spending the previous evening at the hotel bar, I was grateful for the coffee and a little more time to get myself together.

When I arrived at the hotel the night before, I had nothing to do. I was not familiar with New York, and I didn't know anybody in town. Actually, it occurred to me that Elner McCraty might be in town. I had dated her in Nigeria and traveled through Europe with her in December 1965, on my way back to the United States for home leave, before returning to Nigeria just in time for the coup. After my final year in the Peace Corps, I visited her once in Chicago. We hadn't written for many months, and her last letter said she might be moving to New York. I wasn't sure that I could find her, and since I was leaving the next day, I didn't bother. So I just sat in the bar sizing up my life, trying to figure out if I really knew what I was doing.

I knew I was not happy. I was alone. Not lonely, particularly, but alone, drifting, not fixed to anything solid. Did I want to be attached to something, or not? Did I want to have a definite direction, or to remain loose? Perhaps the allure of Biafra for me was that Biafrans had a purpose — a large, desperate purpose, a larger meaning in the whole human context than anything I had yet attached myself to. Biafrans were making a gigantic assertion of their own dignity and identity in the face of impossible odds. At that moment, in fact, they were losing badly. They had just lost three of their four remaining sizable towns, leaving them surrounded and compressed into an area a fraction of their original size. Thousands were dying every day. Biafra might not last until I got there.

And UNICEF. What was UNICEF? What I knew about UNICEF I first learned as a kid, at Halloween. In lieu of candy, people were to give pennies for UNICEF. No matter to me, I still got plenty of candy. We used pillowcases as bags and filled them up till they were hard to carry. I stashed the bag under my bed and took candy from time to time. By Easter it was stale, and I threw away what was left. How pennies got from my bag to the kids who needed them, I don't know.

At the Committee office the next morning, a girl entered about quarter to ten.

"Are you one of the volunteers?" she said.

"Yes. David Koren."

"Hi. I'm Jan Phillips. Gerry will be along soon, and when the others get here we can get started. We have a lot to do today."

"So I'm not the only one going," I said.

"No. There are four of you in this group. Two others are already on São Tomé, and we're expecting four Canadians in a week or two."

São Tomé was a Portuguese island off the western coast of Africa, across from Gabon and about 300 miles south of Biafra. It was one of the major staging points for the airlift. Besides the two volunteers on São Tomé that Jan had mentioned, two others had gone to Calabar on the assignment that I had turned down. Jan showed me copies of some letters that had come back from the two groups.

The guys in Calabar were supposed to be working with a helicopter airlift carrying food from the harbor into the interior where people were starving. The war had swept past those people. Nigerians were firmly in control of the area, and technically those people were no longer within the boundaries of the blockade. However, the war had disrupted all normal commerce, and they were suffering nearly as much as those in the Biafran enclave. The volunteers were having difficulty getting their airlift started. There was some bickering with Nigerian Army officials, who were more interested in fighting the war than in taking care of civilians. But their main problem seemed to be in getting themselves comfortably established. They found quarters, but the rooms were bare of furniture — soldiers had looted everything. The volunteers complained bitterly about their trouble in getting a refrigerator and a car. They requested a thousand dollars from

UNICEF for setting up housekeeping.

The two guys on São Tomé reported trouble getting clearance from Biafran authorities to enter Biafra. They had been there for two weeks, enjoying the beaches, but getting restless at the delay.

I was curious to know who my three companions would be. They were former PCVs from Nigeria, and it was possible that I knew them.

Larry Kurtz was the first to arrive, and I didn't know him. He was tall, neat, wore glasses, had dark hair of medium length, and was affable but reserved. He had been stationed near Abakaliki, in the Eastern Region, now Biafra, considerably north of where I had lived. He had been in the country when I left. He was there when Biafra declared independence and had been evacuated when the war started about a month later. Of all of us, he could be called the most solid, the most respectable.

I didn't know the next one either, Barry Bianchi. He was small, dark, with thick wavy hair and a bushy black moustache, a bright personality and drop-dead good looking. He had been stationed in the Mid-West Region among a people who hated Igbos, the major ethnic group in Biafra. But here he was.

Leo Anderson, the last to arrive, I knew well. He was a short, paunchy, balding, 52-year-old ex-feed grinder and World War II veteran from South Dakota. Of all the people I would have expected to see there, Leo was not one of them. It is hard to characterize Leo: he appeared simple, yet somehow deep. Larry, Barry and I had served as teachers in Nigeria, and Leo had been an Agriculture/Rural Development volunteer.

It *was* a busy day. First, there were the forms to fill out. Every organization has them. Back when we entered the Peace Corps, we spent a solid week taking tests and filling out forms. At that time, the Peace Corps was only two years old, still an experiment. The government had no idea whether it would work or what would happen to all these young Americans they were sending out into the most impoverished regions of the world. They had no idea what kind of people these volunteers were. Who would want to do this? Would they fall apart under the stress? Would they cause international incidents? To find out, they hired psychologists and sociologists to examine us. We filled out forms and took standardized tests for a week. They assembled us in the auditorium to present the results. As a group we scored in the 99th percentile of entering freshmen at Stanford University. The psychologists said that we were more autonomous than astronauts and Antarctic explorers.

UNICEF was merciful with the paper work; it took only about an hour and a half. After all, they were selecting volunteers from a pool of people who had already been tested, on paper and in the field. Next, we dashed over to the UN Secretariat Building for a super-fast medical exam. It was discovered that Leo had not renewed his passport. He had brought his old Peace Corps passport, long since expired, figuring someone would take care of those details for him. It was typical of Leo. In some things he had to be led around like a little puppy. But otherwise, when it counted, he was always *there*: he fought for his country in WWII; he served in the Peace Corps in Africa; he was one of the very few who showed up to help Biafra. While he was rushed to the passport office, Barry and I caught a cab for an army surplus store in lower Manhattan. With a fist full of UNICEF cash, we bought camping gear: canteens, camp stoves, flashlights, hundreds of batteries, Halazone tablets – anything we thought might be useful for living and working in the bush.

Back at UNICEF, the reporters were waiting. We staunchly maintained, as we had been briefed, that we were going to Biafra purely for humanitarian reasons. We had no interest in the political conflict. We wanted only to save lives.

What was our assignment? We would be stationed in Biafra somewhere near the airstrip. We would meet the relief planes as they came in at night and expedite the unloading. Four of us would be stationed at separate parking areas, while the other two, equipped with walkie-talkies, would act as roving trouble-shooters.

Were we afraid? Not too much. Nigerians sometimes bombed the airstrip during the day, but they left it alone at night. If the military situation deteriorated badly, we could always evacuate on a returning relief flight.

I was told there was a telephone call for me. It was from CBS News. Apparently, the same press release that had brought the reporters around had been noticed at CBS, and they remembered our previous conversations. Now that they were convinced that I was actually going to Biafra, they thought that I might be able to do something for them. They felt I was not qualified to act as a correspondent, and they had experienced staff to report on the war. What they wanted from me was a very personal, informal account of my experiences. They would provide me with a tape recorder and a large supply of cassettes. I was to recount my experiences as if I were simply writing letters home to my mother, and through the modern wonders of tape editing, they would be able to piece together a story out of what I had to say. Unfortunately, the budget for this project was very tight, and they couldn't offer me any money. Would I be willing to do it?

Actually, while I was studying broadcasting, I had never intended to be a reporter. I didn't have the deep voice or the particular style that seems common to broadcast reporters. I was more interested in working toward a career in writing or producing, so this proposal of doing a personal account was fine. As for not getting paid – that was disappointing. But my original objective was to get my foot in broadcasting's door, and this might do it.

I accepted the proposal. A messenger was sent over with the recorder, batteries, cassettes, and mailing instructions. The messenger brought two sets, hoping to convince another volunteer to do the same thing. Barry agreed, with little enthusiasm.

Leo appeared. Miraculously, he had a new passport. We received vouchers we could redeem at a bank across the street to pay for incidental travel expenses en route to New York, reimbursement for shots, travel expenses for the trip to Biafra, and six weeks' pay ($75/week) in advance. We squeezed into the bank just as it was closing. I found myself with over $600 worth of cash and travelers checks. It was a fortune, relative to the amount of money I'd seen recently.

Next, we were hustled over to the Office of the Special Representative to the United States and Canada. Had the United States recognized Biafra as a sovereign country, he would have been the Ambassador. Our purpose there was to secure definite clearance to enter Biafra so we could avoid the delay on São Tomé experienced by the other two volunteers. The Deputy Special Representative interviewed each of us separately. It was a formal, and somewhat chilly, interview that lasted about ten minutes. The Deputy wanted to know where I was born, what my Peace Corps experience had been, why I wanted to go to Biafra, was I taking a camera (it was not permitted), did I have any firearms (also not permitted). He granted me clearance.

We beat it back to UNICEF in a hurry. We were to catch an evening flight to Amsterdam, and we had barely enough time to take care of a few final details and make it to the airport in time to check our excess baggage through – there was quite a bit of it.

We were issued walkie-talkies and instructed how to use them. Finally, we were given letters of introduction to key people on São Tomé and in Biafra, and our United Nations identity papers, which looked like passports and identified us as "Consultants," a deliberately nebulous title. We didn't know who we were, in an official sense. Sometimes we were known as "Field Support Officers." We referred to ourselves as "Volunteers," a title we were comfortable with from Peace Corps days. We weren't sure of the United Nations' authority regarding Biafra. *Onye nwe uwa?* Who owns the world?

By this time I was really keyed up. The furious activity of the day, my agreement with CBS, and the impending departure for Biafra, had me in such a state of euphoria that I dismissed the import of the telegram that arrived just then from São Tomé. It was from the two volunteers. It read, "SEND NO MORE REPEAT NO MORE VOLUNTEERS STOP CLEARANCE DIFFICULTIES STOP LETTER FOLLOWS STOP."

"There must be some mistake," we all agreed. "Everything has been arranged. Nothing can go wrong."

All the furious activity halted. As we sat around and discussed this, I slowly deflated. Apparently, the two guys over there were having some temporary difficulties, which would soon be straightened out. We felt that their problems were unrelated to us, since we had just received high level clearance for our mission. Perhaps, even, in the time elapsed since they had sent the telegram, they had received clearance too. Nevertheless, UNICEF decided that we should lay over in New York for a day or two until the matter was clarified. George Orick, another UNICEF "Consultant," would be coming through tomorrow on his way back from Biafra, and he would surely know what was up. Supply planes bound for São Tomé flew regularly out of Amsterdam or Copenhagen, so there would be no problem making connections if we didn't leave that night. UNICEF made hotel accommodations for us in the theater district. We gathered what we would need in overnight bags, and left our suitcases in the office, certain that we would be leaving the next day.

Larry, Barry, Leo, and I took a cab to the hotel. After eating, we drifted into the bar to get better acquainted and speculate on our situation. We hadn't had much chance to learn about each other that day, and now we filled in our various backgrounds, at least superficially. Our service in the Peace Corps together was a strong bond, but somehow we all seemed, strangely, to be a little wary, slightly suspicious of each other. With the collapse of the day's frantic activity, we had a chance to reflect, and perhaps we all felt that we may be doing something rash. Did we really want to associate with people unpredictable enough to pick up suddenly and fly into a starving enclave in the middle of a war? What would motivate them to do that? Was this absurd? You get a different perspective on your own activities when you see someone else doing them.

Supreme Court Building, Foley Square, New York City

CHAPTER 4

Akara-aka

Destiny

In 1968 the one million school children of New York City had been under the jurisdiction of one central school board. It was argued that each local community in New York had its own character, its own problems, and its own needs. As an extremely important element in the community, the local school should relate directly to the community. Curriculum, for instance, should reflect the needs of the children; i.e., black studies in black neighborhoods, remedial English in Spanish neighborhoods, and a racial balance in staff comparable to students. In a city as large as New York, it was felt that one central school board was far too remote from local communities to know what the particular problems were and how best to deal with them. Some community control of the schools must be established. Eventually, three experimental school districts were set up, each with a local board composed of members of the community. One of those districts was Ocean Hill-Brownsville, a predominantly black area of Brooklyn.

1

One by one we excused ourselves, claiming something else we wanted to do. I looked up Elner McCraty in the Manhattan phone directory. I recognized her voice when she answered the phone.

"Elner, this is David Koren. I'm on my way to Biafra, and I'd like to see you before I leave." I waited for a response, but there was silence for a couple of seconds.

Finally, she said, "Uh, what?"

"This is David Koren. I'm on my way to Biafra, and I'd like to see you before I leave. I'm staying at the President Hotel. Could you come over for a drink?"

"Oh. Yes. Yes! I'd like to see you, but I have a nice comfortable apartment. Why don't you come up here?"

"Okay, fine. How do I get there?"

"Are you familiar with New York at all?"

"No."

"Hmm. Where are you?"

"Forty-eighth Street, near Broadway, I think."

"Well, let me think. What subway would be best for you to take? You could take either the IND or the IRT, but I'm not sure which has a stop closest to you."

"What are those?"

"What are what?"

"Those letters you said."

"Oh. They're subways. Maybe you better take a taxi. Do you have any money?"

"Plenty."

"Good. Actually, it won't cost too much. Get a taxi on Broadway, and tell the driver to take you to 82nd Street between Amsterdam and Columbus. The address is 134 West 82nd, apartment 3D." I wrote that down and repeated it.

"Okay, I'll see you in about…actually, I don't know how long it will take, so I'll see you when I get there. I'm leaving now. Bye."

"Bye."

I'd been in New York for about a day, and already I knew how to flag down a taxi. I gave the driver the directions.

Elner and I had arrived in Nigeria on the same date, January 1, 1964, but from different Peace Corps training sites – she from Columbia for science teachers and I from UCLA for English teachers. Elner had been released from jail in Milwaukee to attend Peace Corps training. As a leader of the local Congress of Racial Equality (CORE) she had been working to desegregate Milwaukee schools in the summer of 1963. On August 28 she was arrested for participating in a sit-in, and while she sat in jail, she listened to Martin Luther King's "I Have a Dream" speech.

In Nigeria, we were both stationed in the Eastern Region, but in different schools. I began to notice her midway through the first year when we would cross paths at the Peace Corps hostel in Enugu, the Capital of the region. She was attractive, but what I found most appealing was how she carried herself: the way she walked, how she behaved — mature, together, not like a silly coed. I thought I would like to know her better but guessed she wouldn't be interested in me. A couple of months later I spoke to her as she was walking by. "I know you. You're Elner McCraty." Surprisingly, she sat down to talk. On occasional trips to Enugu, I would run into her again among other volunteers.

At a New Year's Eve party one year after we had arrived in Nigeria, we met again. We ended up sitting on the balcony discussing Dostoyevsky.

We wrote sometimes after that. I visited her on my birthday and she visited me on hers. Toward the end of our second year, I used to visit her often on weekends, traveling the 90 miles from Amaogwugwu to Awka on my motorcycle. She had spent her first year in Ikot Ekpene and her second in Awka. One stretch of that road was later to become a secret Biafran military airstrip, Uga.

At the end of two years, our Peace Corps service was finished. We traveled in Europe together for two weeks on the way back to the States. I left her in Paris because I was returning to Nigeria for an additional year, and I wanted to spend some time at home before going back. We had good times together, but we didn't expect to see each other again. Elner felt that although it was all right in Africa and Europe, interracial dating might be dangerous in the States, especially in those times, in the mid-1960s.

I did see her again, once, in Chicago, after I returned from Nigeria.

Now, as I rode up Amsterdam Avenue, I wondered what we would have to say to each other. We had been very close once, even talked of marriage, back in Chicago. But a long time had passed since then, and we had stopped writing months ago. I was now on my way to Biafra because I had no commitments and no demands on me. I had no love affairs.

"Hi," she said, smiling. "Come on in."

"Hi. I see you're still looking good."

She brought out a bottle of scotch and we sat down to talk. She used to keep a bottle of scotch on hand back in Nigeria, which she got from the regular smugglers bringing it in from Fernando Po.

"You know," she said, "when you called, you and Biafra were the farthest things from my mind. I was so surprised my mind just stopped. I had to take a minute to think: who? what? I certainly wasn't expecting to hear from you."

I told her how I happened to be going to Biafra and what I would be doing there. She told me about herself. She was teaching at Intermediate School 271 in the Ocean Hill-Brownsville experimental school district. As a result of a dispute with the community, the teacher's union, led by Albert Shanker, struck the whole city of New York in September. Some teachers, including Elner, sided with the community, and crossed picket lines to keep the school open. There was violence. She had to walk through as many as seven police lines to reach the front door of the school. It took courage, but she had it. Before the Peace Corps she had been a CORE leader in Milwaukee, standing in the front lines of the civil rights battle in the national news.

Elner filled me in on some gossip about other volunteers we had known. Many were now living in New York.

"Bill Rogers lives here, too," she said. Bill had been a good friend, and I hadn't seen him since I left Nigeria.

"Bill? That's great. Does he live around here?"

"Not too far. Would you like to call him?"

"Sure." Bill was glad to hear from me, and we agreed that if I didn't leave for Biafra tomorrow, I should come and see him in the afternoon.

Elner and I talked for a while longer about Biafra. She too had been quite interested and had been following the course of the war since it started. Years later, she confessed that she had invited me over that night to talk me out of going to Biafra. It was too dangerous.

2

The next day, Tuesday, the four of us reported to the office. Nothing had changed. UNICEF sent a telegram to Pastor Mollerup in Copenhagen who was head of Nordchurchaid, an organization formed of Protestant churches in Norway, Sweden, Denmark, and Finland. Nordchurchaid managed air operations for the airlift: chartering planes and crews, scheduling air traffic into Biafra, ferrying top priority cargo, like medicine, from Europe to São Tomé. It was, in effect, the "airline" serving Biafra from São Tomé. Although hired by UNICEF, we were seconded to Nordchurchaid, and we were considered a part of air operations.

The other major relief "airline" was the International Committee of the Red Cross operating from the Island of Fernando Po, closer to the Nigerian coast than São Tomé. Before the war, Fernando Po had been the point of origin for smugglers bringing whiskey into Nigeria, an illicit trade heavily patronized by Irish priests and an interesting prelude to the subsequent food smuggling into Biafra. Arms flights originated from Lisbon, Portugal, Gabon, Israel, and South Africa.

Mollerup should know the reason for our delay. He was not available when the telegram arrived, but an aide replied that he would have instructions for us in a day or two.

George Orick arrived. The message from São Tomé puzzled him. He felt that the difficulty must be minor, and unless we heard something definite, he thought that we should leave the next day. We were desperately needed over there, he said.

George Orick was a large man, with large ideas, and a large talker with a forceful promoter's style. He was paid a large "Consultant's" fee, too — $1000 per week, compared to our $75. It was he who convinced UNICEF to recruit us volunteers, and he who defined our mission. He had been involved in the early days of establishing the airlift. He colluded with

Father Anthony Byrne, the head of CARITAS, the international Catholic relief organization; Hank Wharton, a shady mercenary who made and lost fortunes flying old airplanes into troubled places; and Swedish Count Carl Gustaf Von Rosen, a colorful and daring pilot. He had flown relief planes into Ethiopia during the Italian invasion, and he had flown for the tiny Finnish Air Force against Russia in WWII. In the very early days of the airlift, Nigeria started firing anti-aircraft shells at the relief planes. No one would fly. Von Rosen arrived, took a flight in and returned it without a scratch. Other pilots resumed flying.

Orick filled us in on the decision to recruit us. He provided more details about what it was like at the airstrip and what we would be doing. Planes from São Tomé and Fernando Po flew in at night blacked out with no navigation lights winking from the wingtips, tail, or belly, because the Nigerian anti-aircraft batteries would fire at all planes irrespective of whether they carried food or guns. No planes had yet been hit, because they flew dark and high.

After crossing the coast, heading almost due north, the planes would follow a simple non-directional radio beacon to the airstrip without radar or any modern ground control approach. Runway lights consisted of two long rows of kerosene lanterns. As each plane landed, half of these lights would be blown out by the prop wash, and Biafran workers would scramble out to re-light them before the next plane arrived.

The airstrip was a stretch of paved road widened to 75 feet. A large four-engine transport landing with its nose wheel directly on the center stripe would have almost six feet of runway left outside of each main landing gear, and the wingtips would extend over the edge of the runway. By contrast, the runway on São Tomé was 200 feet wide.

Eight parking "fingers" extended at right angles from the runway, four at each end. Most of these were paved with blacktop, but some were covered by mat-like metal planking designed in the United States as helicopter landing pads for Vietnam. Somehow they found their way to Biafra. Arriving flights had to land between and slightly above aircraft already parked in the fingers at either end. Orick said it was a frightening thing to watch, both from the incoming plane and from the ground.

Orick had witnessed the slow unloading of the relief planes, up to two hours for each load. The planes were old propeller-driven aircraft designed to haul passengers, not cargo. They had been displaced in commercial service by the big new jet planes and they were available cheap. Wharton bought up several of them — Super Constellations and DC-7s — gave them phony registrations, and flew cargo for whoever would pay his price; arms or food, he didn't care. Because the planes had been designed to carry passengers, they had man-sized doors instead of cargo doors and none of the fast handling capability for palletized cargo. All the items had to be shoved through the doors by hand one at a time. The more time the plane spent on the ground, offloading, the less time in the air. Since Nigerians bombed the airstrip by day, relief flights were restricted to nighttime hours. In those hours, the DC-7s were fast enough to make three shuttles each, carrying ten tons, if their turnaround time on the ground were fast enough. More flights meant many more tons of food delivered to Biafran children. When Orick saw the slow offloading, he saw a way that the United Nations International Children's Emergency Fund could be effective. UNICEF volunteers would organize and expedite the offloading.

The major reasons for the long ground times, according to Orick, were inefficiency and lack of organization. Most of the unloading time was spent with people standing around waiting – waiting for a lorry to haul the cargo away; waiting for someone to move a heavy bale so the next man could move his; waiting for someone to tell everyone else what to do next; or just simply waiting. Often, the tired flight crews would have to do the unloading themselves if they hoped to get back to base that night. This was essential. If a plane were left in Biafra over daylight hours, Nigerian jets would destroy it on the ground. It had happened.

Others, too, felt that something had to be done. Orick met with Von Rosen, church relief officials like Father Byrne, and officials from the Biafran Air Force and Biafra Airways. Biafra Airways had no planes, but its personnel were responsible for the airstrip radio beacon and ground operations for the relief planes. Von Rosen, Father Byrne, and others worked out a plan calling for six to ten supervisors to coordinate the offloading crews, devise more efficient procedures, and generally expedite the unloading. Orick promised that UNICEF would recruit these supervisors. Biafran officials approved the plan, and soon afterwards, I got the call while I was waiting in an optometrist's office.

UNICEF decided that the reason for the delay was not substantial and that we should leave for Amsterdam on Thursday. Nelly Rodrigues, a charming UNICEF girl in charge of transportation, booked us on a flight for Thursday. We were given a $25 per diem for expenses while we were in New York. So I had the whole of Wednesday and about half of Thursday to enjoy the City.

3

I went over to Bill's at 3:30 when he would be getting home from school. He also taught during the strike, at a school in Harlem. Like most ex-volunteers from Eastern Nigeria, he was intensely interested in Biafra, and he was eager to hear what I was up to. Bill's girlfriend, Shirley Ohiri, was there too. She was an African American who had married an Igbo man who had died suddenly just before the war. She was interested as well. Bill brought out some beer and we had a long talk.

After a while, Shirley checked out of the conversation to study. She was working on a degree in anthropology. Bill and I talked about the old days in the Corps. He put on some Nigerian music, and we got real nostalgic.

I called Elner at seven o'clock, and invited her to come over to Bill's. With only minimal coaxing, she agreed to come, but more out of curiosity about Shirley than to see me. Shirley was possessive of Bill, and she knew that Elner and Bill had been good friends. Bill was reluctant to visit Elner after he started seeing Shirley, and Elner wouldn't dare visit Bill with Shirley there. She had heard a great deal about Shirley over the phone and was very curious to observe this woman. With me present she had a good pretext for coming over.

The girls were polite and friendly while studying each other. Soon, Shirley went back to her reading. Conversation fell flat, until Bill suggested we get something to eat. By this time I was hungry, but Elner said she had already eaten and would just go home. She got up to leave and I offered to go with her, skipping dinner.

Back at her apartment we talked about the school crisis. As deeply involved as I was with Biafra, so was Elner involved in the Ocean Hill-Brownsville issue.

Elner had been teaching at a school in a middle-class white neighborhood. She learned of the experiment, of how black people were exercising control over what was taught to their children. She transferred to Intermediate School 271 in the new district and found it wonderful, almost too good to be true. She taught science and Afro-American history.

In New York City schools, discipline was a common and often monumental problem. Elner said there was no problem of that sort at I.S. 271. Students and staff alike were fully aware that they were participating in a significant new experiment: all were highly motivated to make it work.

Although most of the students were black, there were both black and white teachers in the school. Most of the white teachers pitched in with enthusiasm equal to that of the blacks, but some did not. Some showed no interest in the experiment and no interest in the students. Four teachers, in fact, showed racist attitudes toward the students, using the kind of demeaning slurs and treatment perpetrated by white teachers on black students, consciously or unconsciously, all over the country, the kind that undermine one's dignity and self-respect at an impressionable age, the kind that local control of schools was intended to eliminate. The local board exercised their control by firing those four teachers.

The United Federation of Teachers, the union, screamed. Albert Shanker, president of the union, demanded that the teachers be reinstated. He maintained that the local experimental boards had no authority to fire teachers. If they were not reinstated, he said, he would call the UFT out on strike and close all the schools until they were. The community stood fast, and the UFT struck all the schools in New York.

The Ocean Hill-Brownsville board declared that all the schools in the district would remain open. Most of the teachers, white and black, continued to work. To Elner, and to all those who backed the local board, the whole issue of community control was at stake. Elner was animated and eloquent in telling me this. The UFT, because of its size and because of the militancy of Albert Shanker, was one of the most powerful unions in the country. To successfully defy an anti-strike law pertaining to city employees, to keep a million children from their education, as the UFT had done, took power. If the UFT had to negotiate contracts with dozens of local autonomous boards, its power would be fragmented, abrogating the concept of "union." Therefore, Elner said, Shanker meant to kill community control while it was still experimental. Underlying the union argument was a more sinister element of racism. Many white union teachers did not like the security of their jobs depending on black administrators. The habit of racism was so deep in America, the white man so used to supervising and controlling blacks, that the reverse situation was uncomfortable where it was not intolerable.

The children were wonderful, Elner said. They understood what was at stake. They understood what would become of them if the UFT won. They came past barricades, past tall men in dark blue uniforms with helmets and clubs, past union teachers, to come to school. They behaved; they were interested; they learned. For the first time in their lives school meant something more to them than confinement and boredom.

"I just wish you could see them," she said to me. "I'm so proud of them." While telling the story of Ocean Hill-Brownsville, her Biafra, she felt my sympathy and understanding.

"I'd love to see them, but would I be allowed in the school?" I said.

"I think if you went with me, I could get you past the police. Do you really want to go? Tension is so high, there could be a riot at any time. You might be caught in the middle of it."

"Elner, you face it every day. Besides, I was already in a riot. In Syracuse, the day Martin Luther King was shot, I was the only white man around, and I was beaten up. I'd very much like to see your school."

We agreed that I would go to school with her the next morning, Wednesday. If for any reason I had to leave for Amsterdam early, I would call and tell her to go on without me.

We took the "A" train to Brooklyn and emerged from the subway about two blocks from the school. Almost immediately, we encountered the first police blockade. There were hundreds of police everywhere. We were among the first to arrive. The police were just getting set up for another day. After daily confrontations, all the parties to this dispute went home for the night, as if conflict were a regular job. Many of the police were lounging against the barricades with their helmets off. Others were standing in small groups drinking coffee from paper cups supplied by the mobile police kitchen. A large communications truck, the command center, was parked nearby. A strange ambiance permeated the scene, like an army waiting for the order to go out to battle, yet also like office workers lounging around with their coffee before the morning shift. The media hadn't arrived yet, so they missed this languid prelude.

We approached the barricade briskly, looking purposeful, yet unconcerned, as if this were quite ordinary. We passed through a gap in the barricade unchallenged. Six barricades later we reached the front entrance to the school. Someone familiar with the staff was stationed there to admit or bar the appropriate people. Elner nodded to the man and said, "He's with me," and we were permitted to enter. Police were stationed in the halls as well. This felt like being in the presence of an army of occupation, in some ways more intense and threatening than the military coup I had experienced in Nigeria.

Elner punched in on the time clock and took me to her room on the second floor. From the classroom window, we looked down on the scene we had just come through, watching teachers and children walk the same obstacle course.

"You know," Elner said, "I'm scared stiff every time I come through that. I don't mind standing up and fighting for my rights, but I can't stand the thought of having my head smacked open by one of those clubs. This is no way to have to teach your children. Why can't they just leave us alone?"

As time approached for class to begin, no students had arrived in the classroom, although we had seen many of them approach the school. The public address system crackled, and a woman announced that she was now the acting principal and that she was declaring the school closed for the day. She appealed to all the students to go home and all teachers to assemble for a meeting.

"Oh, no!" shouted Elner, heading for the door. "They're not closing this school! Come on!" We ran down the stairs, heading for the office.

The day before, the principal, Mr. Harris, had been barred from the school. The Ocean Hill-Brownsville issue had become too hot for the city school board to handle, and the whole district had been removed from the jurisdiction of the city and placed directly under the administrative control of the New York State Education Department in Albany. A man from Albany, unfamiliar with New York City schools and with the current dispute – to guarantee his impartiality – was appointed to head the whole district. His first act was to bar Mr. Harris from his school. The second was to order the senior assistant principal, the woman who spoke on the P.A. system, to close the school.

As soon as the announcement was made, another assistant principal, who had been gathering the children in the auditorium, grabbed the microphone on the stage while a teacher forced his way into the control room for the P.A. system and threw a switch, giving the man in the auditorium an open mic to the whole school. We heard what he said as we rushed down the hall.

"Children! Listen to me! Don't go home. The school is NOT closed. Mr. Harris has been removed from the school, but I promise you he'll be back soon. In the meantime I want you to stay in the auditorium, behave yourselves, and wait for your teachers to take you to your classrooms."

As we reached the auditorium, we noticed a commotion at the main entrance to the school. People were yelling and shoving. Someone was trying to prevent anyone else from entering the school. Elner told me to "stay back," thrusting her right arm out in front of me, protectively. She shoved her way to the door. She shouted to the children still outside who were being held back by the police.

"Come on in! Don't let them stop you!"

The children surged forward, crawling between policemen's legs, under barricades, and over cars, until the police finally gave up and let them all come. As they reached the door children shouted.

"I made it, Miss McCraty! I made it!"

"Good. Good. Now don't block the way for others. Move on into the auditorium and wait for your teachers."

Some of the teachers began yelling at the few black policemen. One young woman with an Afro hair style shouted, "What are you doing over there? Come over here and join *us*, God damn it! We're doing this for your children!"

Throughout all this, the children were perfect. They did exactly what they were told by their teachers. In the auditorium a woman with an Afro and wearing African beads was standing down front leading the children in a song.

"I'm black and I'm proud! Say it *loud*! Say it *LOUD*! Come on, let me hear it! Everybody! Sing it! Shout it! Tell them we mean it!" And the children sang.

"I'm black and I'm proud! Say it *loud*! Say it *LOUD*!"

When the attempt to close the school failed and things had quieted down, an announcement said that the children could go to their classes. Because of the delay the first three periods would be shortened to a half-hour each. Elner assembled her students in the auditorium and led them to class in perfect order. In spite of the excitement of the morning, Elner immediately began her science lesson on solutions. *We're here to learn*, was her attitude, *and we've already lost time, so let's get on with it*. The subject matter was difficult for children of that age, but Elner presented it well, and the children were attentive.

At the end of the first period I told Elner that I had better check in with the Committee office in case something had come up. She directed me to a pay phone. It was out of order, and I couldn't get to the one in the office, which was jammed with reporters. I told Elner I had better leave. Our situation with UNICEF was so uncertain that anything could break, one way or the other, at any time. I felt uneasy being out of touch. I told her I'd see her after school if nothing came up and if she survived the day.

<h1 style="text-align:center">4</h1>

Jan was the only one in the office. There was no news and she didn't know what the other fellows were doing. Jan and I spent the next few hours talking, mostly about what I had just seen at Ocean Hill-Brownsville. She seemed quite interested by what I told her of Elner, this woman I had been spending so much time with since I came to New York. After that first Monday I had seldom seen any of the others. I would return to the hotel late and leave soon after I got up. Once, Barry asked me if I wanted to go see *Hair*, but I declined because I was seeing Elner.

Jan had some letters to type, and I had nothing to do, so I sat around the office reading the paper, glancing over reprints of articles on Biafra, and going through the Committee files on former volunteers. My name had come out of this file. I knew many of the others. Quite a few had sent in an application to the Committee. With so many applications, I wondered how I had come to be among the chosen few. *Immediate availability*, Jan supposed. That attribute I shared with Larry, Barry, and Leo. Larry, like me, had been in a career hiatus. Barry had arrived dead broke. UNICEF had to send him money to get to the airport in San Francisco. He had been living the life of a flower child, wandering, picking up odd jobs, such as driving a garbage truck during a strike. Leo, over fifty, had not been able to find himself after returning from the Peace Corps. He had never married, had no friends. Tired of the feed grinding business, he took a basic course in computer programming, which astonished me. He had no great enthusiasm for it – it was just something to do. Less than a week on the job he told his boss he was going to Biafra. His boss thought that was a noble thing to do and told him he could have his job back when he returned.

During this waiting period, Leo spent most of his time sitting in the hotel or in local bars. The great city of New York had no attractions for him. Larry went walking, went to museums, exhibits, plays. Barry dug more into the city and what the night life had to offer. He started taking Jan out.

That evening I went over to Elner's again. We rehashed the day. After I left the school, there had been no further disturbances. The school day proceeded normally. Nobody, however, could say what would happen tomorrow. *Onye ma echi*? Everyone thought that the battle to keep the school open that day had been only a temporary victory. Later that night, we heard on the radio that the school would be closed for the next two days, Thursday and Friday, for a "cooling off" period. All teachers were to report directly to the central school board, without loss of pay, for meetings and discussions on how to resolve the crisis. Elner wondered what that meant but felt that she had to comply. Before reporting to the board, however, she would go to the school first to see if anything was happening there. She had told her students to report to school in the morning no matter what they heard on the radio. She would go there, and if there was no possibility of opening the school, she would dismiss any students who did come.

Elner said that after I left the school yesterday, the students wanted to know if I was her boyfriend.

"No," she said. "But you've seen him before. Do you remember the slides I showed you of Nigeria? "

"Yes!"

"He was in one of the pictures. Do you remember which one?"

"Was he the one on the motorcycle with you?"

"That's right."

"Oh, but Miss McCraty, are you sure he's not your boyfriend? He's so cute."

Once again, I entered the office with my suitcase, ready to go to Biafra, but in a much better frame of mind than I had been on Monday. There were no doubts this time about what I was doing. I was much clearer about my assignment. I had a good chance, if I used it right, of starting a solid career in broadcasting. I had a good relationship with Elner; having her to write to back in the States would give me an anchor in the normal world while I lived in the outrage of war and death. I was glad for the delay in our departure. I no longer felt adrift, without direction.

But, God! How precipitously things can change! We were told that we would *not* be leaving that night. Mollerup sent a message from Copenhagen telling us to hold. He was not specific, but apparently he thought the clearance matter was serious enough for further examination. Not knowing what the hell was going on was the most frustrating element in all of this. We did not know what was happening in Copenhagen. We did not know what was happening on São Tomé or in Biafra. These cryptic little messages would arrive out of the aether bearing weighty consequences for my future, and I had no idea what forces were working deep out of sight to determine my fate (I found myself thinking like Captain Ahab). In spite of the modern electronic marvels of instant global communications, I am convinced that the only adequate means of communication is direct and personal. And I'm certain that confusion increases with the square of the distance, no matter the medium of transmission.

We were assured, once again, that we would be leaving in a few days, but my confidence was eroding. Sunday was considered the most probable day for our departure. We were told to go back to the hotel, make the most of our time in New York, and call in from time to time to see if there were any changes.

"No," I said, frustrated and angry. "You call me. If I'm not at the hotel, you can reach me at this number." I scrawled down Elner's number, grabbed my suitcase and left.

When I called Elner, she was shocked that I hadn't left. "The hell with them," I told her. "As long as I'm in New York, let's enjoy ourselves." Friday I took her to dinner at Jack Dempsey's. She had lobster for the first time in her life. Later we went to see *Hair*.

Saturday we spent the whole day together. I went over to her apartment for breakfast, and we chatted pleasantly for a long time over her tea and my coffee. About noon she said, "I have to go to the library in Harlem to look up something for my Afro-American history class. Would you like to come along?"

"Sure."

It was unusually warm for October. The sky was bright; it was a pleasant day for a walk. Elner knew the approximate location of the library, but not exactly, and as we walked down streets of old brownstone houses looking for it, she asked, "Have you ever been to Harlem before?"

"Only once, passing through, about eight years ago," I said.

"Then you never knew what it used to be like. It was a lot different than it is now. Since the riots and since dope took over, it's really gone down. It was well known for its night life, and even many white people would come to hear the jazz. But white people don't come here anymore, unless they can't avoid it, and then only in the daytime." We spent a couple of hours in Harlem, and I never did see another white person.

We found the library, but it was closed. Elner decided that since we were there, she would take me sightseeing. We walked up Seventh Avenue to 125th Street. The scars of the riot were still there — long rows of burnt and broken buildings. Now and then Elner would point to a run-down looking place and try to describe what it meant and how fine it had been once: the Theresa Hotel, the Apollo, the Savoy. We stopped in a bookshop that specialized in black power. The clientele wore Afros, dashikis, black jackets, and beads, but neither here nor in the streets were we given a second glance, even though I was a white man walking with one of the "sisters." There were books by and about Africans and Africa, by and about black Americans. Some of them I had read. Elner picked out a few more for me that she said were required reading if I wanted to know what was going on. *The Autobiography of Malcolm X, Manchild in the Promised Land, Soul On Ice*. Between us, we left the store with a lot of literature.

We walked down 125th Street to Lenox Avenue, looking at the life scurrying all around us. A peddler on the sidewalk was told to move on by two black cops. A few people looked on, but most paid no attention. With the warmth of the day, some people were sitting on stoops. Elner related to me the fine old tradition of stoop-sitting on city streets. She showed me what had changed on 125th Street and what had not. She regarded Harlem with nostalgic warmth from her past experiences there, and with a slight apprehension at the modern decay.

Elner seemed to have forgotten the fear she voiced in Paris about the danger of going together in the States because of race. Or if she remembered, my visit to her school and our walk through Harlem that day had dispelled it.

One thing led to another and we decided to get married.

5

The next day, we had to face something. I was going to Biafra. Neither of us questioned that. It was assumed. I mentioned that because of the deal with CBS, this was a chance for me to build a career that would secure our future financially. But even without that assurance, there was, unspoken, the certainty that I *had* to go to Biafra. There was something so compelling in it that would override even something so compelling as our marriage.

On Monday we learned that you can't get married just any day you want. After waiting in line for over an hour at City Hall, we learned about licenses, Wassermann tests, and waiting periods. We initiated the process. It was like a puff that blew up into a whirlwind. Filling out forms. Finding a clinic to do the Wassermann. Arranging for a Justice of the Peace. We thought we could get it done by Friday.

Jan called from the Committee to say that UNICEF was sending us to Copenhagen Wednesday. Definitely.

Back at UNICEF I sat down with the deputy director, Mr. Hayward, to discuss my plight. He was actually delighted with the news, grinning as I told the story. He couldn't change the Wednesday departure – Leo, Larry, and Barry would go as scheduled – but he could get me on a flight to Amsterdam on Thursday.

Back at City Hall, when it was my turn at the head of the line, I presented my dilemma. "Look, I'm about to ship out to Biafra with the United Nations on Thursday. Is there any way we can get married by then?" I felt silly, like a cliché from an old war movie, where the soldier has to marry his sweetheart before joining his unit at the front. But I shamelessly pushed the analogy.

"Well, if you can find a judge to sign this waiver, the Justice of the Peace will marry you on Thursday."

It looked good for Thursday, then, so on Wednesday I called my brother, Jim, in Boston to see if he could come for the wedding. His roommate, Rob, said he was visiting Paul in New Hampshire, but he would try to contact him. I said he should meet us on the second floor of City Hall by nine o'clock, if he was able to make it. It would be nice to have my brother with me when I got married, but it seemed doubtful.

Thursday morning, October 17, Elner and I and Bill and Shirley made it to City Hall just before nine. Bright morning light flooded the huge window at one end of the hall. Four silhouettes detached from the glare and ran towards us, cheering — Jim, Anne (his future bride), Paul, and his wife Janie. Jim's roommate in Boston, Rob, couldn't reach him by phone last night, so he drove all the way to Plymouth, New Hampshire to give him the message. He arrived about midnight to find Jim, Paul, and Janie just returning from a party out in the new VW workshop. They were tired, loaded, and dirty. Paul and Jim wore full beards and long hippie hair, radical for those days. They brushed their teeth and jumped in Paul's VW mini bus, headed for New York and a nine o'clock appointment at City Hall. They stopped in Boston to pick up Anne.

Paul had modified his VW bus. Outside, it looked ordinary enough with its original green paint, but inside, the rear seats had been removed and replaced with a full-size mattress, wall to wall. On the left side behind the driver's seat was a small potbellied wood stove with the chimney sticking out the side window and up over the roof. The hastily constituted wedding party took turns driving and sleeping on the mattress.

A week or two previously, during the 1968 Presidential election campaign, Jim and Paul had attended a political rally in Plymouth. The candidate at the rally was Dick Gregory, a well-known comedian and the only black candidate for President. Although a very funny guy, he was making a serious statement about civil rights with his candidacy. He had written a book titled *In The Back of the Bus*. After the speech the audience could write questions on a piece of paper to pass up to the podium. Paul wrote, "Do you want to come out for a beer with us afterwards?"

Dick Gregory looked up from that note and said, "Who wrote this?" Jim and Paul meekly raised their hands.

"I don't want a beer, but could you give me a ride to the airport?" I have since heard stand-up comics use a line like that, turning a question from the audience into a request for a ride home to Indiana, or wherever. It gets a laugh. Gregory, being a comedian, either used a standard gag, or he *created* the gag that night, because he *did* ride to the airport with Jim and Paul, in that funky VW, with a police escort. As a Presidential candidate, he was entitled to police protection. But not being a front-runner, and not having much of a campaign chest, he needed to catch rides where he could.

On the way to the airport, he said, "You honkies are gonna get wasted up here if you don't shave those beards." At the airport, he had a rental car waiting for him. It wouldn't start. "Conspiracy," he said, and asked Jim and Paul if they would give him a ride down to Boston.

Not only broke, but dead tired, Dick Gregory slept on the mattress in back of the bus on the way to Boston.

When Jim and Anne and Paul and Janie got to New York, they found a parking place on the street. Tired, grungy, scruffy, hung over, and unwashed, they stood behind the bus and brushed their teeth and freshened up as best they could with containers of water.

People gathered to watch the hippies.

They found the rest of us in City Hall, and we went looking for a judge.

No judge was currently available to sign the waiver. We were directed to seek out a judge at the Supreme Court Building in Foley Square. We scurried over there. Although it was a Thursday, the place seemed deserted. We found someone who said we might find a judge on the top floor. By now I was just repeating our story by rote. To me, it sounded flat.

On the top floor, we all ran down this huge, empty, ornate echoing hall, looking for an open door. We went in an ante room and told our story to a legal secretary. Bill and Shirley stayed outside in the hall with the others, who were concerned about spoiling our chances before a judge with their appearance. The secretary had us wait. (*Chere. Wait small.*) Then she called Elner and me into the judge's chamber. He was an elderly, distinguished looking judge in full robes, Justice Samuel Gold. He listened with his head tilted slightly as we told our story again. Would he please sign the waiver so we could take it over to City Hall to get married?

He turned to his secretary and said, "I'll bet you didn't know you were going to witness a wedding today." Astoundingly, he meant to perform the marriage himself right there in his chambers.

"Do your mothers know you're doing this?"

"Yes."

"Do you have any other witnesses?" I ran out and got the others. When I appeared with my motley gang, the judge lifted his chin and raised his eyebrows.

"Well," he said, accepting the situation, amused.

"Do you have a ring?"

"Uh, no." I hadn't gotten around to that part yet.

"I'm sure we can find one around here somewhere that you can borrow." His secretary rummaged around in a drawer and found something suitable.

He performed the ceremony and we said our vows. The papers were signed. It was done.

Back on the street, we said goodbye to Bill and Shirley. They took the subway to their apartment. The rest of us found Paul's VW parked on the street. Ceremoniously, Paul opened the back hatch. I saw the mattress and the wood stove. Wow. I picked up Elner, as if carrying her over the threshold, and placed her on the mattress where Dick Gregory had recently reposed. I got in beside her. Another crowd gathered to watch. As we rode up the East Side Drive, heading north, Paul threw some firecrackers in the stove, puffing smoke out of the chimney.

That was it. Jim, Anne, Paul, and Janie came up to Elner's apartment for a brief celebration, a glass of wine, then headed off to New Hampshire. Elner and I rode the train to Kennedy Airport. We stared at each other wide-eyed at what we had done. The trajectories of our lives had crossed in New York, at a high angle, and ignited. I flew away on mine; she continued on hers.

6

On the plane to Amsterdam, I sat next to an enormous man who took up two seats. It might have been interesting to hear his story, but I was too full of my own thoughts, trying to understand what had just happened. I got married, and now I was flying off to a war in Africa.

From the airport in Amsterdam, I took a bus to the hotel arranged for me by UNICEF. Just an overnight stay was too short of a visit for such an historic city, so I tried to see as much as I could, mostly from the bus. I remember a lot of people riding bicycles and that the bus stop was labeled *Bushalte*.

In the morning I stood by that sign and caught the bus back to the airport. I found Transavia, the air carrier I would fly to Africa, in the cargo section of the airport. A Transavia representative pointed out to me a plane loading cargo a little distance from the terminal. Transavia had been recently cofounded by Jacob Achterberg as a charter company, and it served the Biafran Airlift from the beginning to the very end. Jacob himself flew the planes and hired crews from all over Europe, including many from Iceland. I walked out on the tarmac hauling my loads and regarded the plane. It was a four-engine propeller-driven DC-6B, once a passenger plane, now converted for cargo. I noted that Transavia's colors, like Nigeria Airways, were green and white, although a different design. I greeted the European crew, and they welcomed me aboard, showing me to a seat in the tail, by the last window. The rest of the "passenger" cabin and the cargo holds were packed with cartons of medical supplies and brown burlap bags filled with food, perhaps flour or rice.

So on the morning of October 18, 1968, I took off for Africa in a zesty soup of emotions: thrilled to be headed to Biafra at last, conflicted about leaving my new wife, and apprehensive about this uncommon, uncomfortable, unpredictable venture. Nothing of this sort, this airlift, had been attempted since the Berlin Airlift in 1948 when American and European allies broke the Soviet blockade of Berlin, which was surrounded by Communist East Germany. But that was a huge military operation, with cargo planes flying around the clock into Tempelhof, a modern airport in a European city. For years, Germans had watched Allied war planes flying over their country; Berliners in 1948 watched cargo planes flying over their city and called them "raison bombers." The Biafra operation was a rag-tag group of civilians, churches, and smugglers flying obsolete aircraft at night onto a stretch of road in an African rain forest.

We flew all day and into the night. The steady thrumming of the engines gave a slight vibration to the whole aircraft unlike the smooth ride of the big jets. I talked to another passenger, a CBS cameraman hitching a ride to São Tomé. We discussed my arrangement with CBS to record my experiences. He thought it was a good idea. CBS would probably use the tapes as a human-interest angle or background for the real stories.

We landed in Tripoli for refueling, another storied city that I touched but wouldn't see. I climbed down the crew ladder and walked some distance away from the refueling plane. I smoked a cigarette and looked around in the African night — only flat darkness out there, but warm. We were clearly in a different climate, a remote place. Somewhere out there in that night, in October of 1968, sleeping or plotting, was Col. Muammar Gaddafi, as yet unknown to the world.

Back in the air, we flew all night while I tried to rest in an old airliner seat. By daylight we landed in Cotonou, the Capital of Dahomey, a skinny country bordering Nigeria. In fact, we were only about fifty miles from the Nigeria border and less than a hundred from Lagos. I wondered if the officials in Cotonou understood the nature of our cargo and where we were going with it. They knew, and they were comfortable with it. We took off for São Tomé and Biafra.

PART II

Mr. Yeager (WCC), Father Anthony Byrne (Caritas), and
Joe Galano (Catholic Releif Services)

CHAPTER 5

Enwere m Nsogbu

I Have a Problem

Eight hours from London by air is a pocket of pain called Biafra where thousands of people die of hunger every day. LIFE sent me to Biafra twice in 1968. Nothing I had seen in Korea, Vietnam or during the Arab-Isreali War was adequate preparation for the agony that waited in the rain forest. Only someone conditioned to stroll fit and fed and unmoved among the living skeletons of slave labor camps could have witnessed the omnipresent suffering of the Igbo children without experiencing compassion – and very likely fury, too. ("How can the great nations of the world stand by and let a generation of kids die?")...There isn't much these days that one man can do – but he can tell a story the way he saw it.

Biafra Journal by Michael Mok (TIME-LIFE book 1969)

1

In São Tomé, on October 19, 1968, I presented my passport and papers to the Portuguese immigration officials. The documents identified me as a United Nations Consultant, a grand-sounding but nebulous title. The Portuguese officer asked me what that meant. I shrugged and smiled and he let me in. I suppose he had to. My UN document contained the statement:

The bearer of this certificate is traveling on the business of the United Nations. You are requested to extend to him (or her) the courtesies, facilities, privileges and immunities which pertain to his (or her) office, in accordance with the Convention on the Privileges and Immunities of the United Nations, and to facilitate by all suitable means the journey and the mission on which he (or she) is engaged.

Biafra, however, did not have to facilitate my journey and my mission, because it was not a recognized country and was not a member state of the United Nations; it was in a war of secession from a member state. Biafra, in fact, did not let me in. The United Nations was not seen as an organization friendly to Biafra, for the UN could not support the breakup of sovereign nations. Yet, UNICEF wanted to help the children in some way. My fellow volunteers and I were a way.

Leo Anderson, Barry Bianchi, and Larry Kurtz met me at the airport, along with Tom Hebert and Jerry Davis, the two volunteers who had sent the telegram trying to stop us from coming. Leo, Barry, and Larry had arrived the day before. We all went up to the Hotel Salvador, fifteen kilometers up in the mountains. It was an expensive taxi ride — $7 for us and our loads. We sat on the large veranda overlooking the town of São Tomé, the bay, the harbor, and the airport — a stunning view. We were exuberant. We had arrived on São Tomé, and we would soon be in Biafra, after a short delay while this clearance thing was straightened out. It was sunny and warm and the world was good. The guys congratulated me on my marriage, and I told them the story. We bought beer.

São Tomé is a beautiful place, part of an island group known as São Tomé and Principe. The islands lie along a deep fault in the earth's crust known as the Cameroon Line, running from the island of Annobon in the southwest through São Tomé and Fernando Po (Bioko) to the Cameroon highlands on the African continent in the northeast. The line intersects the equator at São Tomé. Because it lies on the equator near the Greenwich Meridian, São Tomé is the nearest point of land to the latitude and longitude coordinates (0, 0) – the navel of the world. It is 6000 miles due East of the Galapagos Islands; that is, one quarter of the way around the Earth. It is slightly larger than the Island of Fernandina in the Galapagos and also larger than Molokai in the Hawaiian Islands.

At the time of the airlift, São Tomé and Principe was a possession of Portugal and has since become independent. The city of São Tomé is the largest town on the island of São Tomé, near its northern tip. The town square was paved with ceramic tile, and it looked so neat and precise and clean that I imagined it had been constructed by Walt Disney. The architecture was picturesque Mediterranean style, probably not unlike Lisbon itself. Around the town square were long municipal buildings and a two-spired church, all of them two stories tall. Shops and residences along the side streets were also two stories with red ceramic tiles on the roofs. The buildings were constructed of concrete, painted pastel blues and yellows and greens and pink. Second story verandas were lined with bright white concrete latticework. Many windows and doors were arched and decorated with white trim.

The indigenous people were descendants of slaves taken by Portuguese plantation owners from different parts of Africa, such that the slaves of any one plantation were not related by custom or language to the slaves of neighboring plantations. The Africans we saw were free but poor fisherman, farmers, and servants to the Portuguese officials, hotel owners, and plantation owners. They lived in thatch villages away from the main town. The airlift had a huge impact on the life and economy and future of these people.

Many people in the relief operation stayed at the Hotel Salvador, but it was too expensive and remote for us. Most pilots and air crews stayed at the Hotel Geronimo, also too expensive. Jerry and Tom had found more reasonable rooms in the town. They took us to meet the *patrono* of their hotel, Senhor Lopes, a small, balding, affable Portuguese landlord. He spoke no English or French and we spoke no Portuguese, other than "*Mais cerveja, por favor,*" more beer, please, which I had just learned at the Hotel Salvador. By gestures and meaningless repetitions of our own languages, we expressed the notion that we needed rooms. He shrugged his shoulders and held his hands out, palms up, indicating that he had none. It made sense; the airlift had consumed all the available space on the island. We persisted. We needed something humble and temporary, because we would soon be leaving for Biafra. We had come prepared to live in bush conditions. In one of his boarding houses, he showed us an unused kitchen and adjoining pantry.

Empty. Bare of furniture. Perfect.

He nodded and rubbed his chin, dubious. We negotiated a price of $2.00 per night for each of us. It's amazing how fast you can get things done with people you can't understand. Communication is stripped down to essentials.

We packed in our loads and went to see the town. When we returned two hours later, Senhor Lopes had the place cleaned up, with new screens in the windows, but no beds. We would use our air mattresses. We went through the motions of blowing into our hands to convey the idea of pumping up the mattresses. He seemed to understand, but he looked unhappy, as if he didn't like the idea of us sleeping on his floor. Later he showed up with four metal bed frames with springs, similar to the *vono* beds we had used in Nigeria. There were sheets and covers. The next day he brought mattresses and pillows. So the pantry became our dormitory. We had a two-burner Coleman stove for the kitchen. In a local shop, we bought a frying pan, a pot, utensils, and some bread. Home sweet home.

In the following days, we settled into a glum mood, frustrated that our clearance for Biafra was still blocked. We sat in the Bar Enrique, owned by Senhor Lopes, and listened to Tom and Jerry talk about the various cliques and factions among the relief workers, their rivalries and intrigues. There were Catholics and their subgroups: Caritas and Catholic Relief Services; Protestants and their groups: World Council of Churches, and Nordchurchaid. There were Danes and Germans, British and other Europeans. There were few Americans. As we looked around the bar, we could see the faces of many nations come to work on this great humanitarian airlift, but no Africans. And no women.

"This is the white man's burden's last stand," Tom said.

Tom Hebert had been a Peace Corps Volunteer in Ibadan, Nigeria, 1962-1964, first teaching English in a poor Moslem secondary school, and later teaching drama at the University of Ibadan.

"Biafra's dominant image to the world," he would later write, "was not a political one [built along positive cultural lines], but an image set by the competing relief agencies: starving, pot-bellied Igbo children, dying it was reported, by the millions." Tom wrote of "an earlier chance midnight encounter with Mr. Osuji (Biafra's Special Representative to São Tomé) on a silent foggy street…softly lit by a bent old street light:"

> In a strangely intimate scene, we talked of the war which was not going well for Biafra and the relief effort that chewed up so much money and energy and almost all of the world's attention. As noted, the war had become [in the media] not a fight for independence much like America's own, but of relief planes and children with stomachs bloated from protein starvation — kwashiorkor. Mr. Osuji and I quietly shared a bitterness that night.

2

I discovered a small market in a nearby building, smaller than our village market back in Amaogwugwu. The vendors and shoppers were Africans, speaking their own version of Portuguese. There were bananas, sugar cane, kola nuts, dried fish, and all the things that reminded me of being back in my village, like old times, like being back home. It cheered me up.

We bargained for some empty bottles to carry fuel for our little cooking stove. People were astonished, or amused, to see us in the market instead of wherever Europeans went to shop. A very short lively woman ran up to us. She had a bandage on her foot, one finger missing, and one eye gone. In Pidgin English she asked me what thing we were looking for.

"*Wetin you de look?*" This delighted me; it made me feel closer to

Biafra. So I asked her if she spoke Igbo.

"*I na asu Igbo?*"

"*Ee. I done go Igbo. Por Tarcourt. Aba.*" She was not Igbo, but she could speak it because she had been to Igboland — Port Harcourt and Aba. It was common for many Africans to travel, in trade or for work, all up and down the West African coast where many languages were spoken, including the colonial languages of English and French. Pidgin English, sometimes called Broken English, with a grammar and vocabulary all its own, became a *lingua franca* across West Africa. Within Nigeria itself, where 256 different languages were spoken, it was an essential market language.

So we exchanged simple greetings. I was not fluent in Igbo, but I knew a little bit.

"*Kedu?*" How are you?

"*O di mma.*" Good.

"*A choro m mmanya nkwu.*" I answered her original question by saying that I wanted some palm wine. She took us to the vendor. By now we had drawn a crowd. I was trying to remember how to ask if it was fresh, because if it's not fresh it tastes nasty and gives bad tummy palaver. "Fresh" in English was apparently close enough to Portuguese that they understood what I wanted. A woman poured some into a small cup for me to taste. It was the sweetest, best palm wine I had ever tasted. I indicated that I wanted to buy a whole cup, but I wanted to know how much it cost. So I asked our Igbo-speaking interpreter.

"*Ego ole maka nka a?*"

She translated into Portuguese and listened to the reply.

"Four shillings," she said.

"Four shillings? Four shillings! No, no, no!"

"One and six," she came back with, or one shilling and six pence, equaling one and a half shillings. There were no shillings on São Tomé. The currency was escudos, where one dollar equaled seven escudos. The woman was giving me a denomination she knew, and thought I knew, from Nigeria. To her an escudo was a shilling, and "one and six" would be 1.5 escudos, about 20 cents American, a reasonable price. People stood around watching this exchange, like entertainment. When we left, kids followed us, smiling and yelling, "*Viva Biafra! Biafra! Biafra! Viva Biafra!*"

The Africans of São Tomé liked what the airlift was doing for Biafra. Larry said that after he was evacuated from Biafra when the war started, he was reassigned to Togo. Sentiment there was very high for Biafra. "They are our brothers, and they are being killed." Those people were not Igbos, but they thought the killing was wrong. Larry found the same attitude in

Abidjan, Ivory Coast. I had seen it in Cotonou, Dahomey just a few days previously. Few governments recognized Biafra, but the people of many countries sympathized.

We began to think of our little group of UNICEF volunteers as its own clique, apart from all the others on the island, with a status at the bottom of the totem pole. The exclusion we felt was partly our fault, because we chose to live apart from the other airlift personnel, wear African jumpers, and shop in local markets. Maybe we appeared to flaunt our uniqueness as former Peace Corps Volunteers, with intimate experience in Biafra. Then, too, we weren't doing anything constructive for the airlift.

Our group could also boast of having the only Biafran. He was Doctor Okonkwo, coordinating the distribution of medical supplies. When he was on São Tomé, he hung around with us. We called him "Doc." I told him that I had found kola and palm wine in the market.

"Oh, yeah," he said. "I saw the kola, but not the palm wine. I was going to buy some kola, but I needed to calm down so they wouldn't charge me too much."

"It's good kola, and the palm wine is really good," I told him.

One day, we invited him to come over to lunch. We bought palm oil, plantains, eggs, bread, kola, and palm wine from the market. We fried the plantains in the oil on our little stove. When Doc came over we handed him a kola nut on a plate with a knife and asked him to break the nut into its separate lobes. He did. We said, *"Onye wetara oji, wetara ndu"* he who brings kola, brings life. We served him fried plantain and palm wine. He was incredibly delighted.

Tom Hebert was with us. As a PCV in Ibadan, he had been a city volunteer.

"You bush volunteers are very impressive," he said.

Pilots and missionaries who came and went to Biafra tended to congregate in a few cafés to tell their stories: The Baia, Café Yong, and Bar Enrique. In a few days of listening to them, I learned a lot. The 13 million year old volcanic island of São Tomé punched up out of the Atlantic Ocean two hundred miles off the west coast of Gabon and three hundred miles south of Biafra. Nine aircraft operated out of São Tomé: DC-7s, DC-6s, and one C-46. The first plane took off for Biafra at 4:30 in the afternoon and crossed the Nigerian-held Biafran coast at about 6:00 p.m. in fading daylight. Pilots saw Nigerian jets taking off and landing at Port Harcourt, but the jets didn't come after them. Our planes were seldom bothered by anti-aircraft fire. The flights were becoming routine. Pilots said that the airstrip at Uli was fine – it was long enough and well lighted. Proper runway lights had replaced the kerosene lanterns that George Orick told us about. The radio beacon was strong and clear.

Pilots were paid $500 a flight; copilots and flight engineers got $300. With two flights, a pilot could make $1000 a night, which was good pay in 1968. It was one of the best aviation jobs in the world. It attracted fliers from Australia, Scotland, Germany, Norway, Sweden, Denmark, Britain, the United States, Iceland, and Lapland. Some had flown in WWII and some had flown with Air America, the secret CIA "airline" in Vietnam, Laos, and Cambodia.

Relief flights were making a difference with 200-300 tons of food arriving in Biafra each night. The starvation had been reduced from two months previously. As the food flights were successful, so were the arms flights. According to Johnny Correa, the American mercenary, "the arms basically came from Libreville, Lisbon and Ivory Coast — once a week from Israel, about once every two weeks from South Africa." At the beginning of the war Biafra was getting ten tons of arms per week. By the end of October 1968, they were getting fifty tons a night. The military situation stabilized and Biafra began recapturing some of its territory. Biafrans on São Tomé were elated.

At the beginning of the war, Biafra had food but no guns, and Nigeria quickly captured large areas in the north and south, cutting it off from seaports and reducing Biafra to an enclave. Refugees poured into the enclave, and then starvation became a problem. At that time, all of the planes flying into Biafra carried arms. Some Catholic priests, who had served in Eastern Nigeria before the war, began begging for some space on the arms flights to carry food. The gun-running pilots readily agreed. Eventually, Hank Wharton sold five of his DC-7s to the churches to carry the food.

Missionaries chattered about the famine. At that time, there was a protein shortage causing the condition known as *kwashiorkor* in the children, with emaciated limbs, bloated bellies, and reddish hair. Pictures of these children aroused the world and generated this airlift. Children were more susceptible to protein deficiency than adults, because their bodies and minds were still developing. Permanent brain damage can result from prolonged protein deficiency. What we had been shipping helped alleviate the *kwashiorkor*. One of the missionaries, Father Cunningham, looked ahead to December when the yams, cassava, and rice would be depleted, leading to a carbohydrate famine, far worse for the whole population.

The missionaries felt that the airlift alone, at its current capacity, could not cope with the carbohydrate famine. A land corridor would have to be opened to a port such as Opobo, a town on the coast east of Port Harcourt and due south of Umuahia. Failing a major diplomatic intervention by the United Nations or the United States, unlikely at that time, the corridor would have to be opened by the Biafran military. They would have to fight their way through the Nigerian 3rd Marine Commando, led by Col. Benjamin Adekunle, "The Black Scorpion," the toughest and best-equipped unit facing Biafra. Of course, this would require more arms for Biafra, and not just small arms, but an air force capable of destroying Nigeria's MiGs and Illyushins, which would also allow round-the-clock food flights. An editorial I had read recently in the *New York Times* expressed the opinion that Biafrans should give up the fight to prevent further starvation. But Igbos had witnessed the slaughter of their people and the Nigerian conduct of the war so far, and they had no doubt they were facing extermination. Johnny Correa wrote, "This war continued only because the people felt that there was no survival if they lost the war." They would not give up. A missionary told me that it might sound strange for "a man of the cloth" to be saying such things, but he said, furtively, that maybe we needed more "bullets for babies," more fighting for food.

The BBC reported on October 20 that Nigerian troops had retaken Oguta, putting them within artillery range of Uli and so ending the airlift. A missionary who had been in Oguta saw no sign of Nigerian troops, and pilots who flew into Biafra that night had no trouble. The BBC often gave spurious reports.

On Monday, October 21, my second full day on the island, we toured the warehouses where the relief food and medicine were stored. Since UNICEF had seconded us to Nordchurchaid, Pastor Mollerup wanted us to work in the warehouses while waiting for clearance, which could come in another week. The warehouses containing the relief supplies were a dirty, disordered mess. In the early days of the airlift, when Hank Wharton and Von Rosen were making the first relief flights, there was not much to choose from. But as the relief effort gained momentum, supplies began streaming in through the airport and the harbor of São Tomé. As each shipment arrived, it was dumped in a warehouse with no organization and no inventory. Preparing a planeload of relief supplies was difficult because no one knew what food was available and what condition it was in. The Customs warehouse was soon overwhelmed, and thirteen more buildings in and around the town of São Tomé were designated as warehouses. The first priority was given to unloading the ships and planes and getting the cargo off the docks, out of the weather.

We walked all over the city peering in the thirteen warehouses. There were many tons of food: dried milk, stockfish, salt, flour, and Formula II (corn meal, soy, and milk powder). The fifty-pound sacks of Formula II bore labels depicting a white hand shaking a black hand and saying,

"From the People of the United States to the People of India." The United States Agency for International Development (USAID) had diverted the shipment to Biafra. Although the U.S. government officially followed a "One Nigeria" policy, a lot of the food came from the United States. There were cases of Enfamil and Sego, fudge, kosher mushroom soup, bean soup, beets, peaches, and peanut butter.

After the tour we went out to the airport to witness one of the great social events of the island – the landing of a Transavia Boeing 707 jet. It brought a relief cargo and top officials of the World Council of Churches and Nordchurchaid, including Pastor Mollerup. It was a big aircraft for a small airport, but it landed safely without running off the end of the runway and dropping into the sea.

The next day we were expected to start an inventory of the warehouses. We looked in one of them. Inside the large entrance door was a clear concrete floor, but all around, in the dim light, we saw cases and sacks of different things stacked up or heaved up to the two-story high ceiling. It seemed hopeless. Who could tell what was back in the corners? We were reluctant to get involved because we had no experience in warehousing, and we were enthusiastic about going into Biafra. If our clearance for Biafra came through, we might be bogged down on São Tomé. We felt like we were getting in the way of the Portuguese and Africans who were already working there. So we went to the beach.

Beaches on São Tomé were plentiful and beautiful. There were two large shallow bays between the town and the airport separated by a wide peninsula jutting out into the Gulf of Guinea. On the *Baia dos Sete Ondas*, the Bay of the Seven Waves, sand crabs ran everywhere and small waves lapped into shore. I could wade far out into the bay. Because the bay was shallow, a procession of waves — about seven — rolled in from the Gulf.

That first week I found many quiet little open-air cafés unfrequented by airlift personnel. Tropical birds tweeted and screeched among the tables. I sat alone in one, reading the copy of *The Autobiography of Malcolm X* that I had purchased on 125th Street in Harlem. Tom Hebert also had a copy of *Malcolm*, and the six of us took turns reading them. Well, I'm not sure that Leo did. Every evening around nine o'clock, after we had listened to the stories of the pilots and missionaries, we would go to the airport to watch the planes arrive from their first run to Biafra, reload, and head out again. Many other people came out to watch. The parking lot was jammed. A four-foot high wall separated the public area from the flight line. The top foot was a chain link fence and the bottom was concrete. About every ten feet was an eight-inch square concrete pillar. I sat on top of one of those with my feet hanging over the flight line. Just watching the planes coming in from Biafra and going out again was emotional. I was so close to going there myself.

At night, after returning from the airport and after the others had gone to bed, I sat on the veranda outside our rooms. There was no chair; I sat on the concrete floor among the hungry mosquitoes and listened to the rain falling on the compound beyond the roof. Rainy season was ending in Biafra, but it was still with us on the equator. I could hear planes returning from Biafra, flying in the rain. I began to make my tapes, the ones CBS had given me to record my experiences. CBS thought I had no skills as a reporter, and they weren't going to pay me. I developed an attitude about that, because I'd hoped it would be a career entry, so I didn't try to organize my accounts in any way; I just rambled on, using this medium as a form of letters to Elner. After she heard them and edited out the personal parts, she would give them to CBS and they could sort out what they wanted. As I listened to the tapes forty years later, I could tell that I had made it hard for them.

3

We learned that there were 77 Biafran children on São Tomé, cared for by Irish nuns at an orphanage called San Antonio. They had been evacuated in late stages of starvation when they couldn't walk and couldn't even cry. After a week of good care, they started to respond and two or three weeks later they were running around and playing. The Boeing had brought down a load of prefab buildings for expanding the orphanage. Leo, instead of moping around like the rest of us, helped to erect the new buildings.

I went to see the kids in the orphanage. The main building was a two-story block building with a tile roof and white trim on the windows, doors, and second floor veranda, but plainer looking than the buildings of the town. Dozens of children were standing or walking around eating bread. They wore white shorts or loose white gowns. The weaker ones were sitting and eating. Three or four indigenous social workers were handing out food or sitting with the kids. When the children saw me, some ran over to me, holding my hand or grabbing my pant legs.

"*Fada*," they called me, meaning "Father," a Catholic priest, or anyone who looked like one. I had brought my tape recorder, so I held the microphone out to a boy and asked him his name.

"*Aha gi?*"

"*Peeta*," he said. Peter. But then he jumped back, as if he were afraid of the mic. It was a round black cylinder. Did it look like the barrel of a gun to him? The others backed off too.

"Are you afraid of this?" I smiled to reassure them and played back the tape to show them how it worked. They got the idea very quickly and gathered around again, giggling.

"*Aha gi?*" I asked again.

"Justina."

"Antonio."

"Nicholas."

I asked them where they were from.

"*Ebee ka isi?*" I said.

"*Esi m Emekukwu bia.*" He was from the village of Emekukwu.

"Owerri," was another response.

"Why are you here?" I asked. When I couldn't remember the Igbo, I used English or Pidgin.

"*Butu Gowon.*" I didn't understand that. Gowon was the military leader of Nigeria, but I didn't get the whole phrase.

"*Gini?*" What? I asked.

"*Butu Gowon. Butu Gowon.*" He made a kicking motion with his leg and pointed to his foot.

"Oh. You had kwashiorkor." Kwashiorkor was a protein deficiency that caused feet to swell, and the Biafrans called that Gowon's boot. The kids understood what had happened to them.

"Where is your family?" It was a follow up question to "Why are you here?"

"*My family de for Biafra now,*" said Nicholas. "*I want to see my fada and my moda and my seestas.*"

"I'm sure you will, some day." When the children were restored to health, they were returned to their families to make room for others. These kids were not orphans.

One boy was carrying a toy gun made out of bits of wood and wire and pipe. It looked just like an assault weapon.

"What is that?" I asked.

"*Na gun.*"

"Where did you get it?"

"*I make am.*"

"*Wetin you go do with dat?*"

"I want to take and fight! In Biafra!"

The boy put the gun down. A small girl, perhaps two years old, picked it up and slung it over her shoulder with a casual motion, as if she had been doing it for years, and kept chewing her bread.

I played the tape back. As more children understood what the tape recorder could do, they mobbed me. Individual conversations were no longer possible, so I asked if they could sing a song. They spontaneously erupted into a song, from the smallest kid to the largest. When that song ended, they started another. And another, and another. I couldn't tell who was leading, who chose the songs, but they all sang in unison, loudly. They all knew the words. I didn't. I could hear the names "Gowon" and "Ojukwu" so they had to be military songs, fight songs.

A month previously, these children had been near death from starvation. Had they not come here, they would have died. A month later they would be back in Biafra with their families.

This was a day of high emotion for me. I *had* to get into Biafra and see for myself.

4

Thursday, October 24, started out rotten and ended up good. Tom Hebert came over to our place all agitated because he had just been told by the police to leave the island on the next plane out. He thought he had been torpedoed by one of the church officials for complaining about how the operation was run. Pastor Mollerup had asked the Governor to have him deported. Later Mrs. Mona Mollerup sent a telegram to George Orick at UNICEF saying Tom had been deported "due to demonstrative, insulting behavior and an uncooperative attitude." Separately she expressed the opinion that "Tom Hebert is a mass murderer of children!"

Later that afternoon, in a wonderful juxtaposition of unrelated events, Tom was granted clearance to work in Biafra. He wanted to go in, but that night he was put on an arms plane returning to Lisbon.

The good news for the rest of us was that the same person who arranged Tom's clearance was working on ours. However, Tom's departure threw us into a paranoid fit. Frustrated with the delay, we had been doing some whining of our own. We went low, conservative. I stopped wearing my African jumpers around town. I put away *Malcolm X*. If anybody else knew what was in that book, we could be suspected of fomenting rebellion on the island. We were there to help the Biafra we knew, not to liberate the São Tomé that we did not know. It was a tightly ruled colonial island at a time when colonial rule was crumbling. The Portuguese were watching.

Pastor Mollerup called a general meeting in one of the warehouses. He gave a stirring speech pointing out how vital it was to the relief effort to straighten out the warehouses. He concluded, "Anybody who impedes the delivery of food and medicine to Biafra's children is a *mass murderer!*" He made a mean face directly at the UNICEF volunteers as he said it. He had accused Tom Hebert of being a mass murderer of children; now we were all tarred with the same brush.

Mass Murderers. Well, that surely brought our status among the relief groups to a new low. Recovering our rationality in time, we kept our mouths shut, and we thought that doing something useful in the warehouses would be better than just hanging out on a gorgeous tropical island.

That night, Friday, October 25, Nigerians bombed Uli at night for the first time. A couple of bombs fell but did little damage. A Red Cross plane had a few small holes in it. Still, that was a bad precedent.

Two guys from Transavia who had just returned from Uli after the bombing bought some scotch and wanted to talk about it late into the night. Chris, the copilot, and Ziggy, the flight engineer, were both from Iceland. They had flown for Icelandic Airways. During the course of the evening, as things got pretty loose from the scotch, they insisted that the cheapest way to fly from America to Europe was on Icelandic Airways, with a stop in Reykjavik, the capital. They even taught me how to pronounce Reykjavik after a lot of repetition.

"My heart went all the way down to my knees when the bombs went off," said Chris.

It scared the both of them out of their wits. Just after the bombs fell, they were sitting in the cockpit of their plane, a DC-6, in a parking finger off the end of the runway. There was another plane parked in a finger across the runway. Still shaken from the bombing, they saw another plane coming in for a landing. Incoming planes had to fly right over the parked planes and drop down on the runway just beyond. This plane was coming in low, straight at them. Ziggy tore open the cockpit window and jumped out. He sprained his ankle. Chris and the pilot ran for the back of the plane. The incoming pilot pulled up just in time.

"It was the worst night of my life," said Ziggy.

Chris said that a few nights earlier, they were the last flight to leave Biafra, taking off at about 4:00 a.m. When they crossed the coast at 14,000 feet, heading south toward São Tomé, it was daylight, and they could see Nigerian ships below. They were not a threat. But the night bombing changed a relatively routine operation into a dangerous military situation. Something had to be done. Chris said that if someone could raise $1 million, within three days he could have three F-100 Super Sabers down here with their crews, maintenance, and ground support, ready to fight for five weeks. He seemed to suggest that they would come from West Germany. Over the course of my stay on São Tomé, I heard a lot of such claims, but I never saw any warplanes. According to Johnny Correa, Biafra got some planes after I left for home.

On Saturday night, my vigil at the airport was more suspenseful because of the air raid the previous night. Our planes had taken off as usual at 4:30, but by 9:15 none had returned. Other planes were being loaded; a DC-7 to my left was taking on stockfish. Workers backed a lorry up to the "cargo" door, and some of them got in the plane. Others stood on top of the bales of stockfish and heaved bales into the plane where others stacked them. It took 45 minutes to an hour to load each plane. The loads were carefully balanced but not tied down, as they would normally be, to facilitate faster unloading at Uli. Still, it could take up to two hours to unload in Biafra. That is what we were recruited to do, but not cleared to do.

The sky was clear, bright with stars. There was some heat lightning to the north where our planes would be coming from. The planes were late. Maybe there was a weather delay, or maybe the Nigerian bomber had struck again.

The São Tomé airport tower turned on its rotating light beacon. A plane was coming in. The pilot turned on his landing lights. A DC-7 flew out of sight around the tower and then came in to land. I could identify it as a DC-7 by the tremendous blue flame from the engine exhaust and the deep, heavy sound of the engines, more powerful than the other planes.

The DC-7 taxied over to the terminal and parked. The rear passenger door opened and a ladder was lowered. Some people, including a priest, came down the ladder. A lot of other people ran out to meet them, to learn if there had been another air raid.

Fred Olsen, a contract cargo hauler, provided a C-46 for the airlift. It landed, followed by a Transavia DC-6B, the one I had flown on from Amsterdam.

I met one of the passengers as he came into the terminal. It was the CBS cameraman who had hitched a ride on the same plane from Amsterdam. He had been in Biafra for the last four days. He said that there was a small air raid last night but none tonight. He got some good footage that he would be sending out to CBS, but he had no sound. His tape recorder's batteries went dead, and he refused to pay $6 a battery for replacements, the going price in Biafra. I told him how I had ached to have a camera while I was recording the Biafran children singing earlier that day. He had film of Biafran children, but no sound. He wanted my tape. He begged for my tape.

"No," I said. "This tape is going to my wife. Later, she will send it to CBS."

"Oh, well, give it to me. I'll send it to CBS, and they'll send it to your wife."

"Oh, no. Maybe they will, maybe they won't. I'm not taking any chances…"

"I guarantee it!"

"No!"

I reminded him that he was back on São Tomé where batteries were cheaper, and he could go up to San Antonio and tape the kids for himself. I told him the procedure that I had used to get the kids comfortable with the recorder.

"You can get those kids to sing for you all day long."

"Oh, okay. Good," he said. I didn't have to surrender my tape; he was happy, and maybe CBS would broadcast his recording of those amazing kids. Actually, months later, they broadcast my tape of those kids. More than 40 years later, I shared that actual tape with an ethnomusicologist at the University of Colorado at Boulder. His name was Austin Okigbo, and he had been a child in Biafra at that time. He cried when he heard the songs, along with other grown men. All the songs were known, except for one, and this is the only recording of it.

There was no air raid that night, but the next day Nigeria announced by radio that our planes should avoid the area because they were going to attack the airfield. We flew eleven flights that night, but nothing happened at Uli. Instead, one of the priests came out of Biafra screaming for blankets and bolts of cloth to black out the windows of the hospitals, because Nigeria had bombed a hospital that night.

5

On Monday, October 28, five of us went to work in the warehouses: Jerry Davis, Larry Kurtz, Leo Anderson, Barry Bianchi, and myself. Our first challenge was to unload eight thousand cases of canned milk from a ship anchored in the harbor. The cases were winched from the ship down to lighters, small transfer boats, which ferried the cargo to the docks. We lined up with the African laborers to pass the cases from hand to hand from the lighters to the lorries. We put the milk in a warehouse where a lot of other canned goods had been dumped, most of it in random piles of loose cans. We worked for sixteen hours.

Then another ship came in. I looked at the manifest. There were eight thousand more cases of milk, plus twelve thousand cases of tinned meat, powdered milk, and other stuff. Where would we put it? To make room we worked frantically to clear the loose cans and miscellaneous items out of the canned milk warehouse and put them in one designated for those things. Meanwhile the new shipment was waiting in lighters out in the bay.

Another large ship entered the harbor. Relief supplies were coming in at a far greater rate than what we could move out on the airlift. They were backing up. Pastor Mollerup was right to be concerned.

Before we could move anything more off of the docks, we had to clean up the warehouses. In one warehouse spilled milk powder was a foot deep in places. We worked hard, all day long — long hours. Sometimes we were so tired we just sat and pointed. At other times we had to join in, moving the boxes, sometimes loading the boxes on peoples' heads. Although we would wake up in the morning with sore, aching muscles and swear that we would do nothing but point that day, we would end up sweating our butts off anyway, moving and placing and throwing cartons around. We woke at 6:00 a.m. each day and worked from 7:00 to 11:30 a.m.. At precisely 11:30 a whistle blew all over the island signaling a midday work break. The workers smiled and said, *"Onze e trinta!"* in Portuguese, eleven-thirty. All work stopped, no matter what was happening. During the break we ate lunches that we had packed for ourselves. We developed a camaraderie with the workers. We couldn't keep up with their pace of work, but over time our muscles hardened and our stamina grew. We sat and talked with them in a mixture of broken English, Portuguese, and gestures. They wanted to know about the world outside of São Tomé, things like "The Beatles." They called the group "BeeATElees," but we understood what they meant when they strummed their air guitars. Work resumed at 1:30 p.m. We continued until five o'clock. Sometimes we worked until six o'clock or later if we were unloading a ship.

One night we worked until nine o'clock, thanks to Father Byrne. Father Anthony Byrne, a Holy Ghost Father, headed the Caritas part of the relief operation. He had served as a priest in Eastern Nigeria for the past ten years, and by the sheer force of his personality, he had helped launch the Biafran Airlift, along with Von Rosen, Wharton and others.

Larry Kurtz wrote, "What I remember about Father Byrne was that he was quite authoritative and very Catholic, keeping a chasm between the various factions of the airlift...I was often the inter-mediator between the Catholics and Protestants."

Father Byrne had just returned from Biafra the night before. He demanded that three planeloads of medicine be shipped in right away. The flights and cargo had already been established for that night. The flight schedules were coordinated with other bases such as Fernando Po and Libreville and could not be upset too much. As many as six to twelve planes could be converging on Uli with no radar to prevent planes from colliding in the dark.

"I want three flights to carry medical supplies!" demanded Father Byrne.

"No. You can't do that," said Captain Axel Duch, chief of operations for Nordchurchaid, shaking his head.

"Yes, I can! People are dying in there all the time from lack of medicines, lack of bandages, lack of drugs, and you've got a whole warehouse full of them sitting there, and I want them. NOW!"

Duch just looked at him.

"I will run over anybody who gets in my way," Byrne continued. "By your little bureaucracy, you're contributing to the deaths of many people and I won't stand for it!"

It was beautiful to watch. Nordchurchaid had labeled us "mass murderers." This was like payback.

Father Byrne got his three aircraft. While working in the warehouses, sometimes we sat around for hours, trying to get a lorry, trying to get a crew to move something. In half an hour, he had three lorries and crews ready to work, including us.

Our Nordchurchaid boss was a Dane we called Herr Friedle, an affable but uninspiring leader. He seemed clueless about warehouse organization. He mostly stood around watching us and smiling. We worked with the crew of São Tomé African laborers and a Portuguese supervisor named Edwardo. We came to like Edwardo a lot. He was a slender young man, about thirty years old, pleasant and unflappable, who knew the warehousing business.

Unofficially, UNICEF placed us under the protective wing of Father Byrne. I rode back from the airport with him one day. Although he was forceful and gruff, he could also be kind. He said, "What did UNICEF give you for transportation?"

"Nothing," I said.

"I will send a cable to Hayward (Deputy Director of UNICEF in N.Y.) to see if I can get you something to ride on – will Hondas be all right?"

"That would be very nice." I couldn't believe it.

"How many do you want?"

"Five." We eventually got the Hondas.

Joe Galano, head of Catholic Relief Services out of New York, was another mover and shaker on the island, although he moved more silently in the background. His bald head came up to Father Byrne's chin, and he was a little plumper. I never saw him arguing with the other powers, but he had influence. When we needed something, like the prefab buildings for the orphanage or metal grating for the parking fingers at Uli, they suddenly appeared. We would look at Joe.

"What? I'm telling you: I don't work for the CIA. The only exercise we get around here is jumping at conclusions."

On a ship that had just come in there were two Volkswagens for Caritas. "Take them," Joe said to us. "Just go drive them off. I'll help you get the plates and papers. Why not use them?" Maybe so, but we didn't want Father Byrne mad at us, so we just left them alone.

After we finished work, we would go to the Baia and have an *ananash*, a refreshing pineapple drink, or a beer. We'd take off our shoes and relax a bit, then go get something to eat. We found some quiet little cafés, unfrequented by relief people. Café Palomar had excellent food, much cheaper than Café Yong. Every day, the others walked past the Palomar to get to the Yong. I guess people everywhere follow ruts. Back at our rooms, we would shower and put on clean clothes. After that, we would take a walk, read, or go to bed.

One evening a lower level official from the U.S. State Department came through São Tomé on a fact-finding mission to Biafra. Over a beer at the Baia he said, "What amazes me is how all of you relief people have swallowed the Biafran propaganda about starving children."

UNICEF paid us a subsistence allowance of $75 per week. As in the Peace Corps, volunteers were to subsist, not make a living. UNICEF said that the figure was arbitrary, because they didn't know what was required to subsist on São Tomé or in Biafra. If we felt we needed more, we should ask for it. I kept track of what I spent, and it didn't come quite to $70, but most of the money was gone by the end of the week. I didn't have two pence to send home to my wife, dear wife. With effort, I could have lived on less money, but we wrote to UNICEF requesting $100 per week. Maybe I could save a little money to send home to help Elner get together the airfare to come here. Six months was going to be a long separation.

By the end of our first week on the job, we had established a plan. We would dedicate each warehouse to one or two major items, such as milk, stockfish, or Formula II. We weighed a sampling of bales or bags of each commodity and determined an average weight. As we moved the items into their dedicated locations, we counted them, and therefore we knew the total quantity of each. Edwardo maintained the lists. We named the warehouses A through M. Later, a fourteenth warehouse, N, was added. Warehouse K, which we nicknamed "chaos," was dedicated to all those random smaller items like cans of mushroom soup, beets, peaches, and peanut butter. In response to an appeal by First Lady Pat Nixon, these individual items were donated by people like, say, "Mrs. Murphy" in Connecticut, or "Mrs. Greene" from California, or "Mrs. Rankin" in New York. We called this "missionary food" or "Father food."

The first commodity we moved was stockfish, because it was stinky. There were five hundred tons of it scattered around the warehouses and two hundred tons in the Customs warehouse. We cleared out the Customs warehouse first by taking all shipments of stockfish directly from there to the airport. Two hundred tons could be flown to Biafra in less than a week. The remaining stockfish was moved to the warehouse farthest from town to minimize the smell for the residents. Similarly, sacks of milk powder had been stored in a number of warehouses in varying quantities. If warehouse F had the smallest quantity, we scheduled that milk to be flown to Biafra first, until F was clear of milk. If warehouse D had the greatest quantity of milk, then milk became the designated product for that warehouse, and milk from other places was brought there. The overall plan sorted the commodities into their own warehouses with the minimum amount of movement.

To the jars of peanut butter, cans of beets, peaches, and mushroom soup in warehouse K we added 1000 cases of diet root beer, thousands of cartons of plastic drinking cups, thousands of air mattresses, and many heavy canvas tents. Most of these donations were well meant, but inefficient. A DC-7 carrying ten tons of canned goods would be carrying seven tons of water and metal. A pharmaceutical company sent a shipment of suntan lotion. It was said that they wrote it off as a charitable donation. There was no way we were going to send that to Biafra, but the ship wouldn't leave the port, and make way for other ships, until it was unloaded. So we packed that off to "chaos," next to the root beer. Does anybody remember how bad NO-CAL diet root beer tasted? Could that have been a charitable tax write off?

We were assigned a number of lorries to move stuff from the docks to the warehouses to the airport. They became such a regular part of our lives that we named two of them: "Nellie" and "Jan" after Nellie Rodrigues and Jan Phillips, the two girls who worked in the office at the Committee for Nigeria/Biafra Relief. After Elner and I were married, we went to the office to pick up my ticket to Amsterdam. The girls were waiting for us with a champagne toast.

6

On Saturday, a day off after our first week of toil, I hung out in the cafés and talked to people about the relief effort, even though I was not a real reporter. Maybe that unofficial status loosened tongues. Joe Galano spoke of setting up an entirely American relief operation on the Island of Principe, just north of São Tomé and part of the same island group. It had an airport and a harbor. Joe said he had unlimited resources and money from the New York office of Catholic Relief Services. They wanted to get involved in a big way, and they had six Blackburn Beverlies ready and waiting for orders to go. The Blackburn Beverly was a British cargo plane designed for operation in remote bush locations on short runways. It had a cargo capacity of 25 tons, more than double that of a DC-7 and fast enough to make two shuttles a night into Biafra. The RAF had just decommissioned the planes in 1967. Joe said he had offered the six planes to the church airlift on São Tomé, but Nordchurchaid declined, hoping instead to get C-130 Hercules aircraft from the U.S. government. C-130s would have been an excellent aircraft for Biafra relief, but they were very expensive and not readily available. Since Nordchurchaid refused the planes, Joe wanted to start his own American airlift from Principe, and he wanted us UNICEF volunteers to join him.

Another fellow, a massive Norwegian commonly known as Paul Bunyan, wanted to talk. A former army major, he had been working in Biafra for months constructing and expanding runways. I mentioned Joe Galano's plan to him. He got very upset that Nordchurchaid had refused the planes. I told him that Axel Duch had offered the excuse that the undercarriage of the Blackburn Beverly was too low for the airstrip at Uli.

"Axel Duch has never even seen a Blackburn Beverly," he thundered. "I know those planes very well, and they're perfect for Uli." He said he would stir up some waves and see if he could get some action. I thought that such a very large man could stir up some mighty waves, but nothing ever came of it.

Paul Bunyan was concerned about the coming carbohydrate famine. He felt that the airlift would not be adequate to deal with it. I asked him if he thought some jet fighters would help. Yes, but they weren't necessary. Biafra needed to break out to a port like Opobo, but even if they opened a corridor from the coast to the enclave, it would be difficult to keep it open and keep the food moving. It would require 5000 lorries, he said, and enormous quantities of fuel. The roads would have to be kept in repair. Instead, Biafrans could learn from the Viet Cong and North Vietnamese by transporting a lot of food by bicycle in a steady trickle through the bush. Even at that time much of the water supply for Umuahia was being brought in by bicycle in old kerosene tins.

First, Biafra would have to clear Nigerians out of the way. This too would be done with bicycles, as two-man mortar teams carrying the mortars, base plates, and rockets on the bikes would filter through the bush, attack Nigerian set positions, and fade back into the bush. Paul Bunyan worked for the churches, but he was giving some advice to the Biafran army on the sly.

Paul Bunyan spilled some other interesting information about where Biafra was getting its arms. The French were flying them in, but the French were buying them cheap from the Israelis, who had captured them from the Egyptians the year before in the Six Day War. Egyptian pilots were flying Russian-made MiGs against Biafra, and Biafra was fighting back with Egyptian weapons made in Russia.

The number of people crowded into Biafra was enormous, according to Bunyan. When he was out in the bush he would see people everywhere.

"When you go behind a tree to take a piss," he said, "you find you're not behind it at all, but in front of it." There was a steady stream of people walking up and down the roads, seemingly with nothing else to do. When Egyptian pilots flew over during the day and strafed, they could shoot anywhere, and they were bound to hit a lot of people.

Late in the afternoon, we went looking for a secluded beach. We followed a bush road down to the coast beyond the airport. We found a bay in what looked like an old deserted plantation, a rundown boarded-up old house. It was a beautiful place to swim. The beach faced east, and to the right was the end of the runway. The ground at the end of the runway dropped sharply off to the narrow beach below. We got there about four o'clock. At 4:15 the first aircraft took off, the slow old C-46 of Fred Olsen. Fifteen minutes later a DC-7 took off. We couldn't see the planes until they were airborne, since the beach was below the level of the runway. We could see the tail going overhead, so we could identify the type of aircraft. We heard a third plane roaring down the runway, and we waited to see what it was. It had a large up-sweeping tail with three vertical stabilizers, characteristic of a Super Constellation. When we saw it, we all shouted. It was the legendary Biafran Grey Ghost. It flew from Lisbon to São Tomé, carrying arms, refueled, and took off for Biafra. Seldom seen, it was one of Hank Wharton's original planes, along with the church-owned DC-7s. Sometimes the Grey Ghost returned from Biafra to São Tomé to pick up another load of arms, from a secret warehouse, which we never saw.

We watched a couple more planes take off, swam some more, then walked north along the beach watching the sand crabs. There were also hermit crabs that crawled into abandoned shells to make their homes. Shells were everywhere, along with great rocks. We reached a point where the shore turned abruptly to the west. Out across the bay from there we could see two steep mountain peaks of an island known as *Ilha das Cabras*, the Island of Goats. Toward evening the setting sun enflamed the clouds behind those peaks in an incredibly beautiful display. We walked along into a jungly tangle of trees and heard chattering, like the sound of monkeys. But the sounds were the voices of beautiful white birds, like small flamingos, beginning to roost in the trees for the night. Another DC-6 took off.

As we looked west along the northern coast, we saw *Vrai Afrique*, a vision of what we imagine as the true Africa: palm trees, rainforest, jungle, in the peaceful afterglow of sunset, unlike the vision behind us of that geometric, too clean, too quiet, too regimented little city and the far off nasty little war connected to it.

Later, back at Bar Enrique, I talked to Ziggy, the Icelandic flight engineer. It was his birthday. He had the night off, and he was getting very drunk. He started talking about offloading the planes in Biafra. It was slow. Sometimes they had to kick the food out of the planes themselves so they could get out of there.

"I told all them dumb niggers to get off the plane," he said.

"Ziggy, knock it off! Don't talk like that!" I said. He was a big guy, but he slumped down in his chair, contrite. He said that, in Iceland, there are no black people, so they didn't have any bad feelings about race. He had heard those words from Americans, and because we were Americans, he was talking that way for our benefit. He seemed sincerely ashamed, but I don't know if he actually talked like that to Biafran fatigue workers, or just said he did, for our benefit.

On Sunday, two weeks after I arrived on São Tomé, and after one week of work in the warehouses, we were officially denied clearance to work in Biafra as offloaders. A Telex from Biafra declared us "unacceptable." Our door to Biafra closed.

The five of us sat around a table at Bar Enrique and talked it over. Why were we acceptable before and unacceptable now? Because we were Americans? Because we were with UNICEF? We decided to continue working in the warehouses until they were straightened out, then one by one we would all fade out and go home by various ways. Leo and Larry would probably stay for a while. Jerry had been there about a month and he was going stir crazy. He would leave. Barry would leave. I would leave and go home if I didn't soon find some way into Biafra. We plotted how to get off the island. It looked like that could be as difficult as getting into Biafra. We had sent off a number of telegrams to the UNICEF office saying, "SEND RETURN TICKETS STOP." No answer. Then we sent another: "SEND DOLLAR EQUIVALENT OF RETURN TICKETS TODAY REPEAT TODAY STOP." We got all worked up composing other telegrams as a way of venting steam, such as, "GREEN WEENIE HURTS STOP MIND BLOWN STOP OUT OF BREAD STOP SEND MONEY FAST STOP." We did not send those. I remember the consternation we had felt last month back in the Committee office when we received the telegram from São Tomé saying, "SEND NO MORE VOLUNTEERS." Jan and Nellie and the others were probably shaking their heads and wondering what was going on. We did receive a telegram responding to some previous request we had forgotten about. It no longer made any sense. Long distance communication gets garbled. And frustrating.

Having a dollar equivalent of airfare on a commercial airline would give us some flexibility. There was a weekly commercial flight from São Tomé to Angola to Lisbon to New York. But there were other ways. We could catch a ride on one of the Transavia Boeings going back to Amsterdam and from there an Icelandic Airways flight to New York. When Tom was deported he was put on The Grey Ghost directly back to Lisbon. He was practically broke; it would have been useful to have some traveling money.

Then there was the question of the six-month contract we had signed with UNICEF. To resign, we had to give thirty days' notice. It seemed prudent to me to send in my 30 days' notice of resignation. After thirty days, if the situation on São Tomé hadn't changed, I'd be home for Christmas. If something did break, I could fire off a cable and cancel it. So I resigned. That was the first time I resigned from UNICEF.

As the saying goes, "When one door closes, another door opens." There was the possibility that we could fly as crew, as offloaders, with the planes, help unload them, then return to São Tomé with them. We wouldn't be able to stay in Biafra or leave the airstrip, but we could do what we were recruited to do. Maybe I would be able to send letters from there to people I knew, like Mr. Nsofor, and maybe somebody could meet me there. Hope for that was shallow. Personally, I was very upset. To be called "mass murderers" by Nordchurchaid was a joke; to be "unacceptable" to Biafra hurt.

On Monday, November 4, we learned that flying to Biafra as crew was also impossible. The thirty-day resignation period made sense. Although I was not in the action, I was close to it and I was learning a lot about Biafra and the airlift. My only real function was recording my observations on tape, and something very interesting was breaking, directly related to our exclusion from Biafra.

DC-6 Takeoff

CHAPTER 6

Ana m Abia

I'm Coming

Late in 1968, Nigeria tried to knock out Uli. MiGs would fly down the runway at 50 feet in daylight and drop two bombs. Often the bombs would land sideways and not detonate. When the bombs did explode, it would take hours for Biafran crews to fix the holes, delaying the relief flights. By November, Nigeria tried night bombing. They dropped small bombs by throwing them out the door of a twin engine DC-3, usually missing the runway. Later, they dropped 500-pound bombs from a larger DC-4 flying at 15,000 feet, above anti-aircraft range. These bombs fell through shifting air currents and seldom came near the runway. Relief air crews (like ours from São Tomé) defied the bombs and kept landing. The International Committee of the Red Cross (ICRC) flying out of Fernando Po kept coming. The French Red Cross kept flying from Libreville. (The French Red Cross established Doctors Without Borders for Biafra, and the organization continues to provide medical assistance in places of desperate need today.) Biafran government planes carrying military supplies flew into Uli from Lisbon, Libreville, Rhodesia, South Africa, and Israel. All these planes converged in darkness to a road in the Biafran rain forest. Some of the aircraft disappeared over the ocean without a trace while others crashed on landing. Some bombs found their mark. By a wrinkle of fate, there were no midair collisions in the dark. But over 18 months enough air crews dared the peril to make a dark bush road near Uli one of the busiest airports in Africa, while Nigeria was trying to destroy it.

1

The Biafran Air Force decided to take control of all operations at Uli, everything. According to the missionaries running the airlift, the Air Force wanted to unload the aircraft, put the supplies on their own lorries, take them off the airstrip, and give them to the relief organizations out there. They wanted no missionaries, no Europeans on the airstrip at all, except for the pilots, copilots, and flight engineers, and maybe one representative from each of the relief operations – Red Cross, Caritas, WCC. Up to this point, it had been missionaries supervising the unloading and distribution. When they heard about the Air Force announcement, they went berserk. Missionaries assumed that the Air Force would give the food to the army, not the people.

The Europeans running the relief operation, the Germans, the Danes, the Swiss, the Swedes, the Irish, the Catholics, the Protestants often didn't trust each other, and all together they didn't trust Africans, on São Tomé or in Biafra. They considered the Portuguese only a half-step above the Africans. Only Europeans could be trusted to distribute relief supplies according to their ideas of fairness.

The relief organization insisted that "we are bringing in the food and medicine for the women and children only. The rest of it is not our business." They would not give even a scrap of it to the guys unloading the planes for them, and they paid the workers nothing. They complained that the unloading was very slow, but if the missionaries had observed the custom of *dash*, tipping, it might have gone faster. Fatigue workers, the Biafran soldiers who unloaded the planes, could not work well when they were weak from hunger and debased by European condescension.

The relief services were in a bind, and they had bound themselves. If they raised money, and people gave money, on the premise that it would be used only for women and children, they had to stick to it or lose their funding. It was too rigid. The Nigerian Army attacked the whole population with warplanes, artillery, and starvation. To save the people, relief organizations needed to feed all the people. They needed to compensate the people who helped distribute the food to the women and children and those who defended their women and children. The churches paid white pilots $1000 a night while black fatigue workers got nothing. It would not have hurt to give the workers a stockfish or two a night, or a bale a week for the group of them.

Survival of some of the people depended on survival of all of the people. Life is the main thing. *Ndu bu isi.*

I don't know whether the Biafran Air Force intended to snatch all the food for themselves, or whether they were tired of being treated like children who couldn't be trusted to manage their own lives. Some relief workers I met, missionaries and others, acted with genuine regard for Biafrans as individuals. Others were ramrod paternalistic, compelled by their religion to help the poor and suffering in the name of God. Many of these openly disdained or detested Biafrans. It was an abstract duty, and the objects of their charity were irrelevant.

Here we come to the core meaning of the Biafran Airlift. There is a larger dichotomy than race, a longer spectrum than white to black; race is a subsection of it. Following Biafra, in my path through life, I observed this larger truth: if you are okay within yourself, if you are firm in your worth and if you are content with where you stand in the universe, you have no need to prop yourself up by the denigration of others. Once secure in your stand, you can look out of yourself and notice others with the same grounding, even across a divide of culture or religion. Even in a strange land, a brother may be found.

For some who engage in charity, I think that there is a set of expected behaviors between those who give help and those who receive it. Giving and receiving become one composite event. The givers see themselves as somehow "above" those who receive, and they expect some acknowledgement of that status. Years later, when I worked in a deli on Second Avenue in New York, a man brought a bum in off the street and ordered a "hero" sandwich for him. I piled extra meat on it, knowing what was coming. As the bum ate, he kept his head down and flicked his eyes up to his benefactor once in a while. The giver of the food then expected that he had the privilege, or the burden, to lecture the man on his life and how he should improve himself. More years later, when I worked in a mental hospital, a patient told me that he felt as if the staff did not want him to get better, because then they would not be "better" than he was. Their own needs required that distinction. The race, infirmity, or poverty of others is a vacant excuse to lift oneself out of one's own inadequacies. The bum and the patient were victims of charity.

Biafrans broke the symmetry of that expected behavior by maintaining their dignity and thereby annoying those who expected subservience.

There are times when some of us need help. There must be a balance in giving and receiving aid: giving with humility and receiving with dignity. Both must be done with grace, and trust. In Biafra, I observed the full spectrum of human motivational behaviors. The world is deep.

In response to the Biafran Air Force assumption of control at Uli, the relief groups shut down the airlift. On the night of November 4-5 they did not fly. By coincidence, it was Ojukwu's birthday. There were parties over at Biafra House on São Tomé. We weren't invited, of course.

Jerry, Leo, Larry, Barry, and I remembered the speech directed at us by Mollerup in which he said, "Anybody who in any way hinders or slows up one flight or portion of a flight of food or medicine into Biafra could be considered a mass murderer." Who were the mass murderers now? With a sense of gleeful retribution, we refused to work in the warehouses that day. The previous day we had sweated our nuts off moving things around in the warehouses and unloading a ship. This day we lounged around, read, listened to Larry's radio. I made a tape. No one took note of our little work stoppage, and it had no effect whatsoever on the final outcome.

In a prickly mood, we went looking for Herr Friedle to intimidate him.

"Since UNICEF seconded us to you, it's your responsibility to get us a car."

"Yes. Yes," he said. By the end of the day, he had rented a car for us, a black Peugeot 403 sedan.

After a one-night stand-down, the missionaries in Biafra sent a Telex to São Tomé telling Nordchurchaid to resume the airlift.

I went right to Joe Galano.

"Who won?" I asked.

"Presumably, we did," he said.

"Who do you mean by 'we'?" That backed him up for a moment while he considered the implications of the question.

"The relief operation," he answered.

2

Flights resumed the night of November 5-6. Before the first flight, Nigeria radio warned our planes not to fly, because they were going to attack Uli that night. They had promised that once before and then attacked a hospital. Our planes flew. During the second shuttle, around 1:00 a.m., a bomb landed near one of our DC-7s.

The pilot, Captain Baekstrom, was sitting in the cockpit along with the flight engineer. Father Desmond McGlade, who had supervised the unloading, was still on board. The Biafran fatigue workers were finished unloading the plane and were standing near it with Olsen, the copilot, when the bomb hit.

Twelve Biafrans were killed immediately; four later died in hospital. More were wounded. Olsen suffered extensive wounds to his legs and feet. He was flown to Fernando Po, the Red Cross base, for surgery to save his legs.

Shrapnel ripped through the skin of the plane and hit Captain

Baekstrom in both legs. The flight engineer was unhurt. Father McGlade suffered a slight injury and remained in Biafra. Ragged holes peppered the right side of the fuselage and tail, and one tire was flattened. Two engines were leaking oil badly from damaged oil coolers. While Baekstrom's legs were bandaged, the flight engineer inspected the plane. Number three engine was leaking so badly it was useless. Number four was leaking dangerously, though not as badly as number three. The two men conferred and decided they would try to fly the plane back to São Tomé.

I have no record of what the two men discussed, but one thing had to be this: can a four-engine plane fly with the loss of two engines *on the same side of the plane*? The answer would be *no* or *maybe* depending on which side of the plane. It has to do with the conservation of angular momentum and the moment of inertia of a body in the shape of an airplane. Think of a helicopter. If it had only one large blade above the body, the blade would whirl in one direction and the body in the other, slower in proportion to the difference in mass between the blade and the body. Helicopters have a long tail with a small propeller on the end of it to counter the rotation of the main blades, conserving angular momentum. A single-engine propeller plane has a tendency to counterrotate opposite to the spin of the propeller, which turns clockwise on an American-built airplane, seen from the cockpit. It is a small effect and it is not noticed when the plane is taxiing, because the ground resists the plane's rotation. As it lifts off, the turning propeller and the moment of inertia of the plane cause a slight yaw to the left. But the pilot knows to give it a little right rudder to compensate.

For a four-engine plane, with all the propellers turning clockwise, the tendency of the plane is to rotate counterclockwise; that is, to keep the right wing *up*. With two engines out on the right side, and a lot of help from the rudder, the plane could fly. With two engines out on the left, the left wing would be forced *down* and the big plane would spiral out of control. The DC-7's damaged engines were on the right side.

So it was possible to fly it but also extremely dangerous. Why even try? The plane had been hit by a bomb. It was a casualty of war. Write it off. But this was not a military operation like the Berlin Airlift, where many more planes were waiting to replace the ones lost. There were few planes flying relief to Biafra at that time. Of the original five DC-7s in the airlift, one was in Lisbon, and one was already destroyed on the ground in Biafra, not far from where the crippled plane stood. That plane had been slightly damaged when an incoming plane clipped it on landing. The crew left it at Uli to be repaired the next day, but Nigerian planes destroyed it on the ground and would surely do the same to this plane. If Baekstrom's plane were lost, it would be a significant reduction in the airlift capacity, up to thirty tons of food a night. Captain Baekstrom would be paid $500 for this flight; the engineer, $300 — not enough money for such a risk. Why did they do it? What, other than money, motivates people to risk their lives saving others?

They took off with three engines. When he got up to altitude, Baekstrom shut down number four and flew with two engines on the same side of the aircraft. He set the rudder trim tab to maximum. Nominal flight time between Biafra and São Tomé for a DC-7 was one and a half hours. On two engines it took longer. At 3:00 a.m. the tower in São Tomé received a radio call that the plane was coming in, in trouble. Crash crews scrambled. As he approached São Tomé, Baekstrom started engine four again for landing. He brought the plane in safely. He was taken directly to the hospital for immediate surgery to remove the shrapnel from his legs.

The next morning I walked around the plane with the mechanics and some other pilots, examining the damage. By the spray pattern of the holes in the side of the plane and the engines, we estimated that the bomb had hit fifteen feet from the plane, just forward of the tail. Given the proximity of the impact, the bomb could not have been very large; a 500-pound bomb would have blown the plane to bits. I listened to pilots speculating about the kind of bomb it was and the kind of plane that dropped it. Many thought it was too small to be a bomb at all and must have been a mortar shell. I asked Leo what he thought. He had seen bomb and shell damage in World War II. He thought a large bomb would have made bigger holes and done more damage. A flight engineer who had been in the air at the time of the attack said that he had looked around and saw no other plane at all. Some pilots had seen the outline of it and swore it was a DC-3. Others saw the plane by moonlight and said that it had a big square tail, unlike a DC-3. They concluded it was a Russian LI-2, a World War II copy of a DC-3. It had no bomb racks, so the bombs had to be shoved out the door by hand. And that is the reason they were using twenty-pound bombs. That night and others some of the bombs did not explode. They fell in the bush, and Biafran Air Force ordinance people, working with Johnny Correa, collected them, defused them, and refurbished them. They stockpiled them for use someday when they had a plane from which to drop them. The bombs were twenty to fifty pounds, many stamped "Made in Poland 1941."

One of the Danish mechanics said that he saw the boots that copilot Olsen had been wearing when he was hit. They were shredded. Father Byrne flew to Fernando Po to see him the night after the raid. The operation saved the guy's legs, but his feet were messed up.

Other than the DC-7 destroyed on the ground during a daylight attack, Baekstrom's DC-7 was the first plane hit in an air raid at night. Unlike

Baekstrom, other flight crews were afraid to fly under this new threat. All but one of the Transavia crews packed up and returned to Europe. French arms pilots refused to fly. The night following the air raid, November 6, Captain Tom Delahunt flew a church DC-7 into Biafra with a load of stockfish. Barry, Larry, Leo, and I had used our new car to go to the movies, and when we got out of the show, we heard Delahunt taking off again for the second shuttle. We drove out to the airport. I saw the flight orders for the next day. That DC-7 would try for three shuttles and Fred Olsen's C-46 would fly two.

The church pilots, Captain Delahunt, an American; Captain Mic Nolan, a Laplander; Captain Tangen, a Norwegian; and Captain McCombie, a Scotsman, kept the airlift going with two planes – Tango Alpha Bravo and Tango Alpha Delta. Fred Olsen's smaller, slower twin engine C-46 steadfastly kept flying, a constant throughout all the turmoil of the airlift. Transavia's one remaining crew flew two shuttles every other night, too exhausted to fly every night. After a couple of weeks, Transavia brought down four more crews from Europe to resume flying their three DC-6s every night. Transavia served the airlift for 18 months, from the first flight to the last.

On the night of November 5, a few hours before the air raid, Barry and I had taken our car for a ride along the coast and stopped by the seashore. There was a full moon, a bright night; clouds drifted over the face of the moon, but it was generally bright. We stood on a rock ledge, apart, watching the sea foam in as the waves broke, rolled up among the rocks, the foam shining in the moonlight, shattering in a thousand shimmering patches and hisses. The moonlight glinted along the curl of the breakers. There was no more beautiful sight in the world than that.

We stood there for a long time, just watching the sea. While we were there, an aircraft landed, an aircraft took off. The timing was right – it could have been Baekstrom heading out on his second, and final, shuttle.

I walked up along the beach. I saw something lying there, like a dog or something. I approached it. I heard a big noise of scurrying, scratching. What I saw was a dead pig, a drowned pig rocking back and forth in the roll of the breakers, with a mass of large crabs chewing on it, devouring it. I just looked at that thing, that carcass, and I looked out to sea, and I looked around. I walked back to Barry and said, "Let's go." On the way back to town, I told him what I had seen.

"Perhaps in everything beautiful that there is, somewhere in it there is a dead pig."

The other guys had gotten mail from home, but I hadn't. It heightened my sense of loneliness and frustration. The mail plane from Luanda came in once a week. On Thursday, November 7, it came in on time. After work, I went to the Post Office. I looked through the little glass in Box 202 and I saw letters. But I didn't have a key. I didn't have my own box; it was a general Nordchurchaid mail drop. For two hours I ran around looking for the guy with the key. I pulled out a letter from Elner, and then I was happy. I would have to wait a week and hope for another. I told Elner to tell her students at Ocean Hill-Brownsville that I thought they were terrific, and that she and I would try to produce kids like them and bring them up to be great people.

We also got a long telegram from Fran Koster at the Committee for Nigeria/Biafra Relief. He said that UNICEF would increase our living allowance to $100 a week. They would be glad to send us return tickets or the dollar equivalent, but they wanted to know if we intended to resign, or if we just wanted it in case of emergency. We talked it over again. I decided to stick with my thirty-day notice, a tentative resignation with the option to cancel. Things changed so fast.

I started to make some friends at Biafra House, like Ben Maduke, but I hadn't met the Biafran Special Representative, Mr. Osuji. Maybe I would. Who knows what could happen? *Onye ma echi?*

Driving to the airport one day in our new car, we encountered a strange roadblock where the road ran along the bay. Millions of large crabs were migrating from the interior of the island to the ocean. They covered the road. We stopped. Another car passed us, crunching its way across that wriggling red river. More crabs marched over the crushed shells without pause. We waited. A while later, with no end in sight, we crossed too, slowly, like driving over a rutted road, the tires crunching and popping.

3

After two weeks in the warehouses, urgency gave way to order. The warehouses had been cleaned and the major items had all been sorted and moved to their designated locations. The gross inventory was done. The flow of goods from the port had been regularized. Edwardo and his crews were functioning smoothly. The UNICEF team had essentially worked itself out of a job. One day we stood outside a warehouse discussing this.

"There's no need for five of us here. One man could do this work," I said.

"That would be a mighty man," said Ben Maduke, my friend from

Biafra House.

When we went into the warehouses, we found ourselves with little to do but watch. Edwardo would report on the work and any problems. Edwardo pointed out that the salt in warehouse C was wet, so we had it moved to warehouse J next door, a dry place.

Feeling superfluous, we spent less and less time in the warehouses. We went swimming. I got a bad sunburn, disdaining all the suntan lotion in warehouse K. We hung around. We took our car touring around the island. The car gave us a tremendous sense of freedom, a quantum jump in the possibilities for life on São Tomé. We couldn't get into Biafra and we couldn't get off the island. We watched the big Boeing 707s come and go while we were stuck there. We named our car the *pequeno* Boeing, the small Boeing.

For Portugal, São Tomé island served as a remote location for a maximum-security prison. We never saw the prison, only a guarded gate by a road leading off into the distance. The Portuguese-owned plantations were a secondary use for the island. The African people of São Tomé were impoverished. They made a living as fishermen or laborers for the Portuguese. We felt the irony of all that food we were moving past local hungry people.

The city of São Tomé was on the northeast coast of the island. A road ran from there around the north coast and stopped. The other main road ran south from the city along the east coast to the southern town of *Porto Alegre*. No road encircled the island. The interior consisted of rugged volcanic peaks and deep rain forest. It would have made a great set for the movie *King Kong*. It would make a great set for some future movie.

On Saturday, we set out in our *pequeno* Boeing heading south with no particular destination. We passed breathtaking scenery and squalid fishing villages. For long stretches there were no signs of people, only rain forest. We kept riding, fascinated. Unlike the Hawaiian Islands which formed in a line, one at a time, as the Pacific plate moved over a hot spot below, São Tomé and Principe each erupted independently, eighteen million years apart, along a straight fault line. Out of the jungle on our right appeared a massive rock formation, a tower, a volcanic plug, the remaining hard core of a long eroded volcano, perhaps the one that formed the island thirteen million years ago. Clouds obscured the top of it. It was known as *Cão Grande* (the Great Dog). Africans we worked with had a more phallic name for it. At times, the road seemed like a tunnel through wild vegetation; at times, it followed switchbacks along the coastal cliffs, similar to the road to Hanna on Maui, or the Big Sur in California.

In the forest, a cat darted across the road, too big for a house cat, too small for a leopard. We guessed it was an ocelot or a lynx. There were no turn-offs in the road, so we kept going. We had no sense of scale, no sense of how far along the island we had come or how far it was yet to *Porto Alegre*. It was getting late in the afternoon. We were low on gas. There were no gas stations. Should we try to turn around or press on, hoping we might find gas if we made it to *Porto Alegre*? We kept on, watching the gas gauge get lower and lower. I felt a hint of thrill, imagining the possibility of being stranded in this wilderness. We spotted a bush road turning off to the left, down toward the east coast of the island. We followed it, hoping it would lead to some gas or at least a place to hole up for the night. After a long ride deeper into the bush and a nearly empty tank, we came to a plantation. Individual plantations along the coast ran vertically from the sea up into the interior, their boundaries defined by the switchbacks and jagged contours of the coastline, with no easy means of association across the diverse African populations.

The plantation we found was occupied by a small, old, hospitable Portuguese man. We saw no one else.

"*Bõa tarde, senhor*," said Larry. Larry was learning Portuguese faster than the rest of us. He had already been fluent in French.

"*Bõa tarde*," the man replied.

"*Gasolina?*" Larry asked, and gestured to our car. The man understood. He had a large tank with a hand pump. We filled our tank about half way, not wanting to leave him low, and asked how much he wanted for it.

"*Quanto?*"

"*Nada.*"

He would not take payment, but we gave him some money anyway, with a great deal of thanks.

"*Muito obrigado, senhor.*"

"*Nada.*"

When we passed *Cão Grande* on the way back, it was gray twilight. The Great Dog drifted by us on the left, a massive monolithic shape looming far above us out of the dark vegetation. It was almost terrifying, a huge overbearing apparition out of deep time.

On Sunday evening, we splurged and ate dinner at Café Yong. Most of the European relief workers ate dinner every night at Yong. The menu included croquets, cold cuts, roast suckling pig, hors d'oeuvres, codfish cakes, chicken in the oven and in the spit, chicken soup, appetizers, lobster, shrimp, squid, crab, and other seafood. The waters around São Tomé served up a rich source of seafood. The wines were Rosé, Casal Garcia, Gatão, Moura Bastos, and Casal da Deveza. The beers were Amstel, Heineken, Cuca, Nocal, Laurentina, and Skol. Coffee and brandy were served after dinner. Usually we ate more humbly at Bar Enrique or at Senhor Costa's Café Equador or Café Palomar. But after dinner, we sought out the relief people where they aired all their war stories, gossip, speculation, complaints, and squabbles among the various factions on the island.

That evening after dinner, one of the pilots, Captain McCombie, threw a party for himself, his crew, and all his friends. It was his night off and he was spending a lot of money, about 1000 escudos, which was not a problem since he usually made three shuttles a night. Leo and I and the mechanics joined his party. Captain McCombie was 52 years old and big — wide rather than tall — with an enormous potbelly that crowded the pilot's seat in a DC-7. That night he was boisterous and crude; I was not impressed. He bought drinks for everybody, mostly scotch.

Leo and I and the mechanics drank Cuca beer.

Many people from the airlift were there that night. Heinz Raab, McCombie's copilot, was there with his wife. Raab's wife was a tall, slim, sexy-looking woman, taller by a head than Raab himself. The way she dressed in red and carried herself exuded sex, whereas Raab himself was unremarkable. McCombie was throwing a drunk. He was loud, ridiculing all the "Eskimos" who worked on the airlift. "ESS-key-mohs," he said, drawing it out, referring to everyone born north of Germany, including Captain Mic Nolan, a Laplander, the Icelandic air crews, Captain Tangen and other Norwegians, and virtually all the mechanics, many of whom were Danes, and Arne, the Swede. But they were drinking his whiskey and didn't mind, laughing along with him. He was teasing me, too, because I was wearing a jumper, an African shirt. "Where did you get that wonderful shirt? I want it because all the Biafran girls will look at me when I go over there."

After McCombie wobbled off, the mechanics lingered and talked. They complained that they were badly overworked. DC-7s had the most powerful, sophisticated, high performance engines of all the propeller-driven commercial planes prior to the age of jets. Powerful, but finicky, they required daily maintenance. In addition, the mechanics had Baekstrom's damaged plane to deal with. It was full of holes; it had a blown tire; one engine needed to be replaced, and another one needed extensive repairs.

As they complained, Leo and I listened. With the warehouses in good order, we had little or nothing to do. A bizarre notion bubbled up out of my beer. What if we were to help? We were not aircraft mechanics, but we could turn a wrench. We could work under the direction of the real mechanics and relieve their burden somewhat. They must have been desperate, because they bought the idea right away. They told us to report for work the next morning. They didn't even ask us for any credentials.

Credentials: I didn't know about Leo, but I didn't have any. As a poor college student I had bought an old car for $150. My brother and I shared the cost. It was the worst car either of us ever had, and to keep it running we were forced to become mechanics. Once, with my dad's help, we had to pull the engine, disconnecting everything that mated it to the car. We pulled the valves and rings and pistons and had the cylinders re-bored. Most Cornell students dreamed of standing on the cliffs high above Cayuga's waters on graduation day and throwing their alarm clocks into the lake. I dreamed of sending that car into the lake. But I learned how to turn a wrench, how to use my hands.

On Monday, November 11, 1968, thanks in part to McCombie, I became a junior aircraft mechanic. Igbos say, *Chinyere m aka*. God gave me hands.

I reported to the flight line, stunned by my own audacity. What was I getting myself into now? Jumping into unknown puddles with both feet was a problem that I would face most of my life. The chief flight engineer, a man named Sagwick, signed us up.

The road from São Tomé approached the airport from the south. The runway ran roughly east and west. Visible to landing pilots, large numbers were painted on the ends of the runway, 1 1 (One-One) on the western end and 2 9 (Two-Nine) on the eastern end by the ocean. The numbers told the pilots what their compass heading should be; that is, if the pilot were coming in at the 2 9 end, approaching from the sea, he should be on a heading of 290 degrees. 270 degrees would be due west. The terminal with its tower and the hangars were all to the south of the runway. The two DC-7s that were still flyable were parked near the hangars. The damaged plane was parked out of the way on the northern side of the runway.

"Change the tire on Lima," I was told. The mechanics called the planes by names derived from their registration numbers. When Hank Wharton originally bought these old planes for the purpose of clandestine gun running, he gave them fake registration numbers. When the churches bought the planes from Wharton, they kept the same numbers. This one was 5T-TAL. To avoid confusion over possibly faint or garbled radio transmissions, pilots use internationally recognized names for the letters. Baekstrom's plane was Five Tango-Tango Alpha Lima. The other two DC-7s still flying were Tango Alpha Bravo and Tango Alpha Delta.

Change the tire. I looked at that huge plane sitting there on its landing gear and couldn't imagine how anyone could possibly do that. When a plane is flying, lift generated by the wing holds it up. On the ground the landing gear holds the wing up. If you lift the wheels up to change the tires, what holds the wing up? *How* do you lift the wheels up? Changing a car tire is simple. Our *pequeno* Boeing blew a tire soon after we got it, and

I changed it in minutes.

"Use a wing jack," said Helmut, the chief mechanic. "There's one in the hangar." It was a very tall jack, and strong, but otherwise similar to a car jack. It inserted into a slot in the wing near the landing gear strut.

"One day we parked a plane off the ramp on the ground," Helmut told me. "It rained. The ground turned to mud, and the plane sank in over the wheels. We had to wait for the mud to dry, and then use a wing jack to lift the plane out." That was why, at Uli, it was important to have the aluminum grating for the parking fingers.

After changing the tire, Leo and I pulled the damaged oil coolers out of engines three and four on Lima. The mechanics supervised, but we had to do it ourselves so that we could learn how to remove the coolers from the plane at Uli, where we would have no supervision. Leo and I had volunteered to go into Biafra, recover spare parts from the destroyed plane, and use them to get Lima flying again. The other mechanics refused to do that, because it was too dangerous, and they weren't being paid enough. Leo and I would be paid $50 for each night we worked in Biafra and $25 a day for working on São Tomé. Caritas paid the mechanics.

But even that plan was put on hold because of a new round of bombing at Uli. When Lima had been hit the week before, there was a bright full moon, and targets on the ground were easy to see. There were no more attacks for a few days, then Nigeria started a new tactic. According to Johnny Correa, the MiGs would fly down the runway at 50 feet just before dark, dropping two bombs, just as our first flights were due. The bombs often hit sideways and didn't go off. Johnny's team would defuse them and save them for later. When the bombs exploded, the first flights had to hold while the runway was repaired. Most of them had to return to São Tomé to refuel. Helmut would not allow Leo and me to go in until the situation stabilized.

The mechanics were licensed in categories of Power Plant, Airframe, and Instrumentation. Helmut, the chief mechanic, was Danish. Nielsson was a Dane and a few of the others, whose names I don't remember, ranging in age from twenty to forty, were Danes. Arne was the Swede, Ben the young Israeli, Smyth the Englishman, and Hans the German. Besides the Europeans, eleven Africans worked as laborers and help mechanics.

As I was walking from Lima to the hangar, I noted an African crew working on another DC-7. One guy was standing on a ladder up by an engine and another was on the ground by a toolbox. Both were light skinned compared to the other Africans. The one on the ladder reached his hand down and spoke to the other.

"*Nove semicolcheias*," he said, asking for a nine-sixteenths wrench. I had picked up enough Portuguese by then to realize what he was saying, given the context. Since this was an American-built plane, tool sizes were in fractions of an inch.

"*Wait small*," said the guy on the ground. That was Pidgin English. I stopped and turned around to look at him. He was in his twenties, thin, with hollow cheeks and a small straight mustache. He smiled, showing uneven teeth.

"Are you from Biafra?" I asked.

"No. Cape Verde." The Cape Verde Islands were another Portuguese possession in the Atlantic Ocean off the West Coast of Africa near Dakar, Senegal. I introduced myself.

"*Me name Valario*," he said in reply. He pointed to the guy on the ladder, who was older, heavier, and shirtless, with a bushy mustache. "*Na me broda, Oscara.*" The brothers were working as help mechanics on the airlift. People of European descent came from all over the world to work on the Biafran Airlift. So did people from all along the West Coast of Africa.

After work, I was a sight, covered from head to foot in grease and oil, grimy and grubby-looking. I hadn't had a haircut yet and my long hair was twisted and tangled, full of dirty oil. So was my mustache. So were my khaki shirt and pants and boots. I smelled like oil. I scrubbed up, changed clothes, and went to see Father Byrne. He did not yet know about this job change. Serving in the Peace Corps far from supervision, we had learned to act independently, to do whatever was needed when it was needed. I wanted to inform him, but mainly I wanted to request a transfer from Nordchurchaid jurisdiction to Caritas, as were the other mechanics.

Father Byrne greeted me warmly. He said he was very pleased with the work we had been doing in the warehouses. I told him that the initial organization had been accomplished and that the continuing operation needed only one of us, or at most two. The rest of us had essentially nothing to do. The Portuguese and indigenous laborers were doing all the real work at this point.

I said, "We have heard that five more people were being brought down from Norway to work in the warehouses."

"Wonderful!" he said. "There should be twenty more!" [*I felt that there was some bias involved; that is, Europeans thought that Africans and Portuguese – who were considered only a half-step above Africans – were not capable of managing anything. If a European were not in charge, nothing would get done*].

I told Father Byrne that Leo and I had found jobs as help mechanics with the church's DC-7s. I asked him to cable UNICEF and have us officially transferred from Nordchurchaid to Caritas. Abruptly, that changed his attitude. He was extremely upset. He considered the warehouse organization to be essential.

"What concerns you?" I asked him.

"I want inventory. I want to know where everything is. I want to know what commodities are in what warehouse, what quantities, the tonnage of major items!"

I was surprised. I said, "We already know all that. You mean, you don't know it? We have been passing the information up through channels. If you haven't received it, we will give you a detailed report in the morning."

I said to him, "The only reason we are here is to go into Biafra and help there. We are not here to make money, or just hang around with nothing to do. If we can't work as mechanics or do something meaningful, we'd just rather go home." After a heavy pause, I said, "What do you think?"

"It's not up to me to make the decision. It's up to the Chief of Operations." That would be a man named Erla. Father Byrne could do anything he wanted on São Tomé. He was just dodging the issue. "All I can do is give my opinion." I knew that in his opinion it was a bad idea. From his point of view, it could look like a terrible idea: these untrained guys becoming sudden mechanics. From the point of view of a Peace Corps Volunteer, who had learned self-reliance and easy transition from skill to skill, changing jobs did not feel unnatural.

Later, I went to see Erla, Chief of Operations. He said that he had just come from talking to Father Byrne. I explained to him what we had accomplished in the warehouses and what we felt could be done next with fewer people. Leo and I were no longer necessary in the warehouses, but Larry and Barry could do what was needed now, and possibly only Larry soon. Jerry was fed up; he planned to leave for Amsterdam on the Boeing Wednesday.

Erla said, "When the warehouses were in bad shape, it was necessary for a team of people to go in there as a tour-de-force to straighten things out. Once the inertia was overcome, a few could carry on. If it is your opinion that things are now at that stage, you are very welcome to come to work at the airport. You are badly needed there. As far as I'm concerned, you can do this. I will have to talk to all parties concerned, including Father Byrne."

I thanked him and said, very respectfully, "I want to make it clear that I don't want to be involved in any rivalries, or to cause bad feeling between one group and another." This was a touchy situation. Tom Hebert had been evicted from the island for being uncooperative and critical of the leadership. I was standing heavily in his shoes.

"I understand," Erla said.

Missionaries came in different flavors; they were not all alike. Father Cunningham had been in Biafra a long time and had come out recently to coordinate things with Father Byrne. Where Father Byrne had a large, flamboyant personality, Father Cunningham spoke more softly, but he spoke a lot. He liked to tell us all the gossip and information from inside Biafra. We liked to listen.

Father Cunningham had been at the front recently and had witnessed an exchange between Biafran and Nigerian troops, not of gunfire, but of food. About thirty yards apart, Nigerians were hurling yams to the Biafrans and Biafrans were throwing oranges to the Nigerians. Biafra was surrounded and compressed into an enclave, but Nigerian troops had some problems of their own with long supply lines. They were getting plenty of beer but not enough fruit. Johnny adds, "On Fridays, it was difficult to get anybody to go to the front on either side — the Nigerians were getting entertainment on their lines and we had entertainment too at camp or in town."

The airlift supplied food and medicine to Biafra, but there were smuggling routes as well, overland through the bush and across the Niger River. It was possible to buy a beer in Biafra, at $5 a bottle, about twenty times the pre-war price.

Father Cunningham expressed skepticism about the outcome of the war. Biafrans were getting enough arms, but they were inept at using them without trained leadership. Most of the field commanders, about 250 junior Igbo officers, had been shot during the July coup. Others, however, such as the Fourth Commando Brigade led by mercenary Rolf Steiner, a former Hitler Youth, were capable fighters. Powerful not only against the Nigerian army but also within Biafra, they took whatever they wanted, whether food from the relief convoys leaving Uli or weapons from the regular army. Steiner's commandos commandeered two Red Cross jeeps and placed their skull and crossbones insignia on the hoods, real skulls and crossed human bones. According to Father Cunningham and other sources, friction between the commandos and the regular army led to disasters on the battlefield.

Father Cunningham's dejection affected me. He spoke of desperation and panic in Biafra, ugliness and psychotic reactions. Once-high morale was breaking down. By Christmas, one million people could suddenly die due to the carbohydrate famine. His depression was making me depressed. Did I really want to go into Biafra and see all that happening to my friends and students? I vacillated from day to day. Maybe I should go home.

Maybe I should see if the mechanic job led somewhere.

Tuesday morning Father Byrne got his reports. Herr Friedle and the Chief of Police inspected all the warehouses. The police had been very concerned about the condition of the warehouses, possibly because of sanitation and security. Larry said that at times he couldn't "leave the warehouse because there are workers but no guard and the police are very careful that nothing gets out to form a black market." The Chief of Police and the Governor of the island were very pleased with the situation they found. Mona Mollerup, in her telegram to UNICEF explaining Tom Hebert's eviction, also said, "THE OTHER FIVE ARE DOING AN EXCELLENT JOB ON THE WAREHOUSES AND THE GOVERNOR HAS EXPRESSED HIS APPRECIATION FOR THEIR EFFORTS."

Erla came to me as I was working on the flight line and asked if I was happy as a mechanic. "Oh, yes!" I said.

"Is everybody else happy?" he asked, referring to Caritas, Nordchurchaid, WCC, Danes, Germans, Americans, Portuguese, and all the other cliques and factions on the island.

"As far as I know, yes, but I don't know for certain."

"I want to tell you that we appreciate you being here at the airport as mechanics, very much, and there is plenty for you to do. I want you to be happy here."

But Father Byrne was not so easy to please. He called for some high level people to come down from New York and Europe to check it out. It was not good to have Father Byrne mad at you.

4

On my second day as a mechanic, I worked with Hans, the German, a power plant guy. He was a tall, muscular, blond, blue-eyed Aryan, and a skilled mechanic who worked diligently between trips to the airport canteen to get a beer. There was an oil leak in Bravo's number two engine. Most engines leaked oil most of the time, but this seemed to be a major leak – there was oil all over the inside of the engine, and it was dripping out, puddling on the hot pavement. We removed the engine cowlings and access panels and looked for the leak. Hans thought he had localized it, but he had to be sure. Oscara attached a spray nozzle to a large jar of 140-octane aviation gasoline, highly flammable. Regular car gasoline is 87 octane. Aviation gas, tinted purple, is so volatile that it makes your skin feel cold from evaporation when you get it on your hands. He sprayed the gas throughout the interior of the engine to wash out all the oil. Any new oil that appeared would be the source of the leak.

Hans went up on the aluminum ladder and peered into the engine. He thought he could see the source.

"Can you see that?" he said.

I got up on the ladder and looked in. "Yeah. I see what you mean," I said.

"Do you know how to run the engine?" he asked.

"Uh, no." I said, seriously intimidated by my own ignorance and the magnitude of what I was getting myself into, my second day on the job.

"Okay. Stand here. I will go and start the engine," he said.

"What?" I said.

"Stand here."

I was four or five feet behind the propeller. The huge main exhaust pipe was six inches above my head. My head was virtually inside the engine.

"What?" I said again.

"It's all right. It's all right," he said, shrugging his shoulders as if this were a common part of the job. An hour earlier I had seen another one of these engines start, with great clouds of smoke and flame blasting out. Oscara had just sprayed the interior of the engine with highly volatile gasoline, and fumes were still in the air. I looked at Hans incredulously, probably with fear in my eyes.

"No, it's all right." He scrambled up the ladder into the plane to start the engine.

I thought, well, you ought to know. So we'll see what happens.

Helmut came out of the hangar. He motioned me to get down off the ladder and move it aside while the engine was started.

"Hans told me to stay right here."

"Oh, no. Move away until after we start the engine. Then you come back and look in the engine while it is running."

"Okay," I said. That was fine with me. I got down off the ladder and carried it under the belly of the aircraft to the other side. I stood there while Helmut ran up the ladder to the cockpit. Hans ran back down. He cocked his eyebrow, shrugged, grabbed the ladder from me and took it right back to the engine. He climbed up and stuck his head in the engine just below the exhaust port. Helmut started the engine. Great clouds of smoke belched out, completely obscuring his head for a few seconds. When the smoke cleared, he was holding on as the prop wash blew his hair straight back from his head. For five minutes he calmly peered around in there. He signaled me to signal Helmut in the cockpit to cut the engine. I looked up to Helmut sitting at the cockpit window. I drew my finger across my throat in a cutting motion. The engine sputtered to silence, and the massive four-bladed propeller turned to a stop. Hans got down with oil splattered all over his face and his long blond hair.

Hans had found the leak.

As we worked to fix the leak, lorries began arriving with cargo for the evening's first shuttle. I watched workers load Fred Olsen's C-46, FOP, Foxtrot Oscar Poppa. The cargo was made up entirely of Father Food from warehouse K: onion soup, mushroom soup, jars of beats, peanut butter, boxes of pancake mix. Nothing for starving Biafran children.

"Do you know what they are loading in that plane?" I asked Hans.

"That is not interesting to me. I do not care what is in the plane." He cared nothing about Biafra. This was just another aviation job to him.

Fearless with his head in an engine, he was a bastard with people. In fact, Hans was an overt racist. He shoved the African workers out of his way. When he wanted something from one of African crew, he called, "*Preto! Preto!*" Portuguese for black. "*Preto e estupido!*" he grumbled, shaking his head. I saw him push an African on the shoulder, yelling, "Nigga!" After the third time he did it, I picked up a big pipe to hit him. But I didn't. He stopped abusing the guy in time for me to cool down. He would have taken the pipe away from me and killed me with it. Had I lived, I'd have been thrown off the island for assault. As it was, Hans soon disappeared from the island.

Reverend William Aitken came out of Biafra. He stayed at the same boarding house where we lived. About forty years old, under six feet tall but taller than I was, he was a Scottish protestant missionary in charge of the World Council of Churches operation at Uli, a position similar to Father Byrne's at Caritas. Neither flamboyant like Father Byrne nor pessimistic like Father Cunningham, Reverend Aitken was calm, quiet, and levelheaded.

Larry describes Reverend Aitken:

> I had known him when I visited another Peace Corps Volunteer at his school in Abakaliki before the war. Dr. Aitken was the principal. He was known as a very intelligent, serious man. He stayed in Biafra and led the operations at the airport every other night, then organized the delivery of food to starving women and children. He was at the airport through the bombings, the strafing by MiG jets, and the threat of capture by Nigerian soldiers as they moved in on the airport. The rumor was that he would not eat any more than was available to the people he was caring for. I saw him when he came out of Biafra on one of the last flights before the airport fell to the Nigerians. He was emaciated.

Reverend Aitken had some news for us. Steiner and his mercenaries had been evicted from Biafra. Under guard, they were escorted to an aircraft. Steiner was acting too high-handed with his commandos, stealing relief food and causing dissension between the commandos and the regular army.

Reverend Aitken also had a very interesting perspective on the palaver the previous week between the Biafran Air Force and the missionaries over control of the unloading at Uli. When Aitken and other missionaries went to the Biafran government and said they would stop the airlift, the Biafrans were very, very surprised. They didn't understand it. They had no intention of sidelining the missionaries. Until then the people who had been running the airstrip operations were old Nigeria Airways personnel who had been on the payroll ever since Nigeria became independent. They were civilians with no military discipline, so that when a plane flew over, even one of ours, they would run for bush. Some would never come back. That affected the efficiency of all airport operations, including the unloading. The Air Force sacked the civilians and took over the operation. Some missionaries overreacted to rumors, panicked, and Telexed São Tomé to stop flying. Reverend Aitken said that everyone was relieved to resolve that touchy situation.

On Wednesday, the Boeing came in from Amsterdam carrying cargo, mail, and dignitaries. A man named Kinney from UNICEF and a Monsignor from Germany arrived to check out the warehouses, probably in response to Father Byrne. Jerry was prepared to take the Boeing back to Amsterdam and catch a flight to New York. He was going to take a tape and some letters from me to Elner and give her a firsthand account of our life on São Tomé. But the Boeing was headed for Hong Kong, so he had to wait another frustrating week. I took the tape and the letters to the Post Office.

Leo and I went to work at the airport. I learned how to start an engine and how to operate the wing flaps. In the afternoon, Helmut approached us.

"You're going to Biafra," he said. "Get ready."

After we had spent nearly a month agonizing about getting clearance to go to Biafra, it turned out to be absurdly simple. Erla asked Mr. Osuji at Biafra House if he could send in a couple of "aircraft ground engineers" to recover some parts from the wrecked aircraft.

"Yes."

On the first flight of the evening of November 13, we rode to Uli in the tail of the plane behind bales of stockfish, sacks of Formula II, and 55-gallon drums of petrol strapped to the deck. We had our tools. We were to bring back two oil coolers, hydraulic lines, and wheel cowling flaps to replace the damaged ones on Lima.

Looking out one of the windows on this old ex-passenger plane, I watched as we crossed the coast over the Niger delta in the fading light, a moment of great excitement, going into Biafra at last. I could see it 13,500 feet below me. Stretching inland was the immense rain forest canopy that I had first seen nearly five years ago on my way into Nigeria. Leo looked out a window on the other side of the plane; what he felt I don't know. As darkness advanced down below, I could see dozens of flames from the oil wells around Bugama and Degama, the natural gas flaring off.

We flew north for a while, then turned east to pick up the beacon at Uli. I got out of my seat and came forward to stand in the door to the cockpit. The pilot tried to raise the Biafran controller on the radio.

"YANKEE YANKEE. This is GOLF VICTOR HOTEL. Do you read? Over."

The call letters were YY and GVH, that day's code for the ground controller and the DC-7. There was no response. The pilot repeated the call.

"YANKEE YANKEE. This is GOLF VICTOR HOTEL. Do you read? Over."

The pilot kept repeating the call. The flight engineer turned to me and said, "They don't answer us." Something was wrong.

We flew on through a cloud and some lightening. Turbulence flopped us up and down. I remained standing, holding on to the door frame, wanting to be with the flight crew. Since this was no longer a commercial airliner, no one told me to sit down and fasten my seat belt. Coming out of the cloud, the pilot tried the radio again. He did raise Biafra. The controller said something in response, and the pilot immediately put the plane in a steep right bank. Leo and I were thrown to the floor and pressed there by acceleration, next to the drums of petrol, while he swung that aircraft around and got out of there. Excited before, and so brave, I was now terrified.

The flight engineer told me that the cryptic message from Biafra had said, "No landing lights." It was code for "We are being bombed." The Nigerian Intruder, code-named "Yellow Bar" or "Genocide" was pounding the airstrip again. We moved off to the holding beacon, circling and circling in the dark until we ran low on fuel and headed back to São Tomé. Out over the ocean, safely away from the action, the engineer talked to us. He said that Nielsson, one of the mechanics, had spoken to him about Leo and me.

"Those guys are really good. They really work," Nielsson had told the engineer.

The relief flights were the only conduit for people moving in and out of Biafra: newsmen, missionaries, mercenaries, officials, and politicians. Passengers were common. But the flight engineer talked to us as if we were crew, not just passengers. It was a good feeling of inclusion in the core group of people bringing relief into Biafra, rather than the previous feeling of exclusion as UNICEF volunteers on the periphery, low-life mass murderers.

After we returned to São Tomé, other flights left for Biafra and landed. Leo and I didn't go. We were tired from working all day and depleted from the high emotion of the flight.

While Leo and I were flying, Kinney, representing UNICEF, the German monsignor, Mollerup of Nordchurchaid, Father Byrne from Caritas, and others toured the warehouses. After their tour they held a big meeting. Larry attended. Erla was there, and he told me later what was said. Their report was very favorable about the situation they found in the warehouses. They were pleased with all the information that we had handed over to them. They were completely satisfied that no more people were needed in the warehouses and that we had done an excellent job. We were highly commended for our warehouse work and for our work as mechanics. The reputation of UNICEF volunteers among the relief groups on the island soared.

The Boeing had also brought down medical supplies and another engine for Lima. We had already replaced the shot-out tire. After we changed engine number three, we would need only to repair engine number four and patch up the holes to get Lima flying again. If Leo and I could get the necessary parts from the plane at Uli, we would be contributing directly to the capacity of the airlift, up to thirty tons of food a night, bringing life to Biafra.

Biafra, formerly Eastern Nigeria, my home for three important years of my young life —

I'm coming. *Ana m abia.*

DC-7 Bombed in Biafra

CHAPTER 7

Chinyere m Aka

God Gave Me Hands

Flying into a modern airport at night, like Pittsburgh International, looking out the window as the plane turns onto its final approach, you see lights everywhere. It is beautiful. Headlights on cars define the roadways winding among the hills. Lights of varying color and intensity trace the location of hospitals, spired churches, universities, stadiums, houses, parking lots, suburban developments, and bridges. Wide bands of meandering darkness mark the courses of the three great rivers meeting at the nexus of the city. Pittsburgh drifts by below your window, bright but silent, a jewel of light. The plane's navigation lights blink on the wingtips. You feel a slight lurch as the wing flaps are lowered and the landing gear locks into place. The brilliant beams of the landing lights torpedo the darkness. Your plane glides down the electronic path of radar and modern ground controlled approach to a flawless landing.

Not so in Biafra. You fly and land in darkness because people out there are trying to kill you. Lights below are blacked out against air raids. Occasionally you might see out your window the bright orange blossoming of a bomb detonating or streaks of anti-aircraft fire stabbing at the Nigerian intruder. There is no radar or electronic guidance to bring you in safely. It depends on the skill of the pilots. Some don't make it.

1

The day after our aborted flight to Biafra, Thursday, November 14, I had been married for four weeks. The chief mechanic, Helmut, told us we would fly the next night to recover the oil coolers.

We worked the rest of that day removing damaged parts from Lima. In addition to the oil coolers, we identified other damaged parts: flap cylinders, landing gear doors, pumps, relays, and other parts. Under the direction of the licensed mechanics we removed the parts, paying close attention to what we were learning, because these would be the procedures we would use on our own at night, in the dark, in Biafra.

The next day we would rest, to be fresh for a night's work at Uli.

I woke at ten o'clock Friday morning, did my usual chores, and packed my shoulder bag with food, cigarettes, and Pepsi. We arrived at the airport at 3:30 p.m. Smyth, one of our electricians, met me and said, "You're not going tonight."

"Why not?" I said, sharply.

"Oh, they're sending for the parts, so you don't have to go."

"Who says?"

"Helmut."

I ran over to Helmut. I was thinking that Captain Baekstrom had risked his life to get Lima back here so we could fix it and fly it. The Boeing had already brought down the new engine for Lima. I knew it could probably bring more parts later. But I wanted to go to Biafra. I said, "We need to get those parts now. Otherwise, it will take too long, and this plane will be out of service!"

"Okay," Helmut shrugged. "Go sign in and get going."

Leo and I ran over to the terminal, signed the crew list, grabbed our bags and toolboxes, and climbed the ladder into the plane.

We crossed the coast as before, but this time we were cleared to land. From my position standing in the cockpit door, I could see the forward view. On our approach I saw hundreds, thousands of lights down below, probably from cooking fires. The bush must have been packed with people. In the coming weeks, as the night bomber continued his raids, cooking fires would be extinguished before dark, and no lights of any kind would be permitted near Uli.

Our pilot, Captain Tom Delahunt, was a 52-year-old American Marines veteran who had flown Corsairs in WWII. He landed the four-engine plane on the airstrip — a road in the rain forest — at night, without lights or radar. The flight engineer explained how it was done. The pilots followed a non-directional radio beacon that was mounted in a tree at the center of the airstrip. A needle on a dial in the cockpit told them when they were on the right heading. When the needle flipped 180 degrees, they were directly over the beacon. The frequency of this signal was kept secret and was changed every night so the bomber could not find Uli the same way. The engineer said it would not be too hard for the intruder to find the signal anyway, and he was often waiting.

When the needle swung, Delahunt flew on a certain course for a specified number of minutes, then came to another course for a few minutes, and so on until by dead reckoning the plane should be lined up with the end of the runway. At the right altitude, when he reckoned that we were over the threshold, he called for runway lights. When we had lights Delahunt made hasty adjustments to line the nose up on the centerline, wings waggling seriously. At the last second he leveled the wings and we touched down. As soon as the wheels screeched on the pavement, the runway lights went out. The copilot killed the landing lights. We rolled down the runway in near darkness, about 7:00 p.m. Biafra time. If the intruder were overhead, we would not give him an easy fix on his target.

"This was easy," said Delahunt, "compared to landing on the pitching deck of an aircraft carrier. That was like landing on a postage stamp in the ocean." Delahunt was tall and lanky, calm and soft-spoken.

We maneuvered into our parking finger, nose outward toward the runway in position for a quick takeoff. The crew shut down the engines and all power, including cockpit and cabin lights. When the engines stop, after roaring in your ears for a long time, the sense of silence is magnified. In the dark we opened the door, and immediately we heard the scream of falling bombs.

Whoomp, whoomp, whoomp... about six or eight bombs exploded off the runway in the bush about a quarter of a mile away, with no damage. The bomber had shot his wad with that one salvo, and we were probably safe for the rest of the night. Perhaps the bomber pilot got his fix not from our light, but from the one long skinny stretch of darkness – the runway – amid the thousands of cooking fires all around. Later, when cooking fires were no longer permitted, the dark runway would disappear into the dark bush.

My first landing in Biafra was emotional. The night air was fresh and tropical and familiar, a different flavor somehow than the island air of São Tomé, and much different than the November air of New York. It felt, in a sense, like coming home. I had left Nigeria two years before as the country lumbered toward war, certain that I would never see this place again or the people — almost family — that I had left behind. Their cause, Biafra, their fight for survival, identity, and dignity, was now my fight.

The airstrip was indeed a road. It was not flat, but slightly undulating. The wings extended over the edges of the pavement. It had been one of the main roads in Eastern Nigeria, the Trunk "A" road. On its way from Onitsha to Port Harcourt, it passed through Ihiala, Uli, Mgbidi, and Awomama, where Bob Buckle had lived when he left Cornell to teach in Africa. In his book, *Not For Ourselves Alone*, written nine years before the airlift, he wrote about this road:

The Trunk "A" road goes through the bottom half of the village on its way from Pt. Harcourt to Onitsha. It is not an impressive road, though it is one of the main highways of Nigeria; it is one lane of tar with a smooth sand right-of-way on either side, not more than a street in a small town in America; but it is a busy road, traveled by energetic traders, politicians, and expatriate civil servants. In the early morning and late afternoon the traffic is mostly lorries... hurrying to Pt. Harcourt or making the return trip. These rattling two ton trucks, held together by wire, the driver's kicks, and some mystical bound between driver and vehicle, are solidly packed with oranges, bananas, goats, chickens and people. For $0.56 you can ride to Pt. Harcourt, ninety miles away, in the best seat, beside the driver. Otherwise you pay $0.42 and ride in the back with all the other cargo. The lorries are jaunty trucks, painted in bright colors with mottoes scrawled on the cab, like, "It is in God's hands" or "Ndu bu isi" which means "Life is the main thing."

People walk along the road with jars, baskets, and porcelain washbasins on their heads; most of them are women – some carry tiny babies on their backs, tied up in the material of their dresses. There are bicyclists delivering a table or a board or a coffin, tied on their bikes somehow. They are going to the market with goods for sale, to the stream to wash or get water, or to a customer – a journey of four or even ten miles. Crowds of children are on their way to the mission schools. They walk quickly, very happy to be going. School in session is a mad babble; the children chant and sing their spelling lessons and addition tables. They learn by mimicking the teachers, and somehow they learn to read, write, and figure, though not very well. They learn geography, good health habits, and the parts of a flower. But the most important subject, so far as their parents are concerned, is English. Many are already secretly ambitious, thinking of how they might convince their fathers to pay for one more year of school, then another, and how they might go to a grammar school, and even to the United Kingdom or to the United States, returning to be a great politician or civil servant, to lead and to ride in a very mighty car. The Trunk "A" road that passes through Awomama is a fine road; it leads to the river, the market, the schools, Pt. Harcourt, and the west.

It was a road that became, by night, one of the busiest airports on the continent of Africa, a road known around the world.

"So this is Airstrip Annabelle," I said, as I stood outside next to Delahunt, looking down the runway. Far ahead the dark forest canopy parted where the road pierced it.

"How did you know that?" he asked. "That's supposed to be a military secret."

"I read it in the *New York Times*."

A flight schedule was published every day listing the planes and their arrival times over the beacon in Biafra. At the bottom of the schedule was a notice: "THIS SCHEDULE SHALL UNDER NO CIRCUMSTANCES BE EXPOSED IN PUBLIC." But everybody had a copy; it defined our evening's entertainment. Because we were flying into a war zone, some security was required. However, things were pretty loose, and it would have been easy for a reporter to get information about what was going on. It's not surprising that the *New York Times* knew about Airstrip Annabelle.

2

Reverend Aitken met us and took us to meet the Flight Line Officer. He introduced us and explained our presence as "aircraft ground engineers" who were there to recover some parts. Then he took us to the downed plane. He explained how that plane happened to be there.

After unloading one night, and prepared for takeoff, it wheeled out on to the runway and turned to line up on the center line. It blew a nose wheel. It couldn't move. It sat on the runway, near the threshold where most of the parking fingers were, as a French arms plane, a C-46, came in for a landing. It clipped the big DC-7. There was minor damage to the C-46, and it was able to take off again later. The DC-7 suffered some minor additional damage, but it could not take off. Biafran ground crews towed it to a parking finger well off the runway. They tried to camouflage it with palm fronds. They hoped to repair it the next day, so they didn't drain the wing tanks of precious fuel or remove some valuable spare parts from the belly hold.

In the light of the next day an Illyushin bomber found it. He dropped some bombs, and one of them set the right wing tip on fire. Biafran crash crews and firefighters rushed out to extinguish the fire. Two MiGs followed up the attack strafing with 50 caliber machine guns, making six passes between them. The Biafran firefighters were driven away and the plane burned. The crew returned when the MiGs left and doused the fire before the plane was totally destroyed. The right wing and fuselage were reduced to aluminum slag. The tail section was intact, lying upright on the ground. The left wing with engines number one and two was relatively undamaged. The propeller blades were jammed into the ground, holding the wing up. Remarkably, there was still fuel in the wing tanks.

Leo and I went to work in darkness under a starlit sky. A third quarter moon would rise later that night. The work went slowly: one small screw at a time to remove the wing panels, then one slow nut at a time. The nuts were difficult to reach. By touch, we fit the wrench over a bolt and turned it only a sixteenth of a full circle before it ran out of travel and hit something else. Then we repositioned the wrench by feel, and we made another fraction of a turn. I had cuts on my knuckles and my wrists.

The first flights left, returning to São Tomé. We could hear the roar of the engines as they took off and the diminishing drone as they flew away, but we could seldom see the planes, other than dark apparitions gliding across the star field. It reminded me of the old song, *Ghost Riders in the Sky*. When they were gone, the night got very quiet. The only sounds were ours, banging and clanging with our tools. The cooking fires had been extinguished. I looked out into the dark bush, knowing there were people and things out there, unseen.

Oil started leaking out when we got the seals broken on the oil coolers. We washed the oil off with aviation gas by turning a petcock under the wing tank. We got out three relays and a wheel flap and finally dropped one oil cooler. While I was working up in the engine, I became aware of a presence near me in the dark at about the same time it spoke, scaring the wits out of me. It was Reverend Aitken. He said, "Would you like some coffee?"

I looked down at his form there in the darkness and said, "Man! I would love some!" He set up a thermos bottle and some cups on the horizontal section of the tail, about belt height. The coffee tasted so good.

A fog rolled in. We kept working. We heard the planes of the second shuttle passing overhead as the pilots searched for a break in the fog. There was no radar to help them. We were supposed to go back with the last plane, but as the night wore on and the fog held, we heard no more planes. Leo and I considered the possibility that we may have to stay in Biafra for a day and go back the next night. To me, that was good news. We had no clearance to go anywhere else but Uli. Still, we could see what the place looked like in the daylight.

Reverend Aitken showed up again, after all the planes had left.

"Would you like some more coffee? And some soup?" We were getting very hungry by that time, and it was a welcome break. He stayed with us a little while, then went back to his car to sleep. Though the moon may have risen by then, it was still foggy and we couldn't see it. We heard no more planes.

We had two more bolts to go on the second oil cooler when two more shapes appeared out of the darkness. They were Biafran mechanics who also had been working on this plane by day. I greeted them in Igbo.

"*Ndeewo nu.*"

"*O di mma.*" They responded.

Since Leo and I had been officially labeled "aircraft ground engineers" rather than more modest "help mechanics," that is how we introduced ourselves to the Biafran mechanics, explaining that we were trying to get parts to repair another plane back on São Tomé. We had previously lived here as Peace Corps Volunteers.

"That's why you speak such good Igbo," said one of them.

They were delighted to see us. They had already managed to get some parts off, and had tried to remove an engine. They had got the engine mount bolts loose, but the engine would not detach from the nacelle, with one blade of the prop stuck in the ground. While we talked to them, I continued to loosen the final two bolts, and they helped us lower the cooler to the ground and invert it so the oil would run out.

The Biafran mechanics were in an upbeat mood about the war. They felt that things were going well. Biafran troops were pushing back in Onitsha and around Enugu. "Nigerians are in Aba, but we control the area around it." They talked about politics, how Russia, Britain, and the U.S. were helping Nigeria. "It seems like the whole world is against us." I asked them where they were from. They were from the Mid-West, Yorubas. Responding to my surprise, one of them said, "We are in this together. It is the right thing."

We finished work, tired after working all night. Obviously, we weren't leaving that night. The fog imperceptibly faded from dark to light gray and no planes flew overhead. We told the Biafran mechanics that we would like to stay in Biafra for a few days, but we had no clearance. They begged us to stay.

"We need you here. We will go get the Commandant and he will beg you to stay."

There were so many ways we could help them, they said, like removing the engines. At that point they were hopeful of getting more planes for their Air Force, including jets. They had trained in West Germany with the Nigerian Air Force, which was much more training than Leo and I had gained. I felt awkward; they assumed more than we could deliver. I said that we weren't specialists and had no experience with jet engines, but we would help them in any way we could. With a flashlight we looked up into the engine that they were trying to dismount.

I said, "You have disconnected the engine mounts, but see back here, you've got to disconnect all the leads going into it, all the exhaust pipes, all the electrical leads, all the fuel lines, before the engine itself will disconnect from the rest of the nacelle. If you want to take the engine off, you have to start up in there, way inside."

Enthusiastically, they began their day's work.

Aitken woke up from his nap. We asked if there was a piece of floor somewhere to sleep on. He said, "Oh, yeah. We can take care of you. You can stay back at our store." That is, the place where they stored the deliveries from Uli, and from where they distributed them to local stores throughout Biafra. He would get us a place to wash up and get some food.

I said, "We brought some food – tinned sardines, candy and biscuits."

"No, no," he said. "We have plenty of food." That would be the "missionary food" that we stored in Warehouse K back on São Tomé.

"What about our status," I said, "like permission to stay here?"

"I'll take you to State House and explain that you are here, and why."

We loaded our personal bags and tools and parts into his car. He drove slowly around all the parking bays, flicking his parking lights on and off, checking to see if all the lorries had left the airstrip. Everything was deserted, and still and spooky.

We crossed through two checkpoints, where he presented passes, then on to State House, Mgbidi, which was blacked out. We got out of the car and stood around smoking while Aitken went inside and spoke to Major Akabogu. He came out a short while later.

"It's okay. You are under my care for a while."

No one from State House came out to look us over. I had seen nothing to indicate any tension between Biafran officials and missionaries. The relationship was relaxed and cordial.

So there we were, outside the airstrip, with the prospect of spending a day in Biafra. It was good.

Aitken's place was a former school, now a central storehouse for the World Council of Churches. Food from the airlift was brought to this store, where it was divided up for distribution to local stores around Biafra. He and another missionary stayed in a former girl's dormitory, one big, bare room with a small kitchen.

"Would you like to wash up?" he said.

"Oh, boy, oh, yes!" I said, grimy, greasy, dirty, hair full of oil. He found us some water and detergent. We scrubbed and scrubbed our hands, faces, and hair. There was not enough water for a full bath. He brought us clean shirts, but we still wore our dirty pants and boots. It's amazing how nice a clean shirt can feel.

We sat down. He was saying something to us, but I was beginning to doze off, very tired. I had been awake since ten o'clock the previous morning.

"You can stay here for the day, but I have to attend a meeting in Umuahia." That got my attention. My head snapped up and I looked at him.

"I would love to go to Umuahia!" I said.

"Well, fine," he said. "You can come with us." He offered us a cup of coffee.

"When are we going to leave?" I said.

"In about an hour. We'll have breakfast in half an hour, then we'll go." We had pancakes, with syrup.

We drove to Umuahia with a number of missionaries for the WCC conference. There would be no problem for Leo and me since we were traveling with them. At every checkpoint we were waved through. We headed east through Orlu and on to the Okigwe-Umuahia road where we turned south to Umuahia. I dozed during the ride, but as we got close to Umuahia I began to recognize this turn, that building, that tree. I perked up. I noticed chickens and goats and sheep. I had not expected to see any, assuming they had all been eaten up by then. We came around the final curve uphill into Umuahia, my hometown for three years. What a surge of feeling! When I left Umuahia after the Peace Corps, I thought that I would never see it again. But I did! I saw it as Biafra, less than twenty-four hours after landing at Uli.

We passed the Ridge Club, formerly a British club in colonial days, and the large Government Field across from it, which had been used for celebrations and football games. The field was covered with stakes. They looked like yam posts for the tendrils of the young plants to climb. It seemed like Biafrans were using all extra space to grow food. Yams were an excellent source of carbohydrates.

"Oh, they're planting yams there, too." I said.
Aitken laughed, and so did the others. I think it was the only time I ever heard Aitken laugh. He was not morbid, like Father Cunningham, but he was serious.

"Those are anti-parachute stakes," he said.

I looked again. The tops of the poles were sharpened. Every open field throughout Biafra, every former playing field, was thick with those stakes, guarding against a parachute assault. Necessary I suppose, but an advantage to Nigeria in preventing Biafra from growing more food.

They took us to Queen Elizabeth Hospital, where we met many others, including Mr. Yeager, the WCC representative for the airlift. He was surprised to see us, as were others we had met on São Tomé.

"Oh! You are here!"

After talking with them for a few minutes, I said to Reverend Aitken, "Leo and I want to walk around Umuahia. Do you think there will be any trouble with us walking around with no official clearance?" Because of the long delay by the Biafran government in granting UNICEF clearance as offloaders, I was sensitive to that matter.

"Oh, no," he said. "Well, here. Take these." They were WCC badges we pinned to our shirts.

"When should we meet you back here?"

"Be back at four o'clock."

Mrs. Middlecoop, wife of a WCC official, asked if we had any Biafran money, which we didn't.

"Here, take this," she said, handing each of us a five shilling note. Then Mr. Yeager gave us each a pound note. Pausing, considering for a moment, he then gave me a fist full of Biafran Pounds. He asked us to stop by the Post Office and get some Biafran stamps, two or three complete series.

We began our tour of Umuahia. We walked by the Ridge Club again. We had had many Peace Corps gatherings there. I used to meet other PCVs on weekends to play darts or dance to a High Life band. Each Fourth of July the Umuahia Peace Corps Volunteers hosted an American Independence Day festival, including roast pig or roast cow. On the Saturday before the event I would go to the market to meet the pig farmer, who drove his hogs in once a week. I would order a 100 lb. dressed pig, then collect it in the boot of a taxi the day of the party. For entertainment, we hired the Tex Dandies Dance Band of Umuahia, featuring Tex Ubong Henry, to play High Life music. Up to two hundred PCVs from around the Eastern Region and Mid-West would come, riding out of the bush on their motorcycles by ones or twos or threes, then joining up by the dozens as they cruised through the streets of Umuahia. I try to imagine what that must have looked like to the people of the town.

The Germans from the Golden Guinea Brewery would also come. They got excited every year as they looked forward to it. In their machine shop at the brewery, they fabricated the spit which we used to cook the pig. The spit was a one-inch thick iron rod with holes drilled through it every inch. In the market, I found a hardware vendor who sold me a 22-foot length of rod. I only needed seven feet, but he wouldn't sell a piece of it. Another vendor had a power hacksaw, and he cut it for me. I left the other fifteen feet with him; I couldn't think of any other use for it. I hired a little Morris Minor taxi. The driver and I lashed the rod to the roof and hauled it to the brewery. The Germans machined it, drilled the holes, and welded a crank handle to it. They made skewers that would pass through the holes and pin the meat to the rod.

An American surgeon from Queen Elizabeth Hospital carved the pig for us.

In the year that it had been my turn to organize the event, I was making arrangements to use the large Government Field across the road from the Ridge Club for softball and volleyball, when someone reminded me that July Fourth was in the middle of the rainy season. But it so happened that he knew a rain doctor who would keep us dry. So I paid $15 for a rain doctor. It didn't rain.

Leo and I came to the Umuahia Public Library. This was an attractive two story building of modern architecture, with white patterned blocks defining the second floor and glass panels all around the first. As a PCV I went there often. I borrowed my first book of science fiction, *A Fall Of Moondust,* by Arthur C. Clarke. Eventually, I read all of the science fiction in the library from a shelf about two or three rows back on the right side of the stacks. I still read science fiction to this day, and it led me to a late career in physics and astronomy. Now the building was covered top and sides with palm fronds for camouflage, and it was still lending books.

Next we visited the Post Office, similarly camouflaged, and bought stamps. Some I bought for Mr. Yeager, and some for myself, which I still have.

There was a big tower near the old deserted motor park, once painted white, now covered with scaffolding and painted black against air raids.

Near the entrance to the market we came to Paul Onwuzurike's cold store. It was a favorite place for PCVs. Paul's store had had electricity, so he had frozen foods, ice cream, and cheese. Whenever Paul got a shipment of mozzarella cheese, Umuahia Volunteers knew to head to Bill Christian's house, because he would be making pizza. No more of that now. I walked inside looking at the empty shelves and bales of things stacked along the walls. A young man asked me what I was looking for.

"I was looking for Paul Onwuzurike," I said.

"Oh, ho. He is just inside. Please wait small." Then he said we should go into the back room.

I saw Paul sitting there, and I said, "I want to see *that* man." Paul saw me and jumped up.

"Oh, ho! Oh, ho! Ah, ha!" he said.

"Do you remember me?" I asked.

"Oh, yes, I remember you."

I gestured to Leo and said, "Do you remember him?"

"Yes. I have seen his face, too."

He invited us in and we talked. We explained why we were there and that we were aircraft mechanics from São Tomé.

"Where?"

"São Tomé."

"What is that?"

I explained that São Tomé was the place where most of the relief supplies were coming from. He did not know that. Many other people I talked to that day also did not know that.

But Paul was very happy to see us. He brought out a bottle of kai-kai, distilled palm wine. After a drink, he asked if we wanted something to eat. I looked at him, wondering what to say.

"No thank you. We have just had a big breakfast." But then I remembered that it was customary that if someone offered you food, you should accept. This was awkward.

"Would you like some rice jollof?" he said.

"Well, Paul. I don't need food, and I don't want to take it from someone who may be hungry."

He laughed. "I am not hungry!"

"Okay," I said, "Small-small."

But he gave us large plates of rice jollof with meat. It was delicious.

After the meal, I asked him if he knew Mr. Wilbur Nsofor, the first principal of my school, Ohuhu Community Grammar School.

"Yes, I know him well. He usually comes into the market to a shop in front. He is still big and fat!" He laughed. He said he was working somewhere else now, but he didn't say that it was because the military occupied the school, using it as Intelligence Headquarters, something Johnny Correa told me more than a year later.

Paul also knew Mr. Ibe, the second principal of my school, and many others that I asked about. I asked him to greet them for me if I didn't get a chance to see them this time.

Continuing our walk, Leo said little, looking around placidly, his eyes crinkled up with a little smile. We went by the shop Paul mentioned where he sees Mr. Nsofor. I remembered that he used to park his car in front of that shop to talk to his friend. Mr. Nsofor was not there that day.

I especially wanted to see the market. This was a Saturday, November 16, 1968, and I wanted to compare it with Saturday markets before the war. In *Not For Ourselves Alone*, Bob Buckle gives an eloquent description of a day in the market in 1959. Bob lived in Ben Nzeribe's compound and he became very close to Ben's Grandmother.

Before noon, on a market day, Grandmother Nzeribe and Nnam, Ben's aunt, sit on a mat and paint themselves, on their arms and bodies with a black dye. Then Grandmother puts on her fine blue velveteen wrapper and her brightest head cloth. Nnam helps Grandmother lift up her big white wash basin which is packed with things to sell, topped by a mat and a tiny stool; and the proud old woman starts off with a graceful steady stride; her bare feet hit the sand gently so that the load is not shaken. Grandmother Nzeribe is probably seventy years old, but she knows she is as strong as the younger women, her age has earned her great respect, so she isn't afraid of the bush paths or darkness. Her bright old eyes have seen the coming and going of many men. She has seen the palm cutters fall from the highest trees (eight of her own children have died) and she remembers the sterner days of the tribal wars, slavery and human sacrifice. Grandmother was old when the first bicycle was brought to the village and when the first European came in a motor. She lives in those days as she walks to market; she is proud, for her son is one of the bright stars of the new Africa; and she lives in him and all the toil and market days that sent him through school. There could be rest now, but she will have none of that. Old muscles and the habits of so many years do not easily reshape. She is a child of the Old Africa, and can have little part in the new. She understands the earth, the sun, and the rain; she loves the yam — in a way her children cannot; for her the juju bush, the carvings, the sacrifices are still good vessels for her faith and her hope; the children are making a difficult journey to a new way of life. They are going in bicycles and in cars...and they are struggling with new symbols of faith. So, Grandmother Nzeribe, whom I greet with "Ama," "Greetings, my mother," walks under the bright hot sun to market — perhaps to the kindred's market which is very near, the town's big central market or even ten miles away to the market of a neighboring town. She will meet her friends and walk with them to a noisy market, spread out mats under a low canopy of palm leaves that is divided into tiny stalls, and spend the afternoon gossiping and bargaining. All Grandmother's friends are there; they love to go to market. It is a cheerful, noisy place, with anything one could want to buy. The palm oil sellers have their wares exhibited in earthen pots, bright red and orange palm oil for cooking or for making soap; and next to them are calabashes full of tasty palm wine with bubbles of fermentation spilling out the tops. In other stalls there are bundles of green leaves for fu-fu stew, piles of white cassava fresh from the stream, like snowy mounds; river turtles, dead bats, large snails, rats, chickens, and goats, sometimes dogs — fresh meat for stews; piles of earth-colored yams, clay pots of every size. And in the native doctor's stall one can find bits of fur, feathers, shells, bones, skulls, and wooden images. There are trinkets and mirrors from Japan, school books, bottles of brown snuff — a teaspoon sells for a penny, papayas, plantain, bananas, pineapples, lemons and limes for hardening snail flesh. But the favorite stalls are those of the cloth traders with hundreds of bolts of bright cloth from all over the world. Every lady must have some yards of the shiny brown cloth with "Nigerian Independence, October 1960" stamped over it in bright orange; and many cast covetous eyes on the bolts of cloth with Nnamdi Azikiwe's smiling face imprinted on it a hundred times, two yards would make a lovely wrapper.

Over and through all this buying and selling there is a roar, they talk of all that has happened since the last market and fervent bargainings: "a shilling; no, it is not a good one. You can get one at Onitsha for fourpence. All right; last price, eightpence. Mba (no)! I'll give you sevenpence. O.K. Adinma (O di mma). Finished. Take it." And when the afternoon becomes cool, the women repack their goods and tie their babies on, then set off to their kindreds to gather firewood and cook. Tomorrow they will go to the river or the fields; or, perhaps the women will gather the bunches of red palm nuts tossed down by cutters whom they have hired; the women care for the palm trees in Iboland. They will take the nuts to the oil factory on the river or to a hand press to make oil. The shillings earned from this will be tied into a long thin bag that goes around the waist under two or three layers of cloth that is a part of the ladies dress. A portion of the money will be taken out for the cutter, leaving some for another term at secondary school for the oldest son or for food and drink at the second burial ceremony of a relative.

I wanted to see what commodities there were in a wartime market and the number of people moving about. The market was crowded, every stall occupied, except for the concrete shelter where fresh meat from Hausa cows had been sold. Most of the food carried by our planes was protein – stockfish, milk powder, Formula II – because the starvation affecting Biafra was largely a protein famine, causing the swollen bellies, reddish hair, and brain damage of *kwashiorkor* in children. Because Father Cunningham and other missionaries that I talked to on São Tomé were concerned about the anticipated carbohydrate famine, I looked for carbohydrate foods. I saw some yams, here and there, as well as *garri*, but they were not plentiful.

Women sat on their mats out in front with produce piled on boards – onions, tomatoes, peppers, leafy vegetables, kola, and groundnuts. And there was meat. Chopped up goats. Chopped up sheep. Bush meat from small antelopes or crocodiles from the Imo River. Whole chickens. Some eggs. I wanted to find out what it cost. At one stall I pointed to a piece of meat, probably goat, about two inches long by one inch thick.

"Nkaa. O bu ego ole?" I asked.

"One pound five." Exorbitant! All of the meat was high priced. I saw a leg of goat, from the thigh all the way down to the hoof.

"Nkaa. O bu ego ole?" I asked the woman.

"Pound asato." Eight pounds! I tried bargaining, but she would not come down. In a market, bargaining was an essential part of any transaction. Without proper bargaining, you "spoil the market." That she would not negotiate the price of meat was a sign of the times.

I returned to a pile of kola nuts I had seen. *"Oji, ego ole?"* I asked.

"Sisi." Six pence. Very cheap. I handed the woman the five-shilling note that I was given by Mrs. Middlecoop. She just shook her head. There were twelve pence in every shilling. She couldn't make the four shillings and six pence change. I didn't have the small-small coins necessary for the transaction.

We continued through the crowded market. There was cloth. Tailors sewed the cloth into shirts and trousers. Men were at work in the carpenter section. I had come to them when I was designing our school library at O.C.G.S. They built our tables, chairs, bookshelves, and periodical racks. My fellow PCV teacher, Ric Holt, designed a complete science laboratory, and these carpenters built it. Now, they were making coffins.

There were many people in Umuahia. People told me that the population used to be three or four hundred thousand, but now it was a million or more. But the market itself did not seem more crowded than before the war. There were more people walking along the roads, but fewer lorries and cars, and no taxis.

If you can't get a ride, use your legs and walk. *"Take leg, go waka-o."*

I was surprised that there was as much motor traffic as I saw. Where did they get the petrol? I knew we were flying in some petrol and diesel to fuel the relief lorries and the generators, but not enough to supply all this traffic. Some of it was coming from smugglers across the Niger River. There was a huge black market in Nnewi where anything available in Nigeria was for sale, including petrol, car tires, and batteries. Also, I learned that Biafrans had recaptured an oil field and built their own makeshift refinery from bits of pipes and scraps and material on hand. They couldn't get it hot enough for the best grades of fuel, but they could mix the product at a ratio of two to one with standard fuel, good enough for lorries and generators. While working for foreign oil companies, Biafrans had watched their bosses and learned how to pump and refine their own oil.

As I walked around Umuahia, I noted that the people were not dressed in rags and tatters, but were well groomed and well dressed, the women in clean, bright-colored cloth, hair plaited, some wearing makeup. The overall spirit of the people was upbeat, enthusiastic. There were a very few people begging, but there was not an overriding sense of despair, as I had imagined from listening to Father Cunningham talk back on São Tomé.

Before it was time to leave Umuahia, I found the Doris Palace Hotel on Awka Street. It was a place we had loved to go to eat pepper chicken, drink beer, and talk to Doris. We enjoyed talking about business, politics, philosophy, and world events. Doris was a large jovial woman about fifty years old. By the end of my three years in Umuahia, she was calling herself my Nigerian mother. When I walked in the door that day, I saw her across the dining room to the right, sitting at a table, doing her paper work. She wore a wrapper of good cloth and a fashionable head tie, as she always had. I walked up to the table.

"Hello, Doris." I watched the waves of recognition flash over her face. She jumped up and said, "My son! My son!"

It was very good to see her. We had a long wonderful talk. Her business was doing well. She had strong political opinions. I could easily imagine that the Doris Palace Hotel served as a meeting place for people to talk about the war and the concept of Biafra. Doris reflected the prevailing attitudes. She was full of bright confidence about the future. There was no doubt in her mind that Biafra was going to succeed. People were suffering now so that they could forge their own country, the first African country formed by Africans, not Europeans. They would not give up.

3

At four o'clock we rejoined Reverend Aitken and the WCC group for the drive to Uli airstrip. I slept on the way back. As we approached Uli, at about 7:00 p.m., we heard explosions, about eight booms. We went back to State House at Mgbidi to report our return. A Biafran Red Cross worker came up to us and said that the bombing had hit some people. Three were killed and two wounded.

"Could you help us find a van to take the wounded to hospital?" Aitken's station wagon was full, with Leo and me, our tools and parts, and some other people who were to fly back to São Tomé. Aitken thought for moment, then he started pulling things out of his car. We helped him empty the car and put everything inside the building at State House. We folded the seats up.

I said to Aitken, "Should I go with you?"

"Yes, come along."

We took the Red Cross workers, and they directed us into the bush about a half mile away. Aitken flicked the parking lights along the way. We drove up to a compound. Under the trees Aitken turned on the headlights, illuminating a house with mud walls and a thatched roof. We got out.

There were two children, seven or eight years old, laying over a step, down from the veranda, tangled together, wrapped together, as they had been together when the bomb hit. Their feet were on the veranda, their heads on the ground. Chunks of shrapnel had gone through their heads, back to front, blood and brains coming out their foreheads. Pieces of bomb had also gone through their backs and out their stomachs, intestines hanging out into a great pool of blood on the ground.

I saw a young man lying up against a wall, looking like he was asleep, but with his eyes open. Aitken walked over to him from the car and grabbed his arm to feel for a pulse. He quickly dropped the arm. The man was dead.

Two other people in the same family had been hit by the same bomb. A young woman was lying in the bush. The Biafran Red Cross people picked her up and put her in the back of the car, very carefully. The woman's face was cut up, her mouth bleeding badly. She had been hit in several places.

The Red Cross placed a small boy in the car beside the woman. A piece of shrapnel had gone through his right thigh above the knee, fracturing the bone. His lower leg was sticking out at wrong angles. He whimpered and cried out when he was picked up, but he remained quiet as we drove to the hospital at Awomama, about three miles away. The hospital at Awomama had been started by Dr. Ben Nzeribe eight years before. Bob Buckle wrote about it in *Not For Ourselves Alone*, the book which inspired me to come to Nigeria in the first place.

Clearly, a bomb had gone off in the compound. But there was no crater. It must have been one of those small twenty-pound bombs, made in Poland in 1941.

When Aitken picked up the small boy and carried him to the table in the emergency room, he cried out again. I could see the hole in his leg, and the bone.

The young woman remained limp as she was carried in. She never screamed or cried out, but all the while, from the bush to the car to the hospital, she sang a high, floating, plaintive song.

Uwa di egwu.

Aitken drove us back to State House to pick up our loads. As I placed our stuff into the back of the car, I saw a lot of blood on the floor. On the flight back to São Tomé I slept and woke fitfully, fatigue tumbling memories of elation and horror.

Landing in São Tomé, scrofulous and bleary-eyed, exhausted, we climbed down the ladder to the tarmac with our bags and toolboxes. Quite suddenly, we were surrounded by a lot of people: our mechanic friends, Larry and Barry, people of the air operation. Chief of Operations, Erla, was there and Mr. Yeager, who had just come out of Biafra on the previous flight. Everyone was shaking our hands, saying, "Are you all right? How was it?"

In my fatigued state, this was all very confusing. I wondered, "What's wrong? Why are all these people smiling and shaking my hand?"

Back in the terminal, at the bar, Barry and Larry pumped us for information about Biafra. "What was it like? What happened to you?" I told them in general, with a few details, and promised more when we had rested. Barry and Larry were envious that Leo and I had got to Umuahia, but our mechanics and bosses were scared for us. When they couldn't get a second shuttle into Biafra to get us out, Arne was alarmed.

He said, "Oh, my God, we've got two guys stuck in there. What's going to happen to them?"

Helmut said, "Ah, leave them alone. They'll be fine. Nothing's going to happen."

"You heartless bastard! How can you say that? Those are our boys in there!" Arne was often dramatic, and waved his arms around.

"Forget about it. They've been in there before. They know how to handle themselves."

But we came back, and we brought the oil coolers.

4

The next day, Sunday, after I had finished eating my lunch in a small café, Mr. Yeager called me over to his table. As the head of WCC he was also the paymaster for the air operations. If Leo and I were to be paid as mechanics, he would be the one authorizing it, not Caritas as I originally thought. Because UNICEF was already paying us as volunteers, and Yeager knew that, we thought he wouldn't authorize the additional pay.

Actually, we had never asked for the money. We were just told that we would be paid $25 a day plus $50 a night at Uli.

"Tomorrow morning," Yeager said, "I want you and Leo to come by the office to collect your money."

"Okay," I said.

It came to $300 for the previous week's work. Yeager must have given us the daily rate for Monday through Saturday, plus $50 for our aborted flight Wednesday and $50 for each of Friday and Saturday night. Very generous. I went over to Biafra House and gave Mr. Osuji $100. I sent the rest home to Elner.

In the following week, I flew into Biafra on Monday, Tuesday and Thursday. On Monday, I tried to remove the main landing gear doors to replace those on Lima that were full of shrapnel holes. I worked at it a long time and didn't succeed.

We caught a ride back to São Tomé on a Transavia flight with an Icelandic crew. I was sleeping in the back of the empty plane when I woke up floating in midair. Leo had been sleeping on the floor. He was drifting in midair a few feet away, suspended face down with his hands crossed in front of his face, elbows up, eyes wide. After several seconds we settled back down. I imagined that we were going down, that the plane was plunging into the sea. The flight engineer opened the cockpit door and peered back at Leo and me to see if we were all right. When he saw that we were not hurt, he smiled.

"The pilot wanted to make joke on you," he said.

"You mean, he did that on purpose?" I said.

"Yes! Yes!" nodding with delight. The pilot had arced the nose of the plane up into a ballistic trajectory, and for a brief time at the top of the arc we were weightless in freefall. That is how astronauts train for zero gravity before they go into space. Thanks to the Icelandic pilot I got to experience weightlessness without ever becoming an astronaut.

When I got back in there Tuesday night, after another bombing raid, I found that the Biafran mechanics had finished removing the landing gear hatches and had taken them to their military stores. I spoke to the Flight Line Officer, and he assured me it would be no problem for them to release the parts to me. But I didn't know where they were stored and I couldn't find anybody who would take me there. After wandering around in the dark, the total blackout, for a while, I went back to the damaged plane. Arne came with us that night. While I was struggling to reach up under the wing for a flap cylinder, Arne took a direct approach and chopped a hole in the top of the wing with an ax. We removed a couple thousand dollars' worth of parts.

On the flight back, we carried two and a half tons of lead in the belly hold. Biafra was mining lead and hoped to export it along with large quantities of palm oil in order to build up some foreign exchange.

As we were taking off, a fire broke out on the left wing behind engine number two. Instead of climbing out on the normal pattern, we stayed low, flicking the landing lights on and off to indicate an emergency. About ten miles out we drew anti-aircraft fire from Biafran forces because we were not following a normal pattern. Another flight crew on the ground at Uli could see the tracers chasing us. We were not hit. The fire soon went out, and we flew home. A build-up of carbon deposits on the wing had caused the fire. On takeoff and landing, the engines require a rich fuel mixture which leaves the carbon deposits. In normal maintenance, these deposits are cleaned, but we didn't take the time to do that, keeping the planes flying constantly. On that takeoff, the hot blue exhaust ignited the carbon.

Wednesday I didn't fly. I worked on Lima.

The *Aerogare* (airport) on the volcanic, equatorial island of São Tomé lay along a flat stretch of land by the Gulf of Guinea at the eastern edge of the Atlantic Ocean. Aircraft landed and took off over the bay. Bunches of dry grass grew along the single runway. Beyond the grass, a fence outlined the perimeter, separating the airport from a path used by the African women carrying their head loads to and from the market.

Lima was parked at the edge of the tarmac by the brown grass. I was up on a ladder working on number four engine when I spotted a man walking toward the plane, limping, walking stiffly with the aid of a cane. He was European, about fifty years old, medium build, five feet ten inches tall. I had never seen him before, but I knew who he was.

He was Captain Baekstrom, the man who had flown this crippled aircraft out of Biafra two weeks before. Baekstrom came out on the flight line to see his plane. He had been released from the hospital, but he was still mending. I climbed down off of the ladder, wiped my hands, and walked out to meet him. Somewhat awed by his bravery, I approached him.

"Are you Captain Baekstrom?" I asked, respectfully.

"Yes, I am," he said, smiling.

"I'm David Koren. I'm trying to patch up your plane for you." We shook hands.

"I hope you're recovering okay." I gestured to his legs.

"It's coming along. I'm still pretty stiff."

"That was quite a thing you did, to bring this plane back, wounded and all. What was it like?"

156

"Loud. The wind was screaming through the holes in the fuselage. My legs hurt, so I folded them under me on the seat to keep from passing out from the pain."

I nodded, unable to comprehend what that felt like.

"It seemed to take forever," he said.

He limped around the plane, looking at the damage. He had not seen it in daylight since the air raid. Before too long, they would both fly again.

In the evening, I hung out with two Biafran pilots. One belonged to the Biafran Air Force and the other to Biafra Airways, but neither of them had a plane to fly. Perhaps they were stopping off on São Tomé on their way from Biafra to somewhere else to hustle up some planes. In one of the hangars at the São Tomé airport, I could see the fuselages of two small jet fighters, French Fouga Magisters. They had no wings. A mechanic told me that Biafra had hired Hank Wharton to fly these planes, crated, in one of his Grey Ghosts, to São Tomé. He brought the two fuselages down in one flight. In another flight, he carried the wings. At a refueling stop in Tripoli, Wharton and his crew were seen running from his plane. The plane blew up, destroying the wings. Biafra had paid Wharton to deliver the jets, and Nigeria had paid him to destroy them. Wharton had been involved in starting the arms shipments to Biafra and in starting the relief airlift. After that alleged sabotage, Biafra would have nothing to do with him. That's the official story, but after the war, one of Wharton's pilots told me in a phone interview that it wasn't Wharton's fault.

The effort continued to find planes. Biafran pilots itched to get into a cockpit and go after the MiGs. They hated them. The MiGs and Illyushins flew at will in Biafran skies, strafing and bombing villages and market places.

"Even give me a piston plane," said the Biafran Airways pilot, "and I'll go after those MiGs. I can get them on the ground; I can chase them out of the air. Just give me a plane and I'll go after them. The plane doesn't matter as much as the man in the cockpit, the brains behind the controls. I want to win! I want to kill MiGs!"

I told those Biafran pilots that they could look in the classified advertisement section of trade journals like *Flying* or *Aviation Week* to find aircraft sales for planes like P-51 Mustangs, the hottest piston planes to come out of World War II, before jets. But they probably had better sources. They were hoping to get foreign currency to buy planes from the sale of lead and palm oil. Years later I read in Johnny Correa's narrative that Biafra had twelve T-6 fighters in crates on the docks in Lisbon, but Portugal wouldn't release them.

They told me they had a large stockpile of bombs recovered and refurbished from Nigerian air raids, including some 500-pound bombs dropped by the Illyushins and some bombs that Biafrans had manufactured themselves.

From other sources, I learned that Biafra was making mines, shaped charges they called *ogbunigwe*, "kill in large numbers." These were not the equivalent of what are now called IEDs, improvised explosive devises, assembled from more sophisticated ordinance captured from the enemy. *Ogbunigwe* were terrifying weapons designed and manufactured in Biafra. They came in three sizes and were used against troops and Saracen armored fighting vehicles.

The pilots told me that Biafra had made two guided missiles. They were complicated missiles with complete guidance systems, intended for attacking Lagos. The first missile blew up on the pad. The second lifted off, but they had no idea where it went. They couldn't make any more, because they needed some parts from the United States.

They shared other information. In addition to their one big refinery that turned out one thousand gallons of petrol a day, they had hundreds of backyard refineries producing fifty gallons a day. Some could refine a low grade of diesel, which they mixed with refined palm oil to power generators.

The Biafran government called together all the secondary school principals and asked them to recommend their best science students. Some of my students from Ohuhu Community Grammar School would have qualified. These students joined the Biafran Science Group along with Ph.D. scientists. It was the highest concentration of Ph.Ds. of any comparable-sized area in Africa. The Biafran Science Group developed the refinery processes, built the missiles and *ogbunigwe*, and even provided for the manufacture of consumer goods, like lipstick, that could no longer be imported. Biafra was attempting to build its own self-sufficient society using its own brains and resources. Biafra may have been portrayed to the world as a bunch of poor helpless Africans requiring Western benevolence to survive. The reality was deeper.

On Thursday night, November 21, Barry and I flew into Uli. We flew with Captain Delahunt on Alpha Bravo. Captain Tangen flew Alpha Delta. Barry went off to Customs; he would be staying a few days on business for the warehouses. I went looking for the hatches. After a few hours, I found them and brought them back, looking for a ride.

Captain Delahunt had long since left in Bravo, but Delta was still there from the first shuttle. They had been having mechanical trouble – no bombing that night – but they appeared almost ready to take off. I asked Captain Tangen if I could put the doors in his forward belly hold and go back with him.

"Sure, come on," he said.

This was the trouble: the propeller on engine number two had stuck in reverse. The angle that a propeller blade makes to the air can be rotated such that the force of the propeller can pull the plane forward or push it backward. The propeller can be reversed after landing to slow the plane down on a short runway, or even to push one wing backward to maneuver in a small place. When Tangen was doing just that to get out of his parking bay prior to takeoff, the prop on engine two stuck in reverse. He could take off with three engines, but not with the prop on engine two fixed in reverse. That would cause an unacceptable drag on the left side of the plane. The prop needed to be "feathered" so that it was locked in an orientation to cause minimum drag, but it was stuck.

So Captain Tangen couldn't take off. But if he left his aircraft there, it would be destroyed on the ground as the other DC-7 had been. The flight engineer, Sagwick, went over to the downed DC-7 and pulled a feathering pump from it while I was out looking for the landing gear hatches. A flight engineer from another plane removed the bad feather pump from Delta. Sagwick installed the feather pump, but he did not have the right tools to make a completely reliable connection. Maybe it would work long enough to feather the propeller; then they could take off with the other three engines.

I sat on the ground, under the belly of the plane, smoked a cigarette, and watched Sagwick finish up. I thought that this could be an interesting flight with only three engines. But I knew it could be done, because Baekstrom had done it. Not to worry. Sagwick closed the access panel, and gathered up his tools. We climbed up the ladder into the plane.

I will never forget what the cockpit of an old plane feels like. Sometimes, I can wrap the memories around me like a snug old coat. I can wriggle into the cockpit; smell it; slip into the seat. There is a piece of tape on the seat to keep the stuffing from coming out. Grey paint is worn down to bare metal where hundreds of hands have touched the throttles and the steering yoke for thousands of hours. I remember the tiny thrill of anticipation as I hear "start engines," and then the awful sounds that come next: the whining of the electric motors that turn the propellers, the stuttering, sputtering, coughing as the engines ignite. The sound settles into a steady whir and the plane gently bounces on its shock absorbers.

The copilot read from the checklist as Tangen started the engines in this sequence: number three, number four, and number one, but not number two.

"Three is clear. Turn three."

"Three turning... (*Engine noises: cough, cough, sputter, cough, POW!*) Ignition!"

"Four is clear. Turn four."

"Four turning.... (*Sputter, cough, pop, pop, pop*) Ignition!"

"One is clear. Turn one."

"One turning... (*Brrupp, Brrupp, Brrupp, POW!*) Ignition!"

Tangen pulled out onto the runway, three engines running. He did the preflight run-up and instrument checks. He advanced the throttles for takeoff. We were rolling, accelerating down the runway.

"FIRE IN FOUR!" yelled Sagwick. "FIRE IN ENGINE FOUR!"

Flashing red light filled the cockpit, and clanging alarm bells.

Tangen aborted the takeoff. We hadn't reached the speed where we would be committed to lift off and climb. We taxied back to a parking area and shut down the engines. Sagwick inspected engine four and found that it was leaking badly. In the small, cramped cockpit, in dim red light, Tangen sat in the left-hand pilot's chair; the copilot sat in the right seat. Sagwick sat by his engineer's instrument panel behind the copilot. I stood in the cockpit doorway, watching them scratch their chins, wondering what to do.

Tangen sucked in a deep breath and said, "Oh, boy! This is twice as worse as it was before." Then he laughed.

They decided to start engine number two, hoping that nothing would go wrong with it, so that they would not have to feather the prop in flight. They planned to take off with engines one, two and three. They started number two and noticed that it was leaking oil also. If we reached takeoff speed and lost engine two, we would be in trouble during climb-out. So for back-up, they planned to start engine four, as sick as it was, fire warnings be damned. Tangen, as Captain, made the decision to fly, but the copilot and engineer fully supported him. As for me, this was my ride. They started four, coughing, missing, belching flame and smoke, backfiring. We lined up again to take off. In minutes we were airborne. Number two held out, skipping and throwing oil. Number four continued with low power, nearly quitting twice on the flight back.

We weren't in the air very long before we flew into a violent electrical storm. Embedded in the roiling clouds was a trail of black smoke from engine four all the way back to São Tomé. I sat in one of the chairs in back, buckled in, apprehensive. Lightening flashed almost continually, illuminating the interior of the plane. The big plane bucked up and down, pitching from side to side. My arms flew up in the air, or jerked left and right. I kept looking at my watch by the lightning flashes every ten minutes, then five minutes, then two, in continuous high fear, for an hour and a half.

When we touched down on the runway on São Tomé, the plane rattled and shook, as it always did, a comforting familiarity.

Just as when I returned from my twenty-four hours in Biafra, people came out on the flight line to greet us, shaking our hands and smiling. I collected the landing gear doors, took them to the hangar, and went to the small bar in the airport terminal to wait for the crew because I needed a ride back to town. After they finished their post-flight checklist and wrote their logs – they had a lot to write – they joined me. Captain Tangen bought us all a round of beers.

"Congratulations," I said, lifting the beer.

"It was nothing," he said. "It was normal. Well, not quite normal."

The American copilot had flown with a commercial airline back in the States. He said, "We did things by the book. When you saw that red fire light, you didn't even look at the engine. There was no flight. You took the plane back to the hangar."

The crew talked about the flight. That was the time to swap stories about other memorable flights and to propagate new stories. Tangen had one to tell. Sometime before I arrived on São Tomé, he had taken off for Biafra when an engine cowling came loose and opened up like a clamshell, causing enormous drag, pulling the plane around in a downward spiral. He struggled to gain control and managed to bring it back to the runway. Bolts were missing on the cowling. Everyone talked about that flight for a while. Now there was another story to top that one.

Tangen looked at me with a twinkle in his eye. He said, "So you are learning something about aircraft parts?"

"Well, yeah. I am," I said. I had been learning aircraft mechanics for a week and a half, intensively.

Tangen looked at Sagwick, who had hired me and paid me, and then looked at me again.

"You're doing a terrific job," he said.

A few days later, a Connie from Libreville landed on São Tomé to pick up a load of arms for Biafra. I saw one of the crew sitting at a table in the airport bar, and I went over to talk to him, to glean some information about his job. He spoke up before I did.

"I hear you had an interesting flight the other night," he said.

"As a matter of fact, we did." I said.

"What went wrong?" he asked.

I told him the story. He listened, sipping his beer and grinning. Another one of the crew came up and said, "I hear you had an interesting flight."

"Yeah. I was on that flight."

"We know," they said.

They may have heard about that flight, but how would people from Libreville know that I was on it? They did.

Somehow, after I was stranded in Biafra for a day, and after this flight, flight crews looked at me differently, talked to me differently, as if, because of shared experiences, I had been accepted into a special fraternity.

Leo and I continued working on Lima during the day, even while flying half the night into Biafra, dead tired when we got back. We also worked on the two DC-7s that were still flying, Tango Alpha Bravo and Tango Alpha Delta. When we removed an old part and replaced it with another, we noted the part numbers. The licensed mechanics inspected our work, then entered the part numbers in the maintenance logbook and signed it.

We helped the mechanics with an engine change. With the cowling removed and the prop in a feathered configuration, we attempted to remove the propeller. It was fastened with a large hexagonal nut, which required a three-foot long hex-head wrench to loosen it. I carried the wrench up the ladder and fitted it over the nut. For maximum torque, I pulled down on the end of the handle. The force of my pull multiplied by the length of the handle determined the amount of torque. The nut did not turn. I gripped the end of the wrench and jumped off the ladder, applying a strong jerk force to break the nut loose. The nut didn't budge, and I was swinging in the air, hanging from the wrench. Leo brought the ladder over, and I climbed down. Arne and Leo and I studied the problem. We figured that two of us pulling on the wrench could break the nut free. Arne and I held on to the wrench and jumped. This time there was a result, but not a good result. The nut remained fast, and we bent the wrench, ruining it.

It was our only prop wrench. The plane was out of service until we could get another one. The Red Cross was flying DC-7s out of Fernando Po, and two days later one of their DC-7s landed at São Tomé bringing a prop wrench. When the mechanic who delivered it handed it over to Helmut, he laughed.

"I never heard of anyone bending a prop wrench," he said.

On an afternoon when we had finished working on Bravo, and it had been loaded and the engines started, Father Byrne came to me with a large package. He ordered me to stop the plane and put the package on board. I objected that the plane was already buttoned up and ready to go. We could put it on the next plane. He said that the package was very important and must go on that flight. Captain Tangen advanced the throttles and the plane began to move. I ran around in front waving to him. I pointed to the package, and he stopped taxiing. The plane dipped slightly as Tangen hit the breaks and the shock absorbers absorbed the forward momentum. Helmut helped me put the package in the forward cargo hold. It was sanitary napkins for the Nuns.

Although I worked with Leo every day, he remained an enigma. He seldom spoke. Sometimes he would cock his head to one side, squint, and chuckle. On a hot, dry, still afternoon, as we worked quietly turning wrenches, he said, "In South Dakota it gets too windy to haul rocks."

One other hot afternoon, while I was on top of a flimsy aluminum ladder with my hands stretched way back in the engine, up to my armpits, I looked to my right and saw Leo open the petcock and wash his hands in the 140 octane aviation gas – with a cigarette in his mouth.

"LEO!" I screamed. "Get away from there!"

"Huh? Oh."

The mechanic work was long, dirty, and tedious. Hundreds of small screws held the access panels covering the parts we needed. We often worked without shirts in the hot tropical sun, hotter as the heat radiated off the tarmac and the aluminum skin of the aircraft. Leo got a bright red sunburn on his belly and back. While Larry, Barry, Jerry, and I had been doing a lot of beach time, building a protective tan, Leo had been building the prefabs at the orphanage. After working on the flight line one day, we stopped by warehouse K to check on progress there. A nun named Maria Theresa was sorting a bale of short pants that had just arrived from Germany. Some were khaki and some were blue jeans. Sister motioned us over. She said, "You look like you could use some of these." I was filthy with oil and grease and dirt in my clothes and in my long, stringy hair. I had few clothes and it was difficult to get laundry done, presumably because there were so many foreigners on the island needing the same service. I gave my laundry to Senhor Lopes, owner of Bar Enrique and also my landlord. It took a long time for my laundry to come back. When I had gone a week without any clean underwear, I started referring to him as "Senhor Son-of-a-bitch." He knew enough English to be upset by that. But I apologized and he gave me my clean underwear and we became friends. Sister Maria Theresa gave Leo and I and Arne each six pairs of shorts.

When we appeared on the flight line the next day with our spiffy new blue shorts, the African mechanics we worked with, Valario, Oscara, and others, went, "Aack!" and roared with laughter. Above the blue shorts, Leo was bright red with sunburn, and below the shorts his 52-year-old legs were as white as a newly plucked turkey. The Africans called him *Tio* Leo (Uncle Leo). That day I called him Senhor Turkey Legs.

"He looks like a half-cast between an ESS-key-moh and an Indian," said Arne.

"Red, white and blue," said Leo.

Arne said, "We'll have to get Dave a blue shirt so he'll look like the company." The mechanics wore a kind of uniform with blue tee shirts and blue pants. I was the odd man out.

In the following days Leo got out in the sun enough to get some nice pink legs coming down out of his blue shorts.

"How does it feel?" I asked him.

"Hot legs," said Leo. "Like hot feet, only hot legs."

Bay of the Seven Waves

CHAPTER 8

Achoro m Ila

I Want To Go Home

The Galapagos Islands are on many people's bucket list. They should try to make it, to see the great diversity of life and geology that graces our planet. I will not be joining them, because I have seen such diversity of land and life in São Tomé. It is unlikely that many other people will go there because, although it is at the center of our worldwide coordinate system, it is one of the most remote places on earth. That is one of its great attractions. I feel privileged to have known it.

1

The mail plane from Luanda came in every Thursday. My mail was sorted into Box 202 at the Post Office. Since that box was used by many WCC people, different ones picked up my mail and handed it to me later, often not until Friday. There were letters from my mother and Elner. My mother said she was answering my third letter. If she had answered the first two, I never got them. Elner said Anne Webster, my brother's future wife, was waiting for a reply to her letter. I never got that letter. I hadn't heard from Ric and Marie Holt. (Ric had married his Peace Corps girlfriend, too.)

Communication that did go through lagged terribly. Mom and Elner were both responding to the last letter that they had received from me, saying that I was coming right home because I had nothing to do, and I couldn't get in to Biafra. They had to be utterly confused when they learned next that I was an aircraft mechanic flying into Biafra regularly. In real time, on the Island of São Tomé, things changed rapidly. In the first few weeks, we were very confused ourselves. When opportunities came up, we had to move swiftly. Leo and I had found jobs as mechanics; Larry and Barry settled into regular work in the warehouses with more recognition and authority; Tom had left weeks ago; Jerry had just left, unable to find any meaningful activity. I gave him some things to carry back to Elner personally, like souvenir Biafran money, hoping that would be more reliable than the mail.

Because of the communication lag, it was difficult to carry on a long distance relationship with Elner. There was as much miscommunication as communication, causing frustration, a serious problem. But we were stuck, locked onto either side of an enormous gulf by our strong personal commitments, my Biafra and her Ocean Hill-Brownsville. By letter, I expressed a wish that she might be able to visit me on São Tomé at Christmas vacation. It wouldn't be too hard. If she could get to Amsterdam, she could catch a ride on the Boeing that came down here every Wednesday. I had sent her a total of $300 by traveler's checks.

Things had stabilized somewhat, though we couldn't count on immutability. A popular Mammy Wagon slogan said, "No Condition Is Permanent." We stopped sending baffling telegrams to the American Committee for Nigeria/Biafra Relief, although we hadn't received our allowance money from UNICEF. A new chief of air operations had taken over in São Tomé, a young German ex-hippie named Christopher Gunter. He liked us, and he was trying hard to get us assigned permanently as offloaders in Biafra. If he succeeded, that would be another change.

Long distance, time-lagged communication was often frustrating and sometimes comical. Both Mom and Elner referred to a snowstorm. Mom said that the roads were all jammed up, the schools were closed, and Dad's bowling meet had been canceled. That seemed like news from a distant planet when I was sweating out on the flight line in temperatures that seemed like 150 degrees. To assure that I would get mail more reliably, I advised them to send it to Box 205, because Joe Galano was in charge of that box, and he would get the mail to us promptly.

I met a Biafran family passing through São Tomé on their way to New York. I gave them some things to give Elner, including some Biafran stamps that I had had canceled in Umuahia. I know that they were delivered, because I have them with me now, here in the future.

Elner sent me some articles from the *New York Post* about Abie Nathan in which he was lauded as a hero, gathering relief supplies in New York and Europe and flying them at great personal danger to starving and wounded people in Biafra. It made me gag. On São Tomé he was a nuisance, or worse. He would arrive unannounced with a load of kosher mushroom soup and demand that it be flown in immediately, displacing our normal shipments of Formula II, milk powder, or stockfish. He flew into Biafra strapped into one of the passenger seats in the rear of the aircraft before bombing had started, probably scared out of his mind. He annoyed Father Byrne by misquoting him in the European press, causing many Europeans to be upset with Father Byrne. Father Byrne fired off a cable to Nathan in New York. At a recent meeting of the Coordinating Committee of relief organizations, including UNICEF, we all agreed that the next time Nathan showed up he would be told that his load would be put in warehouse K to wait its proper turn. Months later, a cargo manifest for one of our planes listed a shipment of "Nathan food."

During the week of November 18, the churches negotiated with a company called ARCO to take over the operation of the DC-7s. German Caritas and a group of German churches known as *Das Diakonische Werk* created ARCO for that purpose. The Douglas DC-7 once served as the premier commercial airliner around the world. Sleek, swift, and shiny, with a cruising speed of 360 mph and a long range, it was the fastest and most sophisticated piston-engine airliner ever built. It made regular passenger service across the oceans possible. The DC-8 and the Boeing 707 jets made the DC-7 obsolete. The cockpit of an American Airlines DC-7 ended up in the Smithsonian Air and Space museum to represent the contribution that aircraft had made to aviation. Eighteen leading world airlines dumped their DC-7s on the secondary air cargo market, but because the DC-7s were so sophisticated, they were difficult to maintain, and the secondary carriers preferred the older, more reliable DC-6s. KLM, Royal Dutch Airlines, sold theirs cheaply, and eventually Hank Wharton bought some of them for his illicit blockade running into Biafra. Initially, Wharton's DC-7s and Super Constellations carried only arms and then food and arms indiscriminately. When Wharton was evicted from Biafra for sabotaging the Fouga Magisters, he sold five DC-7s to the churches at a cost of $40,000 each to establish a solely humanitarian relief operation. The churches sold the planes to ARCO for $10 apiece, and they became known as the German DC-7s. The old airline markings were removed or painted over, but inside an overhead luggage compartment, I saw a KLM logo. Outside, the once bright paint had gone dull and scratched: gray on the bottom and white on the top with a blue stripe from nose to tail along the line of windows.

Captain Baekstrom started flying again. He and McCombie, Tangen, and Delahunt had offered to form an operations group and buy the planes from the churches. The churches liked the idea and agreed to sell them for $1 each, including the plane in Biafra. But a lawyer in Germany killed the plan, reason unknown, so the deal went to ARCO.

ARCO took over operations on November 25, and the DC-7s were immediately grounded. Biafra denied permission for them to land at Uli. Biafra was suspicious. A man named Peterson was director of ARCO, and Biafra believed that he worked for Wharton.

That was that. Things had changed again.

Flight crews and mechanics expressed varying degrees of optimism and pessimism about whether the DC-7s would ever fly again. Baekstrom,

Tangen, McCombie, and Sagwick started negotiating with Biafra on behalf of ARCO, assuring that there would be no betrayals. Biafra liked and trusted them, and a deal was possible. The mechanics doubted it. I was disgusted. The convoluted politics and zooming reversals frazzled my nerves. I wanted to go home.

During this hiatus, missionaries in Biafra offered to bring in the flight crews and ground crews, two or three at a time, to tour Biafra for a day or two. They could ride in on Transavia or Fred Olsen. There was a lot of enthusiasm among the crews for this idea; many were very interested in learning about the people they were trying to help.

Other problems loomed. In normal airline operations, by rule, DC-7 engines had to be replaced by new ones every 20,000 hours of flight time. The Biafran Airlift was not a normal operation. The planes flew on punishing schedules and would never reenter commercial service. They would be abandoned on São Tomé or dumped in the sea. (As late as 2012, aerial views of São Tomé showed the hulks of two Super Constellations and other old planes. They are gone now). Though not subject to any regulating authority, ARCO needed to consider maintenance requirements to keep the planes flying and to keep the airmen alive. Of the three DC-7s, Bravo, Delta, and Lima, with four engines each, ten engines were at or approaching 20,000 hours of operation. Used DC-7s could be purchased for $40,000 each, but four new engines for one plane cost $80,000.

The churches had just bought a new engine for Lima, and ARCO would replace engines one or two at a time. In the meantime it was up to the mechanics, including Leo and me, to keep the engines turning. While the planes were grounded, Leo and I dismantled an old DC-7 engine that was lying in the weeds near the flight line for spare parts. We tore it down completely: all eighteen cylinders, all the electrical leads and fuel lines, injection pumps, feathering pumps, oil coolers, everything. The parts went into mechanical stores and would be used on any of the DC-7s. If the planes started flying again, Leo and I and Arne would go into Biafra and tear down the two engines in there.

Perhaps ARCO didn't want to spend the money, because they knew that, deep in the background, another, richer organization was forming – Joint Church Aid. Joe Galano's offer of the Blackburn Beverlies had been rejected, but there remained a strong interest in a North American component to the airlift, including some big planes.

On Monday, November 25, I lined up at the pay table out on the flight line, along with the other mechanics, laborers, pilots, and flight crews. We were collecting our pay for the previous week, when the planes still flew. The currency was U.S. Dollars. I watched as Sagwick counted out the money to each one. I have never in my life seen so many one hundred dollar bills. This was the best aviation job in the world.

On the following Monday, December 2, after ARCO was grounded, there was no pay. Not that there was none due – there would be no flight pay, but the mechanics (except for Leo and me), flight crews, and operations people all got salaries and per diems. Since I had worked three days that week, with no trips to Biafra, I should have received $75. Lack of money wasn't the problem – there was enough money to pay us, but a great palaver erupted between the churches and ARCO over who was to pay what.

What a tangle! What an incredible mess! It is a wonder that the Biafran Airlift ever existed, considering sabotage, sectarian rivalries, disputes between missionaries and the Biafran government, and bureaucratic snafus. The Red Cross operation on Fernando Po was constantly ensnarled as well. I wanted to go home.

Thanksgiving fell on November 28. That mattered to no one but the few Americans scattered among the relief people. To me it was another nostalgic tug from home. For the three Thanksgivings I had spent in Nigeria, American families working for USAID, living in their gated compounds in Enugu, invited PCVs to their homes for dinner.

On São Tomé we arranged to have a proper Thanksgiving dinner at the Café Yong, including roast turkey and all the trimmings. I suspect Joe Galano had something to do with that. Besides Joe and the UNICEF volunteers, Captain Delahunt came, Holtzman (McCombie's flight engineer), and Captain Tangen's copilot (I don't remember his name). There may have been other Americans, but I don't remember them. We invited anyone else to join us.

McCombie and his wife and daughter, Cathy, were the first guests to arrive. His family had recently joined McCombie on São Tomé. Cathy was a beautiful little girl, about six years old, missing her two front teeth. They were looking forward to a traditional American Thanksgiving dinner, including the cranberry sauce. McCombie had enjoyed many of these dinners in American homes. By contrast with the first night I had met him, McCombie behaved like a gentleman, obviously pleased to have his wife and daughter with him. Since that first boisterous night, I had talked to McCombie many times. He was well-educated, and we covered many topics: classical, literary, and political. I became friends with McCombie and his wife. On nights when he was flying, I would talk to her at the airport while she waited for him to return. She talked about him and her family. They had another child in school back home.

I got to know some of the other pilots besides McCombie, even though

I didn't live in the hotels where the others stayed. We talked over lunch or dinner or beers, or sometimes in the cockpit out over the ocean.

I flew with Tom Delahunt, the ex-Corsair pilot, many times and hung out with him on São Tomé. Tall and lanky with a deep voice, he reminded me of movie star Jimmy Stewart. At lunch one day, he scolded me, as a father would correct his son. I talked frequently about my wife because I hadn't seen her since we got married more than a month ago. I also made much of the fact that she was African American. It sounded like I was bragging.

"Stop saying that. We get it that she's black. It doesn't make any difference," he said.

"Okay. Sorry." I apologized for the bragging, but I was not sorry for marrying her.

On one flight into Biafra, after we crossed the coast, I was in the rear of the plane looking out the left side. I could see the oil well fires burning below, near Buguma and Degama. Then I saw lights arcing up toward us from below. They passed above and behind the plane — tracers from Nigerian anti-aircraft guns. I went forward to the cockpit, in the aisle between the sacks of food, and told Delahunt what I had seen.

"Where were they?" He asked.

"Back by the oil well fires."

He pulled that big old DC-7 into a steep left bank, as if he had been peeling off in a Corsair, and flew back toward the oil fires. He was *trying* to draw the anti-aircraft fire so he could locate the position of the guns. I didn't see any more AA, and I wondered if the gunners thought *we* were attacking *them*.

Most of the airlift planes could make two trips, or shuttles, into Biafra each night. With an early start and quick turnaround, the DC-7s could make three shuttles. Delahunt was determined to push it and make three whenever he flew. It was exhausting.

"When I get back in the morning after the third shuttle, I leave three tracks in the dirt – two for my feet and one for my ass."

I heard the story about a Norwegian pilot, flying a C-46, who called the tower at the Port Harcourt Airport, by then in Nigerian control, and said, "This is the enemy." He flew low over the runway, turned on his rotating beacon, and flicked his landing lights on and off before pulling off into the darkness. Just to harass them. I don't know who that pilot was for sure, but I wonder if that C-46 belonged to Fred Olsen.

I asked Larry Kurtz to tell about Tony Jonsson, a Transavia pilot who flew for the entire airlift, and who would pilot the last relief plane out of Biafra, under fire.

I guess the pilot I admired the most was Captain Torstein (Tony) Jonsson. He was a very experienced Icelandic pilot who had flown for the RAF during the Second World War and who had had many flying jobs since in Iceland, Greenland, and Africa. Unlike other pilots, he would fly in salt, knowing the damage it could do to his plane, but realizing it was essential to Biafrans' health. One night after we landed at Uli, a bomb exploded near the plane, ripping holes in the wings and piercing an oil pan. The plane seemed doomed to be left on the airstrip where it would certainly be bombed during the daylight hours. Captain Jonsson would have none of this. He took off his shirt and climbed out on the wing. He cemented the fabric of his shirt over the holes in the wing, his copilot doing the same on the less-damaged opposite wing. He analyzed the oil leakage and determined to fly the empty plane the three hundred miles back to São Tomé.

The next morning, when I returned to base, I was happy to see that he had made it. But his mechanics said that he came in on a prayer, having lost so much oil.

Later in the airlift, Captain Jonsson was badly injured by a bomb. As for others who were injured in the airlift, he was sent off to Europe to be patched up. Then he returned to fly again. He was one of the pilots who agreed to go in after the remaining relief workers as the Nigerians were closing in on the airport. This was perhaps his most dangerous mission.

One pilot I didn't know personally, Augie Martin, had flown a Biafran Super Constellation, a Lockheed L-1049G, a Grey Ghost, registered by Hank Wharton as 5T-TAG. He crashed on landing at Uli on July 1, 1968. Our pilots told me his story. The airmen who flew into Biafra, whether for the church relief, the Red Cross, or the Biafran government, shared a network of information about each other. They all knew what the others were doing. That is why the crew from Libreville knew that I was on Tangen's legendary flight. That is why our pilots knew what happened to Augie Martin.

Augie Martin was a 51-year-old African American veteran of World War II. He had been a Tuskegee Airman with the elite first black squadron of the United States Army Air Corps.

Martin was flying his Connie out of Lisbon with a cargo of food and arms for Biafra (one pilot told me he was flying a C-54). Newly married, he had his wife with him. He arrived over Uli in bad weather. Making his approach, he got a wave-off. As he was pulling up to go around again, he gunned the throttles, and lost two engines. He kept going around on two engines. On his next approach, he hit a tree one mile south of the airstrip. The accident investigation found two fuel selector switches in the wrong position. These switches were a safety measure to prevent running out of fuel on take-off or landing. With the switches in the wrong position, those two engines died of fuel starvation. The flight engineer was responsible for the switches. He had been warned previously for the same kind of lapse. Johnny Correa reported in his narrative that Captain Martin, "an American Negro," crashed to the south of the airstrip on his approach during a storm. Martin, his wife, and crew were buried in Biafra in a churchyard at Uli.

2

On Sunday, December 1, when it was probably snowing in New York, the four of us UNICEF volunteers chartered a boat for a day trip around the island. The tropical waters of São Tomé teemed with sea life: abundant fish, crabs, clams, rays, skates, sharks, sea turtles, squid, and dolphins. The equator runs through the small island of San Francisco just off the southern tip of São Tomé. The boat docked there. We walked up a path through a plantation, the only plantation on this small island of otherwise uninhabited bush. At the summit of a hill was a large marble monument designating the equator. The monument honored Portuguese navigators and scientists. To the south, I looked out over the Southern Hemisphere. I reflected that of all the world traveling I had done, there was still an entire hemisphere that I hadn't seen. Looking north from the hill, across the bay, I saw Porto Alegre, the small town on the southern tip of São Tomé Island. The view was absolutely beautiful.

After re-boarding the boat, we cruised around the island. The amazing natural beauty surpassed anything I had ever seen before. The southern coast was wild, rugged: huge cliffs rising out of the sea, draped with vegetation, dotted with caves, splashed with waterfalls. At the foot of the cliffs, blocks of black rock, great and small, jutted out of the water. Interrupting this ruggedness were fabulous lagoons, great places for swimming, but absent of human presence. This island would be a perfect place for a young naturalist. As I leaned on the railing of the boat looking at the sea and the ancient volcanic land, I felt as if I had been sailing on board the Beagle with Darwin. I saw hundreds of flying fish leaping out of the water ahead of the boat. They flew a surprisingly long distance, actually airborne on fins that served as wings. They whipped their strong, sharp tails underwater, propelling themselves into the air. They unfolded their wings and flew, banking one way and another as they chose. As they came across the crest of a wave, they hit it with their tails again and kept going a long, long way. We saw an enormous sea tortoise wallowing in the ocean swells. A school of dolphins came to play around the boat, riding the bow waves, arcing up out of the water and plunging back in. They played with us for a while, then went on their way. Strange birds – I called them flip-flop birds – flew by us. They flew along straight and level, then all of a sudden they started flipping straight up into the air and flopping down, making a snapping noise, snapping their wings together over their tails.

In addition to swimming fish and flying fish, São Tomé nurtured walking fish. Where an inlet comes in from the sea, these fish — weird, ugly, horrible looking things, about six inches long — came out of the water and walked around on the shore. They crawled up on rocks and logs using their front fins as feet, dragging themselves along. When frightened they ran across the top of the water with their "feet." Not constrained to their native element, the sea, these flying and walking fish cavorted easily in the rarefied air. Natural selection may have molded these abilities as survival skills over millions of years, but at the time I observed them, these fish were not fleeing predators or seeking food or mating, just flying or splashing in the mud because they could, for fun.

Any naturalist would have a rare experience on São Tomé, here at the center of the world, as rewarding as a visit to the Galapagos Islands. There was a strong sense of the passage of centuries, of ages, as great hot forces pushed up the land along a rupture in the Earth far below, and as the pounding sea, the wind, and the carbonic rain eroded the rock formations, the caves, and the cliffs. It was this sense of deep time, long beyond our own lives, that Darwin began to feel on his voyage with the Beagle, a perception of time that he needed to comprehend before he could begin to form a notion of living evolution.

It was refreshing for me to take this boat excursion, a day's vacation. But as I stepped off the boat and glanced back at the name on the bow, "Annabella," I snapped back into my own troubled personal time. "Annabelle" was the code name for the airstrip at Uli and a symbol of all the turmoil.

I wanted to go home.

3

Transavia kept the airlift going while ARCO was grounded, making six flights a night with two aircraft. Fred Olsen was down for a couple of days while the mechanics changed an engine. Otherwise, Fred Olsen's C-46 was one of the most steadfast planes in the airlift. Transavia had a few veteran pilots, some with WWII combat experience, but many of their crews were used to flying their DC-6s around Europe during peacetime. A new crew had come down recently. When they were told that they had to fly into Biafra without navigation lights, they refused.

"That's dangerous. It's against the rules."

"If you leave the lights on, Nigerians will shoot at you."

"Oh. Okay."

While ARCO was grounded, I flew with Transavia Monday night. They needed help offloading a special medical cargo. On the first shuttle we had to circle in the holding pattern while the intruder bombed the airstrip. We returned without landing. On the second attempt we landed without incident.

It was a bright moonlit night, the first full moon since I had started flying to Biafra, so I was able to see what the airstrip looked like. The previous full moon had occurred the night Baekstrom had been hit. Since then Biafrans had built bomb shelters at each parking finger, dug deep and lined with concrete blocks. There were slit trenches here and there. Anytime there was a hint of an enemy plane overhead the fatigue workers went for cover.

"Take cover before they give cover," one of them told me. They had to endure all the air raids, at night and during the day when the MiGs came. They could not fly away and be safe for a time. That night the bombs had fallen earlier, and the fatigue workers were no longer concerned. They went about the business of bringing a lorry up to the plane.

We got the cockpit door opened and put a ladder down. I could clearly see the bunker in the moonlight. I had never noticed them previously, on dark nights. I saw the captain and copilot of that fresh Transavia crew scurry down the ladder, run down the stairs into the bunker, and cower in a corner, covering their heads with their arms. Nobody else was in there. Nobody told them that the bomber would not be coming back that night.

The flight engineer and I helped unload the plane, then closed the rear door, ready to leave. The captain and copilot scampered up the ladder to the cockpit and slid into their seats. The engineer pulled up the ladder and secured the cockpit door while the other two started the engines. With the engines turning they wheeled out onto the runway and advanced the throttles to full takeoff power, no engine run-up or instrument checks. They took off without runway lights or landing lights. Not that they needed them in full moonlight. Not that they would have been a problem, either, since the intruder could have seen them as easily as in daylight.

No longer rookies, they would get used to flying this kind of "milk run." Initially in it for the high pay on this lucrative aviation job, they would, like most crews, develop a bond with the people they were helping to feed. One veteran pilot, Don Merriam, donated all of his flight pay to the orphanage at San Antonio. His crew donated some of theirs, also.

On Tuesday morning, December 3, ARCO got its act together and paid us. The churches would pay the per diem for the mechanics and pilots. ARCO would pay the regular salaries and flight bonuses, and they would pay Leo and me. From the airport, I went to the Post Office and sent a telegram to UNICEF, giving my two weeks' notice of resignation. I had given them a tentative thirty-day notice two weeks ago. This time I made it definite. I would be leaving by the eighteenth, my Dad's birthday, and home by Christmas. Our original contract called for thirty-day notices, for us and for UNICEF, if they wanted to sack us. Barry negotiated a new deal for fifteen days, based on the argument that things changed so fast.

In the evening I was over at the Baia having a beer with Arne, when two Transavia pilots came in. It was their night off.

"The DC-7s are flying again," one said.

"What?" I said, standing up.

"The DC-7s are flying. They got permission."

I saw Friedle. I went over and asked for conformation.

"Oh, yes. They've got permission to fly. But there's some problem."

Arne and I went over to the rooming house and got Leo and the car. We drove out to the airport. The DC-7s were still sitting there. Baekstrom and McCombie had been standing by but had left the airport by the time we got there. I talked to Baekstrom later. He was very bitter, very upset.

"We had gotten clearance for the DC-7s to fly," he said, "but somebody here fouled things up." ARCO and the churches couldn't agree on who would pay for the gas.

"What about tomorrow," I asked him.

"If it's straightened out by then, maybe we'll be flying."

Whether the churches or ARCO paid for it, ultimately the U.S. Government would reimburse 90% of it.

"Conscience money," a Biafran source told me.

Baekstrom, Tangen, McCombie, and Sagwick had worked out a compromise with Biafra that would allow ARCO to fly in spite of Biafra's mistrust of Peterson. The churches chartered Transavia to transport relief supplies. Similarly, the churches would charter ARCO, but on a day to day basis, flight by flight. One day WCC would charter ARCO; the next day, Caritas. Biafra could cancel the charter at a moment's notice. Weird deal, but that's how compromises go sometimes.

Peterson approached me and asked if I would like to be a regular employee of the company, rather than a day by day help mechanic. We had two planes flying, Alpha Bravo and Alpha Delta. But Peterson said he had more planes coming down to São Tomé. There was another DC-7C sitting in Lisbon waiting for parts. It was part of the original deal with Wharton. It would be in service in a couple of weeks. He had a DC-4 somewhere and he had a line on a Super Constellation. ARCO would have six aircraft, including Lima.

"There will be a lot of work to do, and we're really going to need you," he said.

"Sorry," I said. "I'm leaving in two weeks. I could work for you as a regular employee until then. Leo is staying. He would be willing to work full time."

Peterson was willing to hire me for the two weeks.

The usual Boeing came in Wednesday, December 4, with Cliff Robertson, the movie actor, and a film unit. He interviewed Baekstrom and others. Baekstrom was leaving for Sweden for further treatment of his wounded leg, but he told Robertson that he would return to the airlift and fly until the last plane left Biafra. Robertson was going into Biafra that night to interview Ojukwu. He would return to the States to present his information on TV shows like Johnny Carson's. While Leo and I worked on the DC-7s, Larry and Barry continued working in the warehouses and at the airport terminal. Larry wrote:

> Last Wednesday was an incredible day. Tuesday a Spanish princess of French Bourbon stock flew down with a plane load of special cargo. Wednesday the Boeing came, so we were unloading it and trying to get the princess's cargo weighed and sorted and put on planes to be taken to Biafra when she rushed into the warehouse with her entourage and stopped operations for fifteen minutes because some package was missing. Then Cliff Robertson and his camera crew came in and took shots of our work. Fortunately we were very busy and had lots of activity to put on film. Father Cunningham, Barry, and I had lunch with Cliff and his crew. He is very different from what you would expect from an actor. He was the first important figure in the States to take an interest in Biafra and has done much to promote concern. It is he who got

Ted Kennedy interested. He has appeared on such shows as Steve Allen, etc. to discuss Biafra and now he is trying to make a film to show on TV before Christmas. Cliff flew in on one of my flights. He interviewed me as we went in and friends tell me that they saw me in the film on Johnny Carson. He is in Biafra now and may be coming out tonight, but I hope tomorrow's Boeing doesn't bring any princesses or actors.

I met a British Member of Parliament that evening, someone named Dunwoody. Two British Lords, from the House of Lords, about eighty years old, drunk, struggled to get up the ladder into the plane to Biafra.

The Boeing also brought a load of medicine and two Land Rovers.

São Tomé was an international Grand Central Station where people from around the world funneled into the conduit to Biafra, the relief airlift. I met many people, coming and going. I talked to a Japanese photographer. He had spent three years in Viet Nam compiling a big photo essay. He won an overseas press club award for it. He was doing the same thing for the Nigeria-Biafra war, and he had already been to Nigeria, spending time with Nigerian troops around Calabar. Biafra was hesitant to let him in because of the Nigerian connection. I promised to do everything I could at Biafra House to get him in because I wanted to see him do that book. He asked for my address in New York, so he could send me a copy of the Viet Nam book and the Biafra book. He gave me a Nigerian Pound note as a souvenir. Nigerian money had changed since I was there.

In a tape I made the previous week, I more or less apologized for confusing everybody by sending a letter that I was coming home, then following that with a letter saying I was an aircraft mechanic making regular flights to Biafra. In the tape I made for Elner on December 4, the day following my second resignation I said:

> In any case, I'm leaving. I'll stay my two weeks. I'll work hard. I'll get some parts from Biafra. They can carry on without me. The war will not be won or lost whether I stay or go. I've seen enough. I've learned enough about Biafra and about the air operation. I'm coming home.

Martin Luther King, Jr. Memorial

CHAPTER 9

Inwe Onwe Mmadu

Freedom

Suppose a very large eruption on the sun destroyed the electronics on all our satellites. Such a flare hasn't happened in recent times, but it has happened, burning out the telegraph lines along the transcontinental railroad. No cell phones. No internet. International communications would revert to their primitive state in 1968, when there was a huge gap in time between two people trying to connect across the ocean. International telephone and telegraph connections existed in 1968, but they were very expensive and essentially unavailable to ordinary people.

Back in New York, on December 3, Elner made a tape for me. She filled me in on what had happened in Ocean Hill-Brownsville since I was there in October. The citywide strike ended when the four teachers were reinstated at Intermediate School 271, but the tension there remained high. The man sent by the New York State Department of Education in Albany to administer the whole district during the crisis, Mr. Johnson, took direct charge of 271. Elner said:

> We had an overseer in slavery and that's what we have now, because we're like children and we have to be looked after. So our overseer was there from the State, with a crew, to watch us. Everything was going along in a very tense and very electrified atmosphere, but it was going along and there were no confrontations. One guy came up to my room.
>
> "I just can't get over this," he said. "I wouldn't have believed it if I hadn't seen it. You can feel the tension in this room."
>
> "I hope," I said. "I want you to believe it that it is tense."
>
> He was surprised to hear me say it, but I came right out and said to him, "I'm very unhappy. As long as those teachers are in this

building, I will be unhappy, and my children will be unhappy. We will never forget it."

But we went ahead and swallowed it. Of course, as far as I was concerned they could blow that damn school up, because with Mr. Harris out, it was no school. But everybody was scared. I didn't realize it, but that's what it was – everybody was scared for their jobs. So everybody was taking it. I'm far from being a leader in this movement, so I didn't say anything.

I came in Thursday morning [probably November 21, the night I flew back from Biafra with Tangen] — I call it Black Thursday because it was the worst day of my life. I've been in the movement a long time, but that was a hard day to take. The day before, one of the union teachers broke a boy's thumb. That Thursday I came in, there were about thirty parents standing outside the door, and two teachers from other schools who had been active with me in political organizations last year, and they said, "You're not going in, are you?"

"Of course not," I said. "I'm standing out here. No, I will not!"

"We're blocking union teachers today," they said.

"Oh, yes," I said. "I have only ninety pounds to block with, but those ninety pounds will be used."

So we did. We really did. It's amazing what a little faith can do. They say that only thirteen people started the American Revolution. But I wasn't about to let my parents see me going in, you know. But most of our teachers did go in, even the Afro hairstyle girls and the dashiki fellows. They just went right on past us. One guy said, "Are you kidding? I'm not going to put my job on the line."

"Are you kidding," I said. "Before we're free, we're going to lose a lot more than our jobs." I couldn't believe it. And they couldn't believe it when they saw me take this stand. Everybody was very surprised, because I don't say anything. The reason I don't say anything is that I don't want to get involved in leading this fight, because I've been through that before, and that's no enjoyment. I want to have a life, some other kind of life, too.

So I'm purposely quiet. But when they saw me I was mad. I just couldn't hold it back anymore. I was mad. This was my freedom they were fooling with now. To me it was a complete slap in the face. It was saying, "You are under my boot and you're going to be there whether you like it or not." And to me to accept those teachers back in was saying, "Yes sir, boss."

I just couldn't do it. I wish I could. I thought a lot about those teachers going in there Thursday. I wish my Mother hadn't taught me this, but all my life she told us, "You can only die one time." That's the only thing they can really do to me. That job cannot be the end of my life. I can't be afraid for a job. They can't kill me but once. Sometimes, I wish I could crawl, but I can't do that. I'm just not made of that kind of material. And I certainly could not face those children. We've been teaching these children all these months that black is beautiful and they should be proud to be black, and then here they watch you crawl. And that means that they will have to do more than kill me to get that man back in the school.

So we stood there and held the door, the few of us who would hold it, until about noon, and they started immediately having negotiations with the overseer to work out a deal. And what made me so mad was the Governing Board and McCoy and his office was obviously trying to make a deal, and the four teachers who were suspended were trying to make a deal — a deal! We needed their support in order to rally more people from out there and put their heads in front of those police clubs. You can't do it unless you had these people stand there and say, "Yes, we're going to fight for our jobs because we're right." We're not going to have a sell-out to make a deal, because this man's been making deals with us ever since 1619, and I don't see where we have benefited from these deals. Now we might as well stand up there and fight.

The teachers kept backing down, backing down, and around eleven o'clock they started telling us, "Cool it. Cool it." A man from McCoy's office tried to come in and we tried to stop him, and they said he had some reason for going in. And then they came out and started telling us, "Let the children handle this. We've got some big children. Let the children take care of this."

"Are you kidding?" I said. "We are men and women and you want us to hide behind our children? You want our children to see that we are scared to stand up there and face these people? There's something wrong with you. I can't go in there and tell my students that we're proud to be black. I just can't do it."

So I guess they thought — you know we really had been brainwashed in slavery, and we really think that if we treat this man right, he's going to give us a break. I mean, you know, that black people in America are a long way from realizing that they got to take care of their own business. Nobody's going to take care of it for them. They still feel that Mr. Charlie is really good at heart, and if we just be nice, and if we just give him time, he's going to work everything out for us. I think that they must have thought that the four teachers were going to get back in and that Mr. Harris, our principal, was going to get back in.

Well they pulled us off those doors and I was ready to fight those policemen. But I was really hurt when it was our own people who pulled us off those doors. When that man broke the boy's thumb, that was a big issue that we could rally people around. But the only thing that we succeeded in getting in the negotiations that day was that this man, whose name is Malman, would be transferred to another office. He would not be allowed to come back in the school. Now, he did come in the next day and they did work something out. That day he was told to go to the district office, and nothing else.

So I came in. I just couldn't believe it. I could not talk to those people. I thought, "I've heard you stand up there and scream and shout and cuss that you were going to fight since September, and now you're standing up for your jobs." I just can't get over this.

So that day I was so downhearted, in the afternoon, after the confrontation. I went up to my classroom, and it was obvious that I had been through something, and my children thought that I had been hit or something when I was standing on the door. I didn't tell them, but they made plans what they were going to do the next day. What they were saying was, "she's not going to take it by herself." These kids have learned an awful lot in two months. They learned a whole lot more than they would have learned out of any books.

So my children came out; they came to class in blue jeans the next day, ready to fight. They understand the issues, much better than these adults do. And my Afro-American history class got together that night and bought equipment and made signs. They were gonna picket before school and they were gonna picket in the hallway and when they had a union teacher they were gonna hold the signs up. And I'll have you know that our faculty members called them in and chastised them, sent them home to change clothes, locked their signs up, later destroyed them, and then called me in.

So I said, "Well, I'm sorry. We were talking about two different things. I was talking about something else, so we got our wires crossed up." And this woman said, "What?" She was one of those Afro haircut ladies. And I'm supposed to be so damn bourgeois, because my dresses come from Peck and Peck and my hair is straightened and on top of that I'm married to a white man, so I'm supposed to be so Uncle Tomish that you cain't even talk to me. So this woman, with her earrings dangling, black — black for real — tells me this.

So I said, "The only thing I can say is, 'yes, ma'am, and I won't do it again,'" very sarcastically. I walked out. I don't know if I got my point over or not, but I think she felt a little silly afterwards.

So the situation got bad because we had only one administrator in the whole building, the assistant principal. The principal was gone, and all the other assistant principals, and it's impossible to run a school without administrators. And a lot of our teachers are absent — the whole thing has collapsed. It got so bad that it was almost dangerous. I mean kids were getting all out of hand, and you can't tell the children something in one class and not in another. All my discipline had gone, and some really bad children came back — they were out during the strike, but they're here now, setting fires and things and cursing you. You just couldn't believe.

But that is what it is like in a ghetto school. If you cannot be free, they are going to rebel; they know, see. You can't seem to get this over, because they're talking about running an orderly school in the situation that they're talking about. The only way you can have an orderly school, the kind we had in September when we had teaches who were free and we had administrators, we had community people. Well, anyway I think they learned their lesson, because the situation got progressively worse each day.

Plus, part of the agreement imposed on us was to extend the school day forty-five minutes and take away most of the school holidays. We were supposed to be back in school the day after Thanksgiving, and all the Christmas holidays were gone, and all this kind of business. The high school students said, "Hell no, we won't take it." They had rallies. (I was out of town – I went up to Rochester to see Eleanor). They had rallies over the weekend. And I don't know who ever had the guts to do it — because a lot of these same people who said, "Let's take the schools," on that Thursday I was describing were awfully meek and awfully quiet and wanting to make a deal, but I guess they found this man wasn't going to make a deal you can live with, because he's not going to compromise, he's going to have it all or nothing. When I got back to town — it was on the news yesterday — they were going to take the school. There were no two ways about it; they were going to take it.

They called me up and said, "What are you going to do?"

"I'm going to wait and see what they're going to do," I said. Because I know one person can't take that school, and I'm not going to be standing out there by myself.

When I got there Monday morning, the police were hurrying people along; they weren't allowing people to stand around. Now, it wasn't as bad as the day you went. They didn't have that many barricades. You could get up to the school before you reached the first barricade and they had about six policemen standing across the front. One person from the school was standing in the back to let them know who were teachers and who were students, and that was about all. But the two girls I was telling you about who were on that door on that Thursday were there when I drove up, but by the time I parked and came back, they weren't there anymore. So when I got to the door I thought, "I guess they put a stop to this. They aren't going to let anybody in." Well, how do you take a school if you're not there?

So I went upstairs and got ready for classes. The first period, which was about an hour later, I came back down to check on things, and it was quiet. There were the same old observers and State people and people, people, people — I don't know where all these people came from — some of them were plainclothesmen.

The same thing. However, they were sticking to that area around the auditorium, the lobby. They weren't in the classrooms and hallways like they had been sometimes. Things seemed to be rather quiet. I had a hard schedule Monday; I had to teach five classes straight through, except for a break for lunch. Well, at lunchtime I did go down, and I was shocked. There must have been a hundred people in that office. Now, McCoy has been suspiciously silent for the last week or so; in fact, the last we heard of him, he was trying to find a job. But the Governing Board chairman, Reverend Oliver, the minister, has really been great. He was arrested one day for trying to bring one of the suspended principals back, and he has consistently said that we are right, that we should run our own schools, that we have been completely tread on, we have been slapped in the face, we have been insulted, we have been emasculated before our children, and that these teachers should come back in. He has never once moved from that position, whereas a lot of these people have vacillated back and forth, but he has consistently come out with that.

When I saw him, I knew this was business down there. And one day he was even arrested. He came back with ten ministers and they had on their collars. There is not really too much you can do to a man who is pastor of a church in the community, because people say, "There's my minister. There's Reverend So-and-So." Now, how can you say these men are extremists? They are respected men in the black community, and I guess in the white, too. A minister is a respected person. You can't call him a name and get away with it.

So Reverend Oliver was there with his ministers, and I don't know where these people came from — there must have been a hundred of them. I came up to one of the teachers and said, "What's going on?"

"Johnson tried to close the school," he said, "but he can't find anybody to close it. He came to me and asked me to close it, and I said, 'no.'"

"Whaaat?" I said. Then I went on to lunch, and I came back and it was just turmoil and turmoil. People were going in and out of the principal's office. I said, "What are these people trying to do? What in the world is happening?"

I had to teach again, and I didn't get out until the eighth period. When I got back one of the Governing Board parents was having a tantrum, like my mother and I don't know how to have, and I can have some tantrums, but she was having a tantrum for real. She was screaming and cursing and throwing things.

"I mean, god damn it, everybody get out of the office!"

She put all the State people out, saying this was her school. She was sitting in Harris' chair herself. I thought, "No. I don't believe it. They did it." How they got in the building, or why, I don't know, but they took that school.

There have been all kinds of reports. I think I will send you this article so you can read it yourself. I don't know how much of this is true. We never get a fair shake in the news. It's gotten so bad now, we don't even let the news people in. There's reports that Johnson was actually locked in the closet to prevent him from closing the school. I don't think that's true. I heard that they wouldn't let him have the microphone — they won't let anyone have the microphone. But I don't know about locking him in the closet. Those secretaries down there would push you down before they'd let you do that. I would knock you out of the way before I would let you do that.

These people have never seen people before who say, "No, I'm not going to do it!" It takes a pretty strong man who would come up and hit a woman, especially a white man hit a black woman in a situation like this, so I don't think they had to lock him up. Another thing that was brought up in the Times is very true: how can they lock him up when he has plainclothes guards and patrol guards and people all around that building? I don't see how he could be locked up. But they're reporting — and this is true — that some of the parents hit the union teachers.

Also, yesterday, the high school children walked out of school, protesting the extension of schools, and let the teachers cool their heels. So the high school students were hanging tough, because most of them who are applying for colleges, most of them have lost their chance for the top schools. They have been thrown into all kind of turmoil. So they said, "No, we're not going to stay in here so you can make up the money you lost by screwing on us."

So about 400 of them descended on our school. And I mean it got bloody. I got kind of scared, because I don't go for getting my head beaten in or anything like that. The police beat up a newsman, but we didn't know that he was a newsman or that the police had done it. All we saw was this man coming in bloody and everyone was scared. It was a very tense situation toward the end there.

In any case, we did leave at three o'clock, and the school wasn't closed.

But then last night on the news — the poor overseer has had it; he had such a bad day yesterday, and the two weeks he's been at Ocean Hill, that he has resigned. Now, he told us before that things were going smoothly, and that things could be worked out, and we'll handle things, and we'll get things together, but yesterday he asked to be removed. Now we have a new one, and he's coming in rough and ready and telling what he's done so far. But Johnson resigned and now we have a new overseer.

And 271 has been closed.

This morning my alarm went off. I had planned to get there early, but knowing that I don't have to be at work, it's hard to get up and be about early, so I was a little late getting there. We went over to McCoy's office and they don't want to have anything to do with us. Now it's the 271 faculty who are the rebels. There's no one else out there — Reverend Oliver was out there; he's always going to stand by you — but most of the community people were absent today and all the principals. It's amazing. They would not let us meet anyplace. We were standing on the streets. We can't get in the schools. It's pretty warm now, but it's too cold for me at least to be standing in the streets.

So I went to McCoy's office, but they won't let you near him. They start immediately, "Oh, are you from 271? Well, there's a room down there for you to sit in." They don't want you around him.

"You'd think we had leprosy the way people are running from us today," I told them.

By the way, 271 faculty has been very meek ever since those four teachers were suspended. Not us. The Governing Board and the community have rallied to their support.

We went in there and sat for a while. Mr. Harris said he would arrange for us to meet at somebody's school. I knew we couldn't meet at one school because they are afraid of us. One teacher I know said the principal would have a heart attack if they knew 271 faculty would come near him. But this Chinese principal, we thought he might help us a little bit. I went over there.

When I went in the door a policeman and another man asked me if I was from 271.

"Yes," I said.

"Oh, you can't come in."

"What's wrong with you?" I said. "I'm not going to do anything. I just came in here because my principal, Mr. Harris, said we were coming in here for a meeting."

The policeman — he had the braids; he was the general of something — said, "No, you can't come in this door. I'm sorry. No one can come in this building." The other man was from the Board of Education. I just looked at him, and I said to myself, "You know that I'm from 271 and you think that somebody from the Board of Education is going to make me move? I thought you knew better than that. You're wasting your breath with that."

So they got all uptight and everything. I was calm.

"Look," I said, "You ought to be humane for once. It's cold out there. They told us we were going to have a meeting. I'm not going to do anything to this school, and no one else is. I'm not here to make any kind of trouble. I'm not going to stand out there in the cold. You said that Mr. Lee is coming down. Why don't you let me stand here and wait for Mr. Lee?"

Well, the Board of Education man ran. I'm not joking: he ran. I'm standing here alone, in my loafers, no lipstick, and my trench coat and my pocketbook. Now, I know that if you don't look at me very close, I don't even look like I'm an adult. So he ran from this little person standing here. And this big general, this policeman, went out and got a patrolman to watch me. So I went and stood by the door, me and my paper. The policeman went to make a phone call, and when I changed feet — I was standing on one leg, and when I went to shuffle on another foot — and turn my paper, you should have seen him run. He ran out to see what I was doing.

Then the Board guy came down and said, "We have gotten Mr. Harris on the phone and told him that you — he — cannot have a meeting at this school."

"Okay," I said. At that point no one else had come, so I just left. I went over, and it was pitiful: our whole faculty was standing out in the streets. There was no place. We can't go in McCoy's office. We can't go to any school in the district. Fortunately, our kids — most of them — did not show up, because I did not want them to see this side of what was happening.

Harris said, "This can't be right. No. We're going to get in one of these schools." He went around to a few of them, and he came back and said, "No, we sure can't get in them."

"I can tell you, we sure can't," I said. Right now they aren't going to let 271 people anywhere near any of these schools.

Finally McCoy and them opened a room in the basement, a boiler room, no chairs, not anything: just a room. Harris said we've got to talk to this new trustee, because he's the one who put the rule out that we couldn't get in any school. Now, what I can't get over is that they are really letting us sink, that they are letting us drown alone.

How can one man run your school? That's why 271 had to be closed. Because when these people come in to our school, they don't run it. Nobody, the children, the teachers, the assistant principals, the principal — nobody does what they tell you to do. If they tell you to do something and you don't want to want to do it, they can't just replace you, especially if you're a professional. They can't go right out and get somebody else to do it. You just stand around and say, "Hell no, I'm not going to do it." But these people didn't do this. They wanted to get 271 completely isolated, away from everything.

So we have our little meeting, and I walked out of it cursing. Because, I don't know how to say this, David, but most of the white faculty members are going to go with us up to a point, but most of them have turned back now, because they feel that now we have to try to educate our children. We can't get the point over to them that we are fighting for something that is so important to us — something that they have and we don't have. We can't get them to see this. They are talking about improving their schools. We cannot improve our schools unless we have freedom in our schools. And the fact that those teachers are back in there is contradictory to the fact that we are free. We're not. We're still slaves. We can't get the white people to see that. So they start taking up a whole lot of time with: What are you interested in? Politics or educating your children?

"Fuck you!" I said, and walked out.

I came home and tried to find a bank. My school check wasn't in "Koren" so I had to keep my account in "McCraty." I had to find some way to negotiate the money that I have here from you. I feel a lot closer to you talking to you on this thing. I still haven't had my breakfast and it must be around two o'clock now. I'll probably go down to KLM or someplace this afternoon and work on going to São Tomé. That will be good for me.

Tomorrow I'll go down to the Board and asked to be transferred over here. It just isn't worth getting up, traveling for an hour in the morning and an hour in the evening for that bullshit those people are talking about over there. I just can't be bothered with it. A lot of the black teachers — black people are so pitiful — you talk about racism, what it has done to both peoples, both races, it's so pathetic. First of all, there are those who are scared. I don't understand you being so scared. I remember the days when I first started sitting in, and the police would come in — this was in the South — and I would be afraid. But I have never been so afraid that I wouldn't act. I've never been that afraid. My knees might be shaking, but my voice was steady, my eye was steady. I always looked them in the face. And of course, my size was quite a help, because you don't just pull your brute force on someone less than one hundred pounds. I guess I've always used that. Anyway, I just could not be afraid. I just could not. I feel like there is something I could do. Hell, I could teach in Biafra before I would be afraid, and Lord knows, I don't want to go to Biafra. There's always something. I just wouldn't be scared.

But there's these people who are afraid of their jobs. They just can't see this whole thing we're in together. I always make this analogy, and people forget it as soon as I say it: In Germany back in 1939 there were Jews who went around talking about politics. "I don't want to be involved in politics. Oh, no. No. I don't know anything about politics." That is the way the professors in the University of Munich were talking. Sure enough, the people selling vegetables on the corner were being picked up, but this doesn't affect me being in politics. But before it was over, everybody went. They didn't ask you how many degrees you have. They didn't ask you how clean your nose is and how many white ancestors you had. In the final analysis, everybody's going to go. If they're not free down there in Ocean Hill-Brownsville, I'm not free sitting up here in a mid-town Manhattan apartment, with a white husband, you know. I mean, I'm still not free.

I don't understand that this is the way people think. But they don't understand this. They feel like, "I'm just the victim of a circumstance." So I don't see anybody over there, white or black, that I can work with. In fact, those that are taking a stand are so crazy — they're so unreasonable. They are so affected, too. So I haven't found my little niche as far as people are concerned, so I'm going to just find me a job. I hope to do day-to-day substitute. I don't want to take a regular job, because, after that beautiful school we had for two months, I'd hate to go back to the same old sixty-six. But I'll probably do that.

Well, that's enough bad news from Ocean Hill-Brownsville. It's pretty bad in a way. But one thing, I finally made them come down in the end. Stand and fight like men. If you're going to fight, do it like Biafra.

I was so excited when I received your letter, because I was beginning to feel not being cared for, and I like to be pampered, and have a little special attention paid to me. And every time someone says to me, "How's your husband?" Well, you know, he talks about DC-3s and DC-7s. My sister says she doesn't know a DC-3 from a DC-7, and I don't either.

And she says, "Well, what else did he say?"

"He didn't say anything else."

So when you said you wanted me to come see you for Christmas,

I was so excited. I called her. It was so funny. She said, "What do you mean, Amsterdam? Amsterdam is in Holland."

"Yes," I said.

"Well, everybody's not able." She was a little jealous and happy for me, too, to be doing this.

I have an awful lot of tape left. I can't do like you. I can't take forever and a day to say something. I have a tendency to want to get things over with. I need to fill up this tape and I don't have any music here. I want to mail this right away, so it might be kind of empty. Is there anything else that has to be said?

Well, you said you just wanted to hear me talk, so I guess I can go into detail about my trip to Rochester. I went up Thanksgiving morning and came back Sunday morning. It was welcome. I don't like New York the way I might seem to. It's nice once in a while to breathe unpolluted air. So every chance I get, I try to get away.

Eleanor was a wonderful host. She's a pretty bad cook. I'm a bad cook, but she's worse than I am, so it's really bad. But she tried to fix a turkey dinner. Her fiancée is in Thailand working for an American company, unfortunately for the wrong reasons, because he's making communications systems between Viet Nam and Thailand. He's an engineer. He's doing this for money. So we were feeling sorry for ourselves. We sat and talked about how our men don't care anything about us [laughing]. So we had a good time consoling each other. Neither of us, of course, were interested in going out with any fellows or anything, so it was good to have each other. She couldn't go home because she couldn't get airline reservations. It doesn't do me any good to go home because my sister won't be there and my mother isn't really a family kind of person. So I don't think about that. But anyway Eleanor and I had a good time.

You know, my attitude and commitment toward Biafra and Africa are different from yours and Eleanor's is quite different from mine, because the life she lived as a volunteer, I would personally be ashamed of and she's very proud of. Her school paid for her membership in the English Club. She didn't have any Nigerian friends and was proud of it. And as far as the Biafra-Nigeria situation, she was so pro-Nigerian that we almost went to blows — almost had a fight. That's why I haven't made too many attempts to get in touch with her, because it really made me angry when she would give pro arguments for Nigeria. But her Peace Corps life was so different — she rubbed elbows with the British, and their position is safe by Nigeria beating Biafra. She doesn't understand about black people being free from under the boot. For all these years she hasn't had any comprehension of this at all because she has escaped it. She makes a lot of money and all the amenities of life and people don't call her horrible names and things like that. She's kind of out of it. But the atrocities and so forth have awakened her, and so she even gave some money to Biafra while she was here. But she doesn't have any feeling for the situation. She is willing to concede to me that the Nigerians are wrong in the genocide. Everyone who has been in West Africa will agree whole-heartedly that they know how people feel about Igbos. Some people think the killing is justified and some people think it's not. But everyone admits that Biafra has to fight to win. There is no question about that.

She was telling me her experiences in the North, noticing how the Igbos were discriminated against, and she said, "Oh, I know if they ever get a chance to, they'll wipe them out." I got her to agree to that much. So we didn't have that argument.

There are many other things that we don't see quite eye-to-eye about. We've had such different kinds of backgrounds and experiences. Even our students in Nigeria were so totally different. Certainly we have enough in common to get along. And she has come over the years, since we met in training, to respect me a lot. She disagrees with my point of view, but she will certainly respect it. She thinks I'm an intelligent person. And we have come to have a real tight bond. She makes more money than I make because she has her Master's. However, she has more expenses than I have, so we come out about even. She's always asking me if I need money. She was telling me how her fiancée sent her $50, and I said my husband sent me $300, so do you need any help?

That reminded me of another interesting thing. There was a teacher at my school who had spent two years in Ghana — Accra — with a university, and he did that for Afro-American history. He knows that as a field, the way I know Biology, and I don't know it that way. I have to teach from my own feelings, and I feel this way about — what one of the history teachers said — we aren't really teaching Afro-American history, we are teaching them to rise up off their knees, we're trying to get them to understand that they are not inferior people. So I don't really go so much for African history. I was really surprised when my students were telling me some of those things. I haven't paid that much attention to African studies in training, because they were too cold — black people have soul; I have soul. I sit there and turn you off when you start talking to me about cold facts about something that means so much to me.

I was talking to that teacher about something. Let's see, how did that conversation get around? We were talking about Africa, the course of study. He was telling me what he was doing in his class. He has asked his class, which is smarter than my class, to do a research project, papers on different groups of people — I don't even know their names, I guess the Hottentots — not just tribes, but major groups of people. "The thing I'm doing," he said, "is to show that they are not really that different. They have so much in common."

He's going to make a chart of all of their findings and he wants to show that these people are not different. And I said, "Well, I think just the opposite because, as far as I'm concerned, it's amazing that these people have one flag, and they all look essentially alike, because they are different. It is true, I have read, for instance, this book I have on Igbo culture written by an Igbo who was here working on his Doctor's, so it's very good. I read this book and I think in terms of living in the village in Efik land — I didn't live in a village when I was in Igbo land. Some of the processes are very similar — that's true — certainly outlooks and attitudes are very similar. But the people to me are miles apart. I can't imagine saying that Efiks and Igbos are like one people.

"Well," he said, "I can see how you feel that way, but if you went to the rest of West Africa, you would find the rest of the people not so far apart."

"Okay," I said, "That's enough. You can get out of my room now."

Anyway, getting back to Eleanor, we went to see Dick Gregory. He was really great. He was on a fast again. He said he was drinking distilled water. He has a new line, at least new for me hearing it, kind of precious.

"I stopped drinking on Thanksgiving," he said. "One Thanksgiving I was putting my knife into that turkey, and I started thinking: Now suppose we run up on some of those other people from those other planets who listen to us talk, saying, 'please don't do this, don't do that,' and they hear, 'gobble, gobble, gobble, gobble' and we end up on a plate as somebody else's turkey dinner."

The way he told it, it was really hilarious. And, like I told you — I think it's the second or third time I've told you — he wasn't needlessly cruel. I don't believe in telling jokes about white people that are unnecessary. And I don't get any pleasure about making anybody suffer. It doesn't make me feel good to call people those names they have, so I don't go for that kind of stuff. I believe in taking care of business. Calling people names doesn't give me any kind of lift. And I don't want anybody to call me a name. That's one thing I dropped early from my vocabulary: these derogatory names. I don't use them in any sense. I just don't want to hear them.

I've got to get up now and get something to eat and see how I'm going to get to São Tomé.

I sent my telegram of resignation to UNICEF on December 3. Elner mailed that tape to me on December 3, before UNICEF could notify her, if they notified her at all. I can imagine the following scene:

JAN (opening the telegram): It's from Koren. He says he's resigning again.
GERRY: Yeah. Just ignore it. He's not going anywhere.

The soonest Elner's tape could have reached me was December 12 on the mail plane from Luanda. Unaware of the bombshell headed my way, I continued my mechanic work, expecting to leave soon.

DC-7 Bravo Charlie Whiskey

CHAPTER 10

Ndu Bu Isi

Life Is the Main Thing

In the closing days of 1968, the continuing mass starvation in Biafra frustrated those outside of the conflict who felt compelled to "do something." Either stop the war or stop the starvation, but Biafrans wouldn't quit in evident fear of genocide. Nigeria wouldn't quit with the powerful backing of Britain, who wanted control of Nigeria's oil, and Russia, who wanted political influence in Africa. The United States government was twisted in knots over what to do. Henry Kissinger's State Department ardently promoted a "One Nigeria" policy in support of Britain, America's strongest ally, while the Nixon Administration and most of the American people were sympathetic to Biafra. The U.S. sent no weapons to Nigeria, but most of the food aid for Biafra came from the U.S.

The relief airlift had dramatically reduced the rate of starvation, but the anticipated carbohydrate famine was expected to be far beyond the capacity of the current relief effort. The safe passage of a water corridor up the Niger River was proposed by the churches and rejected by Biafra because of the possibility of Nigeria sneaking troop ships along with the aid and breaching their enclave. The Vatican, the church relief agencies, and an unnamed U.S. congressman attempted to negotiate a protected air corridor for round-the-clock relief flights. That failed because Nigeria insisted that the churches were smuggling guns along with the food, a nonsensical political statement – Biafra's own transport planes were delivering plenty of weapons to the military and the churches needed all their capacity for food. The bottom line was that Nigeria was using starvation as a legitimate weapon of war. Relief aid impeded their effort to starve Biafra into submission.

1

We changed all the spark plugs on Alpha Bravo. The R3350 engines (3,400 horsepower, each) on a DC-7 had two banks of nine cylinders each arranged radially around the propeller shaft. Each cylinder had two spark plugs. When we changed plugs on a plane, we changed 144 of them. The plugs in front were easy to reach with a simple socket wrench, but the back plugs on the second bank of cylinders required major contortions. We used a socket wrench with three separate flexible elbows. I gripped the socket in my right hand, leaned forward with one foot on the top of the ladder, stretched my arm way back in the engine, and, by feel, fitted the socket over the plug. Carefully, I withdrew my hand. I gripped the wrench handle with both hands, and began to turn the wrench. I had to use enough force to break the plug threads loose in the cylinder, but not enough to jerk the socket off the plug. If the socket did pop off, I had to insert it all over again. I turned the handle slowly until the plug came free. I reached in and pulled the plug out. Then I removed a new plug from its wrapping and reached it back in, carefully catching the threads in the hole, so as not to strip them, and turning the plug down hand tight. I stretched back in and slipped the socket over the plug, seating it properly on the hex nut without cracking the ceramic insulation. Then I turned the wrench with just enough torque to tighten the plug. I reached in again and deftly slipped the socket off the plug. With one more reach, I slipped the electrical lead over the end of the plug and snugged it down.

I was working up on engine number one. Leo was to my left on engine number two. At the end of a day's work in the steamy heat, he was working on the last plug. He dropped it. He climbed down the ladder. He picked up the plug, cocked his head the way he does and squinted at it. He puffed at it a couple of times, blowing on the spark gap. He climbed the ladder again and successfully inserted the plug. We buttoned up the cowlings, collected our tools and called it a day.

Soon afterwards, the crew arrived and prepared for the first shuttle to Biafra. I watched them taxi out to the west end of the runway. They throttled up the engines, brakes set tight, the plane rocking gently, while the flight engineer checked his instruments. But instead of taking off, the pilot throttled back the engines and taxied back to the hangar. I went out to see what was wrong. The flight engineer, studying his oscilloscope, could see that a spark plug on engine number two was misfiring on one of two cylinders, either top or bottom. I knew which one. We changed the plug, and they took off for Biafra with ten tons of food.

That incident scared me. Leo and I were help mechanics, three weeks on the job, doing serious maintenance work. With the heavy workload on the licensed mechanics to keep those old planes flying and delivering life-giving relief, Leo and I were needed. But it was a serious responsibility, not like a hobby to occupy our time until we could be assigned as offloaders or until we went home. If we made a major mistake, we could lose one of those planes, and the crew.

On Friday, December 6, we washed Alpha Delta. There were two reasons for that. First, we had recently had a wing fire due to a buildup of carbon deposits behind an engine. Second, the accumulated dirt on an aircraft increases skin friction, robbing air speed and increasing fuel consumption. Speed was necessary for the DC-7s to make three shuttles a night, a significant tonnage of food. A lower weight of fuel per shuttle meant more capacity for cargo.

Turning wrenches in the equatorial sun is hot, dirty, and tedious. Washing a large airplane is totally fun. All the mechanics: Africans, Americans, and Europeans, got involved. We stripped down to our shorts. We dragged long hoses out of the hangar. We got out the ladders and long-handled brushes and lots of soap. There were suds everywhere, water spraying everywhere. We got soaking wet, shouting and laughing. It was like running through the lawn sprinkler on a hot summer day, times ten.

The sunny days were hot and humid, and the rain fell more often on São Tomé as we approached the height of the rainy season. In October, when I first came to the island, the rainy season was beginning to taper off in Biafra and beginning to escalate in São Tomé. They say that the rain follows the sun. As the world rolls through its seasons, the sun slides south across the equator and by December, the rain intensifies on São Tomé. My room leaked like crazy. Water ran down the walls and across the floor. It was damp and horrible. Barry, Leo, and Larry had moved out of our original, temporary space and found individual rooms at Senhor Costa's Café Equador. I remained, hoping that I could fix it up and that Elner might join me on São Tomé. When the room got wet, I found another place to rent for the two of us at about half the cost — $18 a month. But when I decided to leave in two weeks, I stayed where I was.

UNICEF had still not sent our living allowance. We were given an advance of $500 to last five weeks. We were then in our seventh week. Larry and Barry were getting rather destitute. Larry was flat broke. He was running up a tab for his room and meals at Costa's that he would have to pay at the end of December. I was helping him with some of my mechanic's pay. Leo was rolling in dough, but he wouldn't get up off of a dollar. He wouldn't even take any *dash* into Biafra. When Barry and I went into Biafra we took a carton of cigarettes, soap, or razor blades. Not Leo.

When Barry went into Biafra on business for the warehouses on November 21, he came out a few days later with news that Nnewi was in danger of being overrun by Nigerian troops pushing down from Awka in the north. That would have been bad because Nnewi was a huge black market center, replacing Onitsha as Biafra's biggest market. Goods were smuggled across the Niger River from the Mid-West Region of Nigeria, where there were people sympathetic to Biafra, as were the two Yoruba mechanics I had met at Uli. Anything available in Nigeria could be found in Nnewi, but at black market prices. Missionaries talked about the need for a land corridor to the coast at Opobo, but Biafrans had already established a corridor through Nnewi funneling food, petrol, tires, batteries, and even some luxury goods.

Barry saw a lot of lorries lined up, full of petrol, waiting to evacuate people with their loads if Biafran troops could not halt the Nigerian advance. Barry went back into Biafra the following week and found Nnewi no longer threatened. Biafran troops had pushed the Nigerians back to Awka, in the process capturing a lot of weapons. The weapons were mostly old rifles, given to Hausa boys with little training, the same people who had slaughtered Igbos before the war. This time Igbos could fight back, and they established a static front line near Awka.

2

What is worse: that cold moment when you sense something terribly wrong or that moment when you learn the terrible reality?

On Sunday morning, December 8, 1968, I went to work at the airport. We had been doing one hundred hour engine checks on Alpha Delta, changing spark plugs and oil filters and checking all systems. After the scrubbing we had given it on Friday, it looked pretty spiffy, like an old man dressed up in his best twenty year old suit. We had completed the checks on two engines Saturday, and we wanted to work a half day Sunday to complete another engine. I greeted the security guard, who knew me by now and no longer checked my ID, and I walked out on the flight line. I saw Bravo there in its usual parking place, and I looked over to where Delta always parked, and should have been, but wasn't. I looked around the airport and counted planes. A Transavia plane was missing, too.

I got an uneasy feeling in my stomach. It's true that strong emotions can manifest themselves physically. I felt it in my knees. I shuddered. This was something bad. There had been a rumor that Nigeria meant to begin a series of intensive bombings at Uli, lasting three or four days. The night before last would have been the first such night. They did drop more bombs than ever before, but as usual, they didn't hit anything. Maybe last night they got lucky. Worse, maybe there had been a mechanical failure due to my mechanical inexperience. These thoughts swirled through my mind, and came out through my knees.

I saw no one around. I walked toward the terminal building looking for someone to tell me what had happened. I saw one of our Danish mechanics sitting at a table. At a distance too far to talk, I spread my arms out, palms up, and shrugged my shoulders in a gesture that said, "What happened?" I pointed to where Delta should be. He signaled with his hand palm downward, moving it toward the ground, meaning, "Down."

I broke into a run. Sitting at the table with a cup of coffee, looking dejected, the Dane said, "All we know is that McCombie crashed in Biafra."

He crashed going in on the second shuttle. With him were Raab, his copilot, Holtzman, his American flight engineer, and another American named Thompson, who was along as an observer. There were no bombs. Another pilot who was in the air at the time reported hearing Raab radio that he was on downwind leg, ready to come up on final approach. A team of Biafrans, sent to look for it, confirmed that a plane had crashed. The Transavia plane flying an air-sea search soon returned.

A team from São Tomé was selected to go into Biafra Sunday night to investigate the crash site: McPhee, a Canadian expert in air-sea rescue; Father Cunningham; Barry, because he knew some Igbo language; and me for the same reason, and because I had some familiarity with aircraft parts. We packed enough food and supplies for a couple of days. Before we could leave, a message from Biafra said that the plane had hit a high-tension wire, and that no investigation was necessary.

"No investigation necessary." That raised suspicions. We knew of no high-tension wires near the airstrip and we grumbled that Biafran authorities might be covering up a Biafran ground fire incident that caused the crash. Of course we would have to investigate the crash. But Barry and I did not go; McPhee and Father Cunningham went anyway. Reverend Aitken and Father Butler, already in Biafra, joined them. Delahunt flew Bravo that night. Remember, it was Delahunt who flew the night after Baekstrom was bombed.

All the planes flew. Transavia flew two planes; they didn't have enough crew to fly their third plane. Fred Olsen flew, of course. And another new charter company, Braathen, flew their DC-6B. A friend of mine from Biafra House thought it was scandalous to fly that night, that the airlift should have been suspended out of respect for McCombie and his crew. Biafra would not die if we missed one night, he said. I told him that continuing the airlift was the best way to honor them, because they would always fly no matter what, bombing or bad weather, to take care of those still living. He said that was a good way to think about it.

Ndu bu isi. Life is the main thing.

I thought of Elner hearing on the news that a DC-7 had crashed in Biafra with two Americans killed. I started to send her a telegram, but fortunately I thought that through before I did. What if she heard the news, and the next thing there was a kid at her door handing her a telegram? Instead, I sent the telegram to Gerry Schwinn, UNICEF, 866 UN Plaza, New York: "UNICEF VOLUNTEERS NOT IN BIAFRA AIR CRASH." Gerry could call her; she wouldn't have to fumble open a telegram to learn my fate.

McPhee, who was also a photographer, took his equipment with him. Later, I saw the pictures: a clearing in the forest of burned, unrecognizable rubble. The tail section. An engine. A landing gear strut, ripped from the plane and standing alone, upside down with the tires still intact. "You can tell the incredible force of the impact by how that strut was torn away," said Helmut looking at the pictures. The strut must have been ripped out of the wing before the plane burst into flames. The investigating team gave their report.

McCombie was on the downwind leg flying parallel to the runway but in the opposite direction, 3½ miles from Uli. As McCombie banked into his turn to come upwind on final approach, the right wing, between engines three and four, struck an iroko tree, shearing off the wing. The plane veered sideways, bounced a couple of times, and blew apart. The bodies were found in the impact area, some with the backs of their skulls missing. Nothing like a cockpit was identifiable. The investigators found an altimeter that read four hundred feet. At the crash site, there is a rise in the ground of about two hundred feet. The iroko tree, a giant of the rain forest, with long fluted roots, may have been two hundred feet high, enough to account for the crash. The other pilots said McCombie liked to come in low and level, rather than come in high over the runway and drop down. But four hundred feet at 3½ miles out is very low. There was no radar or ground controlled approach to let a pilot know he was on course and on glide path. It was dark. The pilots of the Biafran Airlift depended on dead reckoning and their own cockpit instruments.

So McCombie, a Scotsman, was gone, along with copilot Heinz Raab, a German, flight engineer Holtzman, an American, and Captain Thompson, an American who was flying as an observer that night. I had talked to Holtzman a few times on the flight line as he was getting in the aircraft, reporting on what work we had done on the plane that day. Captain Thompson had flown as a U.S. Air Force pilot during the Berlin Airlift. He was observing the flight so that he could fill in as other DC-7 pilots took time off for Christmas. I talked to him as he was entering the aircraft for the first shuttle that night. He was standing up in the door and

I was down on the flight line.

"This is a little different than the Berlin Airlift, isn't it?" I said.

"Oh, yeah. Quite a bit different. There we had a plane landing every three minutes."

At the time of the crash, McCombie's wife was there on São Tomé. Raab's wife and Thompson's wife were also there. Holtzman was unmarried. He was survived by his mother back in the States.

On the Monday afternoon following the crash, the Biafran Air Force, Army, and Navy held a full military funeral in Biafra, attended by the Archbishop and relief workers. It was held at the church at Uli, just off the road along the approach to the airstrip. Landing planes passed right beside it. The church, with its two tall spires, was clearly visible out the windows on the right side. I could see it in the landing lights as the plane rushed by on final approach, waggling its wings to line up with the runway. I could see it in the moonlight. McCombie and his crew were buried there, alongside Augie Martin, his wife, and crew. By the end of the war, 35 airmen would die. Nigeria bulldozed the graves.

On São Tomé, we had a memorial service on Tuesday, a joint Protestant and Catholic service. Reverend Aitken represented the Protestants, giving a brilliant, moving speech. Father Byrne, Father Cunningham, and Father Kennedy performed the Catholic Mass. Father Byrne spoke about the crew. He said that they were international, that they came from all over the world and gave their lives doing this marvelous humanitarian service, flying food to Biafra so that nine million people could survive.

Soon after, Mrs. McCombie surprised me by thanking me for being a friend to her and her husband. She gave me a Christmas card addressed to "Mr. and Mrs. David Koren." She gave me an eight-inch tall statue of a Buddha, finely carved from heavy wood. It was a jolly Buddha with a big smile and a huge belly sticking out of his robes. It looked just like McCombie.

I recorded my tapes in various locations. On them you could hear different backgrounds, miniature environments. Rain drenched the setting of my first tape. Others were recorded in quiet or noisy cafés, with tropical birds screeching or tweeting beside me, or children playing, or people eating and drinking, or motorcycles going by, or airplanes in flight. Once there was a piercing siren, as if an air raid were in progress, but I ignored it. It must have been the *onze e trinta* whistle signaling the mid-day work break on São Tomé. Once there was a Strauss waltz, the one from Stanley Kubrick's *2001: A Space Odyssey*, a movie just released in 1968. But when I spoke of McCombie's death, I was in an enclosed space, a small hard place, sound rebounding from hard walls unbuffered by soft curtains, soft furniture, soft rugs – my own empty room.

On the morning of December 11, Leo and I and Arne went out to work on Lima. It was late in the morning, because we really didn't feel like working that day. The sun was well up, dodging in and out of rainy season clouds. It was hot and sticky. We had to remove a damaged aileron so we could fix it, and that required removing about 120 small screws, turning each one by hand.

A friendly Portuguese soldier, who often talked to us while we were working, stood by. Two Portuguese policemen in blue uniforms with nothing else to do on a languid day joined us. Then some of the mechanics wandered out to watch us. Pretty soon, there was a crowd standing around. Somebody went and got some beer. On the Boeing that morning, someone had brought a bottle of cognac, and one of the mechanics had it. He passed it around. Everybody was sipping. They started laughing and hooting at us working up on the wing in the hot sun. Arne came down and had a sip. Leo came down and had a sip. Then I came down for a sip while Leo went back up. We kept going up and down until we had removed the aileron.

Lima was parked near the fence that ran around the airfield. An African woman was walking by on the path outside the fence with a basket on her head. She was selling coconuts. Someone bought the whole basket full and brought them over. We drank the coconut milk and ate some of the meat. Leo drank a little bit of the coconut milk from the husk, then poured a lot of cognac in it. We tasted it. It was awful. Another mechanic, named Vaughn, drove out from the hangar in one of the Caritas Volkswagens that Joe Galano had tried to give us. He saw us drinking from the coconuts, and his eyes lit up. He really wanted some of that good coconut milk. Leo offered him his.

"Nyuuk!" he said. "I didn't know they tasted that bad. It's a familiar taste, though; I can't quite place it. Cognac?"

Tuesday night, all of our planes flew into Biafra in spite of Nigerian bombing. Several of our planes had taken off as usual when it was still daylight on São Tomé. They hadn't gotten far when they were called back because the runway at Uli had been damaged. They waited a couple of hours while the holes were patched, then they all flew two shuttles.

But Wednesday the airlift halted. One of our planes flew from São Tomé and one from Santa Isabella on Fernando Po carrying delegates from the churches and from the Red Cross. The delegates were to meet with Ojukwu to protest Biafran ground fire that was sometimes directed at our planes. The McCombie crash had been correctly ruled an accident, but one night Biafran troops had fired their guns in the air in wild celebration of a rumor that France had recognized Biafra. The need for hope was high; Biafra felt alone against the world, but the rumor was false, and some bullets struck a plane. The previous week a Red Cross plane had been hit by small arms fire. There was no serious damage, but the delegates wanted Ojukwu to enforce better discipline on his troops to avoid friendly fire incidents, deadly ones.

While they were dealing with that, Arne and Leo and I found a little restaurant that sold cans of Danish bacon. We had the cook fry us some of the bacon along with eggs and potatoes. The waitress served these with mushrooms and onions and lettuce and tomatoes. After we ate, Leo and Arne wrote letters while I made a tape. Arne complained that his communication back and forth with Sweden was as bad as our mail with the States. He asked if we could get him in the Caritas mailbox.

Arne. Of all the people in the airlift and their associations with different groups, Arne chose to hang around with Leo and me. He was short, like we were, and between our ages, with a craggy face. He was the only mechanic who would come into Biafra with us. He laughed and talked boisterously. But one night while we were drinking in a café, he lowered his voice.

"I know how we can make a lot of money," he said.

I looked at him. Leo watched me.

"One of the Red Cross DC-7s on Fernando Po needs a part, and their mechanics can't find one. It's a landing gear locking latch. When the gear retracts, the latch locks it in place during flight."

I thought I saw where he was going with this. We would get the part from the DC-7 in Biafra and sell it on the sly to the Red Cross mechanics. I didn't like it. It sounded underhanded, profiteering from starvation. If the Red Cross needed the part to get their plane flying again, we should give it to them. But that's not quite what he had in mind.

"We could take it from Lima when we're out there working on it. Nobody will know."

"Arne! We're trying to get that plane flying again. Taking that part out would be dangerous!" I said. Leo looked on.

"That old crate will never fly again," said Arne.

"Yes it will! That's why we've been working on it all these weeks. Leave it alone," I said.

"I already took it out," Arne said.

"Shit! Put it back!" He said he would, late some night.

On December 12, the mail plane brought Elner's tape of Ocean Hill-Brownsville. Things changed as fast a striking rattlesnake. She was coming to São Tomé and I was going to New York. I fired off another telegram, directly to Elner this time, telling her to come on. I would stay here. She could catch the Boeing from Amsterdam or Copenhagen. I sent her $500.

For the next two weeks I had no days off work, and I met every Boeing that came down, not knowing which one she might be on. Besides the regular Wednesday flights there were sometimes extras. I didn't tell anybody why I was there, but everyone knew that I was expecting Elner. Everybody, all the people I worked with, including the Portuguese and the Cape Verde Islanders, kept asking when she was coming.

Mrs. Mollerup, wife of Pastor Mollerup, head of Nordchurchaid, saw me waiting for a plane that was due in at midnight and didn't come in until about five o'clock in the morning. She knew that I'd stayed up all night, then went home and changed clothes and went to work. She told her husband. Without saying anything to me, he made a reservation for Elner on the special Boeing coming down on Saturday, December 28.

Between time at work and time waiting for planes, I worked on preparing our apartment. Senhor Lopes even got excited that my wife was coming, and he threw himself into the effort. And it required effort; it had never been intended as a living space, but as a pantry and kitchen for the guests in his rooming house. At the time we rented it as a temporary UNICEF dormitory, it had been used for storage. He patched the leaking roof. He brought in a double bed. We scrubbed and polished the ceramic tiles on the kitchen walls. I told him I would do the painting. The walls had been whitewashed long ago, and the kitchen walls above the ceramic tile were a faded sickly yellow. It seemed that everybody was pulling for me. My bosses at work were ready to give me a day off when she came, but when each plane came and went, they got more skeptical. My friend Oscara, the aircraft help mechanic from Cape Verde, added some extra electrical outlets in the apartment. I ordered a wardrobe, so we wouldn't have to hang our clothes on nails in the wall. I planned to get a table and a cupboard, glasses, cups and saucers, plates and silverware.

About a week before Christmas, I was sleeping in my bed, when about four o'clock in the morning I heard a loud rapping on my door.

"Whaaat? What's going on!"

Leo and Arne were at my door. "Get up! Get up! You've got to go to the airport!"

"Oh, God. What's going on now?"

"You've got to go to the airport. Dr. Okpara is out there waiting to see you."

"Dr. Okpara? Wow!"

I jumped into my clothes, and we raced out there and sure enough, there was Dr. Okpara. He had been the proprietor of my school and the Premier of the Eastern Region of Nigeria before the coup, when he was arrested along with other politicians. Now he was assistant head of State in Biafra, behind Ojukwu. Dr. Okpara had come on the Grey Ghost, making a refueling stop in São Tomé on its way from Biafra to Lisbon. He was traveling with the Ambassadors to Portugal and Tanzania on a diplomatic mission.

Leo saw him in the terminal and recognized him from the last Fourth of July party we had in Umuahia. He spoke to him.

"By the way," Leo said to him as they were talking, "do you know David Koren?"

"Yes! Is he here?"

"Where will you be staying tomorrow, so he can contact you?" Leo asked.

"Well, I'll be leaving here in forty minutes."

"We can go in and get him for you, if you want."

"Oh, please do."

So they came and got me. It was a great reunion. He looked so much better than the last time I had seen him, when he had just been let out of prison in 1966. At that time, he had lost all that fire and energy, whatever dynamism that he had had before. As I knew him personally, I knew he had a genuine desire for seeing the development of his place, his Region, and all his country. When I saw him again he looked a bit thinner – still rather stout, but thinner. The energy and delight were back in his eyes. He looked fine.

I told him that I had made it down to Umuahia one day, and he got a little annoyed that I hadn't come to see him. I told him that there was a transportation problem.

"Nonsense," he said. "Tell *anybody* that you want to see me and they will take you right out. They'll arrange transport and petrol, somehow. When I come back from this mission, which will be about three weeks, I want you to come and see me."

"Well," I said, "There's a little matter of clearance. We haven't been cleared to work in Biafra."

"No, no," he said. "Nonsense. You just go to Mr. Osuji and tell him that I asked you to come and visit me for a few days and there will be no problem."

It was really good to see him and to learn that Mr. Ibe and Mr. Nsofor were well. He confirmed something that I had heard about my students.

"In the early part of the war, when things were really bad, all the Form Four and Form Five boys enlisted immediately. I doubt that many of them are alive and well now."

I had brought my class book along with me to São Tomé so that I could refer to it in Biafra, to be sure I got the names right when I asked about them. After talking to Dr. Okpara, I was not sure I wanted to ask about certain individuals.

He had to leave, and I drove back to town with Leo and Arne.

"How did you happen to be at the airport in the middle of the night?" I asked them.

"For some reason," Arne said, "I woke up and went and got Leo up and said, 'Hey, we gotta go to the airport.' 'Why?' said Leo. 'I don't know. I just have a feeling that we're needed out there.'"

Bull. I think they were out there putting the landing gear latch back in Lima.

Here is another coincidence, perhaps. Right after I met Dr. Okpara, and two months to the day since we arrived on São Tomé, UNICEF volunteers were granted clearance to work in Biafra as offloaders. All four of us had already managed to get into Biafra, one by one, by signing on as aircraft crew, but then it became wide open and official.

Larry and Barry started working in Biafra almost immediately, just before Christmas. They flew in with the first flight, worked all night and came out with the last. It was tiring. By the end of three days, they were absolutely shot. They were going to request that they be allowed to stay in Biafra rather than waste time and energy flying back and forth. On their first night, bombs fell around them as they crouched near a bunker. Larry related this:

> One got used to the bombs. You could hear them fall. I got so I would just lie on the ground and listen to them. [Barry was] with me on our first night in. The bomber was overhead. We were sitting on the edge of a bunker with the soldiers. Suddenly we heard the bomb falling and the soldiers jumped into the bunker. I was the last one in. Dirt from the bomb threw in on top of me. We were then saying, "What the Hell are we doing here?" But we got used to it.

Leo and I didn't go. We were still working every day as mechanics, because many of the regulars had gone home for Christmas. I didn't have any Christmas, really. I worked Christmas day. We had to get Bravo flying, and we did. I got the next day off, my first in two weeks, which was no use as far as the dinners and parties that I missed. In the morning, I ran around buying cleaning products like pails, sponges, and detergent, but I couldn't find a scrub brush anywhere. Life on the island was full of anomalies. In the afternoon, I was going to buy more Christmas presents for Elner, but Leo and I were told to stand by at the airport. ARCO wanted

Bravo to make three runs that night, and they wanted Leo and I to go along as offloaders to reduce the turnaround time. The DC-7s could make three shuttles in a night, but we really had to push it, crossing the coast coming and going with light in the sky. But after we wasted half of our day off waiting around on standby, ARCO flew only two shuttles, abruptly changing plans involving Bravo's mission the next day.

It didn't look like I would get many more days off in the coming weeks, nor would I be working in Biafra as an offloader. With Elner coming to São Tomé, it would be better for me to stay on the island.

4

The mail from Luanda came in as usual on Thursday. Hayward, Deputy Director of UNICEF, sent me a letter dated December 16, which arrived on the twenty-sixth, accepting my resignation. Although Elner, Jan, and Gerry hadn't taken my resignation seriously, Hayward did. He said he hoped to see me home again soon and thanked me for all my hard work on the DC-7s. Elner had blabbed to him that I was making a lot of money as a mechanic, and he was furious.

So my UNICEF allowance of $100 a week was cut off. I had accepted Peterson's offer to work as a regular employee for ARCO, but he never followed up on that, and I was still making $25 a day as a help mechanic, not so much for a married man. Things would be tight. I would have to stop doing some things, like donating money to Biafra. For Christmas, I had given Mr. Osuji $100. I would have to eat crow and write to Hayward requesting reinstatement in UNICEF.

On Friday, December 27, I received a telegram from Elner saying she couldn't leave New York until after January 2. She didn't say why, but I presumed it had to do with I.S. 271. I was disappointed, but at least I knew I wouldn't have to meet the Boeing on Saturday. When Senhor Lopes heard the news and saw my dejection, he bought me a couple of drinks in his own bar.

In one letter Elner had complained about the absolutely confused picture she was getting on her side of the Atlantic about what was happening on São Tomé. I told her that if she got the total picture, she would be three times as confused. We had a saying, a watchword, which we repeated to ourselves: "This is not a normal island." Doc Okonkwo had uttered it first, back in our early days. He was sitting at a table, looking down, shaking his head, when he said it.

"This is not a normal island."

We stopped talking and looked at him, then resumed talking, not realizing the tremendous thunderclap of understatement we had just heard.

In Peace Corps days, working alone far from our own culture, we had to depend on our internal resources, to be agile and creative, to be self-sufficient. But the mushy, quivering reality on São Tomé challenged our capacities to keep up, to keep sane and stable. It was like walking a tightrope, or standing on top of a little ball which had a tendency to roll.

As Elner knew little of what was happening on São Tomé, we knew little of what occurred outside of it. I had been fascinated with the space program since before the Soviet Union launched the first earth satellite on October 4, 1957; it grew out of my interest in aviation. Hearing snatches of information about an Apollo mission to the moon frustrated me. It had launched. It had reached the moon. It had splashed down in the Pacific Ocean on December 27. Had I been able, I would have followed every minute of it. Unknown to me, Apollo space craft in low earth orbit preparing for trans-lunar injection passed right over our island.

We worked hard throughout that Friday preparing Alpha Bravo for a very unusual flight, converting it from a stinky old cargo plane to something like the airliner it had once been. We had to extract every particle of old milk powder and Formula II and salt and the stink of stockfish, which permeated the whole cabin and cockpit. We totally fumigated it. We installed regular airline seats. We worked from morning until the scheduled flight time of about 8:00 p.m.

The mission was a big secret. There were rumors flying about, but they were totally off the mark. We knew what it was, and we were told to keep quiet. It started about a week before when Father Byrne received a Telex from Rome at one o'clock in the morning summoning him immediately. He left four hours later. He came back in four days and went right into Biafra. We knew something was up. Count Carl Gustaf Von Rosen, who had helped start the whole airlift and had urged George Orick of UNICEF to recruit us, landed on São Tomé and followed Father Byrne into Biafra. When they came out of Biafra, together with an American congressman (I don't know his name), they told ARCO to prepare Bravo for a special mission, and keep it hush-hush. Von Rosen, the American congressman, and other passengers were flying to Addis Ababa to meet with Nigerian representatives for the purpose of negotiating a humanitarian daylight air corridor into Uli. They chose Bravo for the mission because the DC-7 was the fastest plane on the island and it had the range to fly all the way across Africa.

When the lorries came out to load the plane as usual during the day, Helmut told the workers that we were fixing the floor and they would have to wait. They went away to load another aircraft. The Shell tanker lorry came out to fuel the plane.

"How much do you want?" the Shell representative asked Helmut. The amount of fuel varied from flight to flight depending on the cargo weight and the amount of time allotted for holding over Biafra. The weight of fuel and cargo should total the same for each flight.

"Fill it up," said Helmut. For Helmut and the Portuguese Shell guy, English was not their first language, nor their best.

"Yes, but how much do you want?"

"Full," said Helmut. The man looked at him and scratched his cheek.

"But how much do you want?"

"Full!" said Helmut. At this time I intervened.

"*Total*," (toe-TALL) I said in Portuguese. This amounted to about 2,500 gallons. The man's mouth dropped right open. It was comical. We didn't normally carry anywhere near that amount of fuel.

"Biafra?" he said.

"Yes. Fill it up," said Helmut.

That was enough fuel for fourteen hours flight time, nine hours to Addis Ababa with five hours reserve.

To make the flight legal, we had to paint the legal registration letters on the plane. It was last legally registered in Bermuda as VR-BCW. It had been operating on São Tomé under an illegal – or non-existent – registration, one made up by Hank Wharton, 5T-TAB. The only two places in the world the plane could land were Uli and São Tomé. It needed a legal registration to land in Addis Ababa. We painted the new registration on it.

As we were admiring our neat paint job, the new ARCO chief, a man named Joseph, came out of the terminal.

"We have to put the old registration back on," he said.

"What?"

"We have to put the old registration back on, because, well, um, because the plane is recognized here as Tango Alpha Bravo, and it will not be allowed to take off with any other designation."

"Oh," I said, "And it won't be allowed to land anywhere else without the real registration on it?"

"Yeah, well, that's the way it is." It was not a normal island. The Portuguese governor, the only one who could approve a change of registration, was not due back until midnight. The lieutenant governor would not take the responsibility.

Smyth, our ingenious electrician and instrument guy, smiled wickedly, and winked. He went to the hangar and came out with some white paper, tape, and more paint. He painted the old registration number on the paper, just as neatly, and we taped it over the legal one. The plane would take off with the old designation on it, and at a certain airspeed, the paper and tape would be ripped off, allowing the plane to land legally in Addis Ababa. Joseph went away shaking his head.

Meanwhile, Shell had completed the long process of fueling "Bravo." Joseph returned a little while later.

"How long will it take us to de-fuel?"

Again: "What?"

"How long will it take us to drain enough fuel down to our normal capacity for a trip to Biafra?"

"What is going on?"

"Well, I've just been to the Caritas office where we talked to Von Rosen and the American congressman and Father Byrne and Father Cunningham. No one wants to pay us for this flight. Caritas thought the American was going to pay for it and the congressman thought Caritas was going to pay for it, and Von Rosen thought both of them were going to pay for it. None of them was prepared to do it. The congressman is not really on an official U.S. Government mission, he claims, and Caritas does not want to foot the bill for a round trip across Africa, so we have to de-fuel. How long will it take?"

"Six hours," said Helmut, disgusted. Draining that much fuel, so we could load cargo, would leave enough time for only one run to Biafra.

"Don't worry," I said to Joe, "I know who is going to pay for this flight, and you don't have to worry about it. I know how it's going to be paid, although you may not. But don't worry – it's going to be paid. We will not start draining fuel until you know definitely and for sure that it won't be paid."

What he knew was that the churches paid ARCO for flights to Biafra, just as they did for Transavia, Fred Olsen, Braathen, Sterling, and any other charter company. What he did not know was that 90% or more of the cost was reimbursed to the churches by the United States government. Furthermore, the U.S. government donated over 50% of the dollar value of the food going to Biafra. The United States was in the ridiculous position of proclaiming its support for "One Nigeria" while working under the table to subsidize the Biafran Airlift. It was not a normal island.

Back away. Back far away from the island. Move your viewpoint far above the equator, out into orbit around our planet. Not normal? Are the affairs of that little island at the navel of the world so different from what we know of the world as a whole?

Such was the secrecy of the mission that we were all hustled away when our work was done, before anyone boarded the plane. We didn't see the passengers, and we didn't see the crew. Tom Delahunt was our chief pilot at that time, but his personal log showed that he flew Bravo into Biafra on December 26 and again on the night of December 30. It is unlikely that he made the long flight to Addis Ababa in between. Von Rosen was a famous aviator. He had flown relief missions for Ethiopia when Mussolini attacked that country, and he had flown one of our DC-7s from São Tomé to Uli back in August. I wonder if he flew the mission himself. I will never know.

Alpha Bravo took off for Addis Ababa on December 27 and returned three days later as Bravo Charlie Whiskey. The mission had failed.

Our work done, Leo and Arne and I went to the Baia for a beer and a bite to eat, a hot dog-like thing called a *salsicha*. From our table in the outdoor part of the café we could look north out over the bay. We saw the winking lights of a plane lowering over the bay and coming in for a landing at the Two-Nine (eastern) end of the runway. Watching planes land and take off was one of the main entertainments of the island, along with drinking, complaining, rumoring, and speculating. We knew all of our planes and we had the evening flight schedule. No plane was due. We headed for the airport to check it out. There sat a C-46, painted white with one red and two blue stripes flowing from cockpit to tail, and blue highlights on its nose, cowlings, and the edges of the tail surfaces. It had an American registration, N69346. No other American plane belonged on São Tomé. The crew had already left the airport.

We came to know the crew later. Bob Hall, the owner of the plane, chose to associate with the UNICEF guys. He roomed and ate with us at Costa's boarding house.

The arrival of the American plane set off a wave of speculation among the airlift watchers. It was said that five more large American planes would be coming to join the airlift under the operation of Joint Church Aid, with overt backing of the United States and Canadian governments. The Portuguese were preparing by expanding the parking areas at the airport. This was significant for two reasons. One was the sad fact that the DC-7 fleet was now down to one operational aircraft, Bravo Charlie Whiskey, with one plane bombed in Biafra, Delta crashed, and Lima battered and under repair. The second reason was the anticipated carbohydrate famine in Biafra. Until now, protein was the principal nutrition deficiency, most serious for developing children. When the supply of yams and rice and cassava dwindled, a widening crisis could be expected. We would need a greatly expanded airlift to cope with it. At the same time, Nigeria was increasing the bombing pressure at Uli. Yellow Bar, the intruder, was now a larger plane, perhaps a DC-4, and could drop heavier bombs. Though no more planes had been hit, the presence of the intruder disrupted the airlift, causing the planes to hold off landing or to spend more time on the ground as offloading crews sought shelter in the bunkers, thus making fewer shuttles.

A lot of speculation involved getting fighter planes for the Biafran Air Force to shoot open an air corridor for the airlift. But Caritas and WCC and, surreptitiously, the United States government, were working on a different option, a secret, diplomatic one, just then on its way to Addis Ababa, to open a daylight air corridor. If we could fly more planes around the clock without interference from Nigerian fighters or bombers, we could move more food into Biafra. But Nigeria claimed that the church planes were carrying arms, so they killed the idea. Biafra would continue to look for warplanes.

In the final minutes of one of my tapes, I made a cryptic entry. I said I knew where to get between four and a dozen P-51 fighter bombers, five F-86 Saber jets, 32 Hawker Hunter MK-50 jets, and wings for the Fouga Magisters. I said nothing about how I knew that, but I sounded quite definite. I said we needed to find money to pay for them. I have no memory about my source, but the information likely came from Biafra House or the Biafran pilots that I had met.

With our plane away, I had Saturday off. I sloshed around in the rain, damp and dingy, buying things for the apartment. Also, I bought myself a radio so I could listen to the rest of the world, reducing my isolation. Biafra, the airlift, and São Tomé dominated our whole lives, like a huge moon filling our sky, and I needed some contact with a wider universe. It upset me that I had missed the Apollo moon shot. I had missed the U.S. Presidential election, learning later that Nixon had won. Big events were taking place at home and around the world as 1968 evolved into 1969. The radio cost $50. I had earned double time for working Christmas day, so I bought myself a Christmas present with the extra pay.

Our mechanics returned that Saturday with some more licensed mechanics from Europe hired by ARCO to work on its DC-7s. There was now one plane flying, Bravo Charlie Whiskey, and one, Lima, under repair, and eleven ground mechanics. Leo and I were laid off. And Elner had not yet come to São Tomé.

Bomb Fragment from Runway Crater

CHAPTER 11

O Di Naka Chukwu

It's in the Hands Of God

Falling bombs take a few minutes to hit the ground. You may have time to take cover in a bunker or a ditch when you hear one coming. But when a plane is strafing – shooting machine gun bullets at you – you have almost no chance because the bullets are coming so fast. Hit the ground immediately or dive behind something. No time for prayers.

1

No problema. Nsogbu adighi. Since we had finally been cleared to work as offloaders in Biafra, we jumped over to that job. Barry, however, couldn't do this job with us because both of his feet were in casts. It had happened in a fall when he and Larry were at the beach on New Year's Day. It could have been a disaster, but Barry felt himself slipping and thankfully managed to get his legs under him. He landed on the crags with his feet, breaking them both. He could still ride his Honda around Sao Tome, but he couldn't work in Biafra. So, Larry, Leo, and I worked out a rotation where two of us would be working every night, while each of us worked four nights in a row and had two nights off. As an official load-master, I worked on the ARCO DC-7, four Transavia DC-6s, and one Braathen DC-6. I never worked on the smaller Fred Olsen C-46.

I left home at 3:00 p.m., drove to the airport on my Honda, and picked up my copy of the cargo manifests and the evening flight schedule. With two UNICEF volunteers flying, one took the first flight and the other took the second. I scanned my copy of the schedule to see what plane I would be riding and what ones I would be meeting at Uli. Checking the manifests, I inspected the loads on the planes of the first shuttle. I checked that the cargo agreed with the manifest and that the distribution of the cargo was safe and secure within each plane. We learned this skill under the tutelage of a young German named Rudi who worked for *Das Diakonische Werk*. The load had to be secure against shifting, especially during violent maneuvers. In normal operations, cargo would be secured by netting, but that would impede the offloading, so proper stacking was even more important. Barrels of petrol, however, were strapped down. I made sure there were full plastic jerry cans of water and drinking cups for the fatigue workers who would unload the cargo. I chatted with the crew as we all signed the crew list, and then I climbed the aluminum ladder into the cockpit door on the right side of the aircraft.

I carried a personal bag on each flight. It was rectangular, like a letter carrier's bag, made of heavy dark green canvas with several compartments and an adjustable shoulder strap. Tom Hebert had purchased it in Copenhagen and passed it on to me when he left São Tomé. In it I carried sandwiches or other small food items, cans of Pepsi, cigarettes, an air mattress, and things to trade at Uli in the quiet periods between shuttles. We took off about 4:30 p.m. GMT and usually arrived back at São Tomé by 5:00 a.m. the next morning. By the time I returned to the apartment, I'd have been gone about fifteen hours.

As I was checking the cargo one day, Father Byrne swept on to the flight line with his white priestly robes flying about him. He was in a rage. It was a real dandy rage – his face was bright red, and he was screaming. Rudi was cowering and getting red as well.

"Yes, Father. Yes, Father," he said bobbing his head up and down. The priest had learned that WCC had used its designated night to fly all the medical supplies into Biafra. After Father Byrne had commandeered all the medicines for Caritas back in November, more medical supplies had been gathering in the warehouses. WCC had shipped them all into Biafra the previous night. Father Byrne ordered all the food to be removed from one of the planes. The workers reloaded the lorries and drove them back to the warehouses where the food was exchanged for car batteries – all the batteries, so the Protestants couldn't get any for their lorries.

Because I handled the cargo, and because I checked the manifests, I knew what the planes were carrying. One day I was lying on my bed listening to a BBC broadcast on my new radio. It was a lengthy report about the Biafran Airlift. The report described how Caritas was using the cover of relief flights to smuggle arms to the Biafran Army. The reporter read aloud from the cargo manifests, listing all of the guns and ammunition. He had details, like the make and model numbers of the weapons, and the tonnage, and he gave the dates and the aircraft on which they were flown. Those were *my* planes, and *I* was on duty those days. *I* had checked the cargo on those planes in São Tomé or unloaded it in Biafra, and I never saw a single weapon or bullet. Not those days or any other. The reporter accused Caritas of this deceit, but not the World Council of Churches, which flew on alternate nights.

Larry and I shared the same responsibilities. He confirms my observations: "Though some have tried to say that our planes carried guns and ammunition, I am absolutely certain that they did not. I chose flights that I would fly on; I inspected cargo on the planes; I inspected manifests; and I was never kept from entering a plane."

During my broadcasting education at the University of Pennsylvania and at Syracuse University I had learned, and had believed, that the BBC was the world standard in journalism for accurate and unbiased reporting.

No comment.

No. Wait. I do have a comment. Through the British Broadcasting Corporation the British government asserted that Caritas supplied weapons to the Biafran Army. That this was untrue did not matter; the accusation alone forced the churches to spend considerable time and resources denying something they were not doing. They had to avoid any appearance of aiding the war effort, including feeding the troops. In this war, women and children were military targets. They were bombed and shot in their homes, their markets, and hospitals. They were the primary targets of starvation. The massive worldwide humanitarian effort to protect the women and children from starvation could not interfere with the killing. Biafran men were the only ones defending their women and children. No one helped them. The accusation worked. A hungry Biafran Army lost the war.

Words can be weapons of war.

2

Larry wrote a letter home dated 16 January, 1969:

> Have been very busy. Now that we are deeply involved in the airlift, the island is no longer the peaceful sanctuary that it was in the beginning. You can't sit down to read or write without being disturbed. There are many problems with the airlift, problems with codes, friction among groups, accusations of conspiracy, bombings at the Biafran airfield, conflicts of interest, problems with offloading cargo in Biafra, etc. Many times our planes are not able to land and must return to Sao Tome, which means a waste of fifteen to twenty thousand dollars. The operation is growing. We should soon be lifting over 150 tons of food a night. The Red Cross has been expelled from Fernando Po, so food for Biafra depends on us, but the problems are innumerable...

The most scary times on the airport in Biafra was when the MiG jets strafed the runway. On one occasion, we were unloading a plane. I had a flashlight hung from my belt to provide a little light for the workers. Suddenly a MiG was shooting down the runway coming straight at us. Of course it was very fast. I scrambled to turn off the light, as though it would have made any difference, and Biafran soldiers jumped on top of me, their instincts telling them that the light was a danger. The strafing miraculously stopped right outside the door. Another second and it would have cut right through us. I can still vividly see the sparks approaching the plane. It was terrifying. I must give credit to the young soldiers for going right back to work and getting the plane unloaded.

As a defense against MiGs flying down the runway at 50 feet, Johnny Correa devised a steel pot packed with a mixture of dynamite and gelatinite with a vertical jump range of 150 to 300 yards. A soldier hidden in the bush beside the runway would detonate it remotely by wire when he judged that the MiG was in range. It was tricky, but Johnny thinks that they knocked down one or two MiGs that way.

Biafran Air Force fatigue workers offloaded the cargo, directed by one of their team leaders and me, Larry, or Leo, and sometimes joined by the copilot or flight engineer. It was usually a frantic scramble. The first planes were trying to turn around as fast as possible in order to make three shuttles, and that is when the bombs usually fell.

The bombing pressure at Uli intensified in January. Instead of the old DC-3 or LI-2 dropping twenty-pound bombs, the intruder was now a four-engine DC-4 with bomb racks able to drop six five-hundred-pound bombs all at once or selectively by ones and twos. I know that Nigeria Airways had a DC-3 and a DC-4 because I had flown on them. I flew on the DC-4 from Lagos to Enugu when I first came to Nigeria in 1964, and I flew on the DC-3 to Port Harcourt in 1966 after the first coup.

Johnny Correa: "Nigeria started using the DC-4 as a heavy bomber, but usually missed because they dropped the bombs from 15,000 feet down through two or three different types of wind currents."

The accuracy of the bombing improved, probably because the intruder was getting braver and rolling his bomb load from a lower altitude. Though the intruder had not hit the runway since December and most bombs still fell off in the bush, some were coming close, nicking our planes with bits of shrapnel.

One night, I was flying in on the first plane, a Transavia DC-6B. We crossed the beacon at 4000 feet and came around for our approach. We were on final; then short final; then landing configuration: gear down, landing lights on, wings dipping left and right as the pilot made last second corrections; runway lights on. We got a sudden wave-off from the ground controller. The pilot killed the landing lights, pulled the gear up, and shoved the throttles forward, moving out on a flat, fast climb. Looking out the right side of the plane I said aloud, "Watch for the bombs!" although I was alone in the cabin. Sure enough, there were two great bursts, big orange fireballs, side by side. Seconds later another single fireball bloomed, closer to the runway. All three bombs fell near one end of the runway where we would have parked, had we landed.

As soon as the bombs detonated, the runway lights went off, and the Biafran gunners opened up with anti-aircraft fire. I watched closely to see if we would catch any of this fire, since we were low and in the vicinity. But no tracer came our way; all were directed at the enemy. In one burst, I saw three tracers come out of the Bofors gun, about thirty degrees from the vertical and out ahead of us. The third tracer caught up to and passed the first two. Was that normal? Or was it an example of poor, old ammunition?

Johnny Correa was in charge of air defense at Uli. "At Uli, we had always 3 AA guns, usually two working. There were Bofors 40/60 mm, renovated barrels firing up to seven thousand feet, plagued by stoppages and malfunctions. There were ten 30 mm and ten 50 caliber machine guns around Uli, plus four new Orlicons from Rhodesia."

As the intruder was improving his accuracy, Biafran gunners were becoming more consistent. Since the delegation from the churches and the Red Cross had appealed to Ojukwu for better fire discipline, there were no more incidents. Some pilots complained that they were fired on, but I was on the ground at the time of those incidents, and I observed that the fire was directed at the intruder. There was a time when the gunners waited until after the bombs fell and the intruder was some distance away before they came out of the bunkers and started firing. By then the bomber was well out of range. But lately they commenced firing as he approached. While in the plane, unloading, the AA fire was the first indication that I would have that the enemy was near. I could look out the window and see the tracers going up all around the plane. The muzzle flashes of the guns lit up the interior of the plane like strobe lights, giving a surreal motion to the fatigue workers hustling sacks of food. The Bofors antiaircraft gun (*egbe tuum*) had a distinctive, complicated sound, a low-throated pulse, "thoomp, thoomp," with a kind of twang wrapped around it. Once, I was out on the ground when I heard the intruder coming. The AA started long before he got to the airstrip and continued as he made two passes, dropping three bombs each pass, nowhere near the field. Maybe the persistent fire spoiled his aim.

Since the intruder had started dropping the heavy bombs, he had not yet hit the runway. If he were to hit the runway with one of those heavy bombs, he would stop the airlift for at least a day. Ministry of Works kept a bulldozer and tipper lorries full of sand and laterite on standby in anticipation. Yet even without a direct hit, the threat of it disrupted the relief flights and cost the churches hundreds of thousands of dollars for which no relief was delivered. When the ground controller knew the intruder was in the area he would wave off our planes and direct them to a holding beacon about twenty miles from Uli. When the controller thought it was safe, he would call the planes back to the airstrip beacon, but by then some planes were low on fuel and had to return to São Tomé. In some months 25% of the flights didn't land, but the churches still had to pay for the fuel, flight pay, and landing fees in São Tomé.

After my plane landed, we taxied to a parking finger at one end of the runway. I usually worked at the Three-Four end. Huge white numbers, 3 and 4, were painted on that end of the runway to tell the pilots that they were landing at a heading of 340 degrees relative to due north, which was 360 degrees. Therefore I was at the southern end, near the town of Mgbidi. The town of Uli was at the One-Six end. Planes coming in on a landing pattern from the North passed the church with the twin spires at Uli, landed, and taxied to parking areas on the south end. A marshaller with flashlights in each hand, which looked like mini red light sabers, directed the pilot to a designated spot. These parking fingers were lined up perpendicular to the runway, like fringe on a belt.

When the engines stopped, I opened the main cabin door, which was about two-thirds of the way back along the left side of the aircraft. I yelled out for a lorry. When the lorry backed up, we placed a slide board from the door of the plane to the bed of the lorry. Most of our planes had once flown passengers, so they had narrow man doors rather than wide cargo doors, restricting the flow of food sacks. About a dozen fatigue workers entered the plane by scurrying up the slide board or climbing the ladder to the cockpit door at the front of the plane.

Workers threw the sacks of food or the bales of stockfish onto the slide, and others moved cargo from the front or rear of the plane toward the door. I urged them to work faster; I held the flashlight; and sometimes I joined in. It was a frantic activity. The earliest flights tried to make three shuttles, so turnaround time had to be fast. In the early days of the airlift, it would take an hour and a half or more to unload a plane. Now we were doing it in twenty or thirty minutes. Some special cargoes, like heavy sacks of salt, took forty-five minutes.

The threat of bombing added urgency to the job. The sooner we got the plane unloaded, the sooner we could get to the bunkers. One such night our pilot stayed in the plane with us. He kept a vigil by the front door, listening for the bomber. From back in the cabin, we couldn't hear a bomb until it was very close.

"Enemy aircraft in the area!" he shouted. Some of the fatigue workers wanted to head for the bunkers.

"Keep working! Keep working!" I said. "It's all right." The fatigue leader, who was working very hard by the door, throwing sacks out, picked up what I said.

"Neva mind!" he said. "De bombs are not for us! Dere is God!"

O di naka Chukwu. It's in the hands of God.
But: *God dey; Man dey.* There is God and there is Man.

We kept on working. The pilot told us when he heard the bombs falling, and I yelled, "Get down! Lay down on the floor of the plane!" We did, and when the plane stopped rocking from the concussion, we got up and started heaving sacks again, with AA going off all around us, lighting up the inside of the plane. I was scared. They were scared. But we kept on working. I told them, "If you are in a bunker when the bombs start falling, stay there. If you are in the plane, stay there. If you try to run from the plane to the bunker, while the bombs are falling, you will be outside with no protection when they hit." I remembered the children who had been hit by the bomb when they ran outside of their home in panic the night Reverend Aitken and I took two of the survivors to the hospital at Awomama.

When the first plane was unloaded and on its way, I met other planes of the first shuttle and helped unload them. My wait time between finishing one plane and meeting another varied from ten to thirty minutes. If seven planes made the first run, I typically met four of them. Then I waited for the second shuttle and repeated the work. The wait between shuttles could be from one to three hours.

Barry asked me to do him a favor. He still couldn't fly because of the casts on his feet, but before his accident he had made an arrangement with a Biafran contact to trade some items during the lull between shuttles. For a carton of American cigarettes, his contact would give me some Indian hemp, a potent form of cannabis. Before the war, in the wild political days, gangs of political thugs high on hemp would zoom around in pickup trucks intimidating voters.

Barry was a red hot ladies' man and a streetwise wheeler and dealer. He came up out of San Francisco in the early 1960s in the days of the flower children. Just before he joined the American Committee for Nigeria/Biafra

Relief, he told me, he went to see the new Stanley Kubrick movie, *2001: A Space Odyssey*, which was loaded with never-before-seen special effects, mind-blowing special effects, like a waitress walking up a wall holding her tray. Barry saw it while high on Mescaline. And away he went.

Barry's contact found me in the dark as I was sitting on my air mattress eating a sandwich. He approached me reservedly, loosening up a little as he assessed me, and I told him what Barry had said. I gave him the cigarettes and he gave me the hemp.

"Do you want to try some, to see if it's okay?" he asked.

"No, thank you."

"Are you sure?"

"Yes. I don't want any. I have to meet these planes when they come in."

"Do you mind if I roll one?"

"No. Go ahead."

He did. I could see the glowing tip in the dark. After a few minutes he handed it to me and said, "Here, try a hit."

Well, I did. I got so high so fast, I felt like a disembodied phantom in the dark, just when the flight line officer came over and wanted to get acquainted. I think he asked me where I was from back home, but I'm not sure. By the time he finished a question, I forgot the first part of what he had said, so I tried to answer based on his last words until I forgot what I was saying. I figured that I was screwed, and I would be thrown out of Biafra.

But he just went away, dissolving into the night. I sat down hoping the feeling would go away before a plane landed, and I would have to do something. Meanwhile, a bomb fell. It hit across the far side of the runway, a little to the north. A tower of sparks shot up. I thought it was the most beautiful thing I had ever seen, like a fountain of fireflies. *Umumuwarri*, as they are called in Igbo.

Streetwise Barry had read my copy of *The Autobiography of Malcolm X*. We had discussed it. He was intensely interested in news from Elner about Ocean Hill-Brownsville. I gave him the articles she had sent, and I played parts of the tape for him. Malcolm talked about Western cultural definitions of white and black: how white was supposed to embody all that was pure and good while black stood for things degraded or evil. Black people had to learn that that was not true, that black was beautiful. Afro-Americans had to learn it, because they had been told the opposite for so long. To Africans, shouting "black is beautiful" made no sense, since it was fundamentally obvious.

Elner described her disagreement with her friend Eleanor about Biafra, in which they almost "came to blows." That represented a much wider split in the American black community about the war. Malcolm preached, at least early on, that white people were responsible for all the problems of blacks, and that blacks should stand together to solve their problems, even go back to Africa. White people shouldn't be involved in an African war, trying to break a black nation apart. When Elner reminded Eleanor of the genocidal massacres of Africans against Africans that led to the war, she relented. It was a strong dilemma for black Americans, a wrenching ambivalence.

White people could take no comfort in their association with that hue. By 1968 I had read *Moby Dick*, one of my all-time favorite books, four or five times. Chapter XLII, "The Whiteness of the Whale," fits here. Ishmael says that in spite of all its stellar associations, "It was the whiteness of the whale that above all things appalled me." Pallor. Apparition. Mist. Frost. Wraith. Veiled, half-seen, nameless things. Blankness. Death.

All those words of color, black and white, words that form some temporary bond or barrier, make slippery associations with people. The meaning of a person, of a people, arises from within, down amid shifting complexities and gelid anchors. The world is deep. *Uwa di egwu.*

3

January 2 had passed, but I still didn't know when Elner was coming. Pastor Mollerup made her an open reservation on any relief flight from Amsterdam or Copenhagen. I continued to meet planes.

Returning to São Tomé on Bravo Charlie Whiskey one night, exhausted as usual, I fell into a sound sleep in one of the old airline chairs at the back of the cabin. Sometime during the flight, the propeller on engine number three came loose and slashed into the cabin behind the cockpit door as it spun away. I slept through that. When we landed, I saw the hole. I looked at the flight engineer and pointed to the hole. "What is that?" He grinned and shrugged. Just another night on the Biafran Airlift.

In the middle of January, a Canadian Super Constellation bearing the name Canairrelief joined the airlift, followed shortly by two American C-97s. These planes had greater capacity than our DC-6s and DC-7s, about 14 tons, and large cargo doors. Each one also had a load-master as part of its regular crew, so UNICEF volunteers were not needed.

The Canadian Super Constellation, NAJ, November Alpha Juliet, looked sleek for its large size. It had a blue stripe swooping along the fuselage and up to an impressive tail with three vertical stabilizers. It was the same kind of airplane as the Biafran's Grey Ghost. The crew called it their "blue canoe." Later they would name it "Snoopy's Doghouse." They wrote to Charles Schultz, the cartoonist, for permission to paint Snoopy on the nose of the aircraft. Permission was granted. So Snoopy sat on top of his doghouse wearing a leather helmet, goggles, and a dashing scarf, imagining that he was a famous World War I flying ace. Captain Patterson and his crew were used to flying in Canada's far northern bush country, so they easily adapted to flying the Biafran Airlift.

They hired an African steward to look after their laundry and cleaning. Once, when the Canadians took Snoopy's Doghouse for a test flight around São Tomé, they brought the steward with them. Patterson invited him to sit in the copilot's seat. He showed him the plane's controls, how to hold his hands on the steering yoke and put his feet on the rudder petals. Surreptitiously, Patterson slipped the plane into automatic pilot. He told the steward to keep the plane straight and level, then he excused himself and abruptly left the cockpit. The kid was terrified. But he stayed at his post. The crew came back and congratulated him. From then on they called him *"El Commandante."* Wherever the crew went on São Tomé, he walked with them, practically swaggering, his chin high.

The Blue Canoe was the first of many planes that were to come to São Tomé from North America. It was a big event when it landed on the island. I sat on the airport terminal steps along with Ed, one of the American C-46 pilots and watched it come in. It signaled the beginning of many changes. The Canadian government provided it through a group of Canadian churches called Canairrelief. It would become part of a larger group called Joint Church Aid, JCA, and nicknamed "Jesus Christ Airways." Rumors had it that the United States was sending some Boeing C-97 Stratofreighters.

Curiously, the American C-46 that had landed just after Christmas never joined the airlift. It just sat out there on the tarmac, off by itself, not flying. Bob Hall, the plane's owner, was not a part of JCA or Nordchurchaid. He came to São Tomé as a freelance operator, intending to hire his services to the airlift. He had recently flown for Air America in Viet Nam and Laos. Back in the States, he had heard about the Biafran Airlift — a high risk, high paying way to make money, if he had an airplane. He borrowed $30,000 from his mother — her life savings — and bought the C-46 in Ft. Lauderdale, Florida. In the Miami-Ft. Lauderdale area, hundreds of propeller planes were available, put out of service by the new jets. One of his pilots, Art, was small, slim, dark-haired, serious, and quiet. The mechanic, Colin Greenwood, was tall, fluffy-haired, slow moving, soft talking, and looking half puzzled most of the time. The other pilot, Ed, was a large young man, like McCombie. We would sit on the steps by the terminal, where missionaries and airlift officials passed by, while he talked about what he would do to a Nigerian MiG if he could just get a

P-51 Mustang.

"I'd slam the throttle to the firewall, dive out of the sun at him, and kill the son-of-a-bitch!" He sounded remarkably like the Biafran pilots I had met. More than forty years later, in a telephone interview, he told me that he *was* a Biafran pilot. He flew the Grey Ghost. That was one of the many things I learned as a result of publishing the first edition of *Far Away in the Sky*. Art also was a Biafran pilot. Bob Hall's C-46 was like their cover. Colin Greenwood was a Canadian with some B-25s he wanted to sell to Biafra, but the Canadian government wouldn't release them. I had no idea. Anyway, with all those planes coming from JCA, Nordchurchaid wouldn't need a C-46. Bob Hall was losing a lot of his mother's money.

The Canadian plane and its crew quickly integrated into the airlift and into the life on São Tomé. Hopes were high now that North America seemed to be taking an interest in Biafra. Until now it had been a European operation with a sprinkling of Americans, such as UNICEF volunteers and some flight crew. But not everybody was thrilled about the impending changes. Some Europeans speculated the Americans were just dumping some old cast-off Air Force planes — junk that nobody knew how to fly anymore. They felt the planes would be in bad shape and difficult to maintain. By then, January of 1969, I identified thoroughly with the existing operation after my total immersion in the airlift. So I participated in the doubts. Interesting that we denigrated the expected quality of the American planes after the magnitude of the problems we had faced with our planes: loose propellers, massive oil leaks, faulty feathering pumps, and flaming engines.

One night shortly after the Canadian plane arrived, Larry and I flew back to São Tomé on Bravo Charlie Whiskey. We landed at 5:00 a.m. Where BCW usually parked, there sat a C-97. Another one occupied the place where Delta used to park, the best spot on the airfield, next to the big hangar. We climbed down the ladder from our plane and walked around the newcomers. They were big. I was impressed. C-97s were reconfigured B-29s, outfitted to carry cargo instead of bombs. Except for the bulbous fuselage, they looked like B-29s with the same wings, engines, tail, and cockpit. B-29s had dropped the atomic bombs on Japan.

In the next few days we talked to some of the crews, and we gently raised some of our concerns.

"What kind of shape are these planes in?" I asked an engineer.

"They're in great shape. They're real good. But that doesn't matter. If one of them goes bad, we'll just get another one."

"Oh?"

"There are a lot more planes where those came from – bigger ones, better ones, newer ones."

"Oh, yeah? What kind of planes?"

"Ah, um...newer, better," he dodged.

"Hercules, maybe?" I said.

"Well, you know..." Much later the crews admitted they would prefer Hercules.

The landing fees were exorbitant at São Tomé, $250 for each landing of a DC-7, the heaviest plane here so far.

"What was the landing fee for the C-97s," I asked.

"We don't know. We don't care. Just pay it. This is not a shoestring operation. There is a lot of money, a lot more planes. We have twenty crews waiting." These were U.S. Coast Guard crews. Military. They wore parachutes, and carried full survivor gear in case of ditching in the ocean. Our church crews had no such things.

The C-97s had fresh paint jobs with new lettering: "Joint Church Aid – USA." The outline of a fish, the symbol of JCA, was painted just under the cockpit window. Thinly painted out but still visible were the letters "U S Air Force." After talking to the crews, we began to feel that something big might actually come of this.

Activity around the airport exploded as São Tomé prepared for a massive escalation of the airlift. Bulldozers pushed dirt everywhere. Gangs of workers made new parking places. Special Boeing 707 flights brought sixty tons of aluminum planking for parking ramps and ten prefab buildings for parts stores and offices. The man directing the airport construction, a Portuguese and life-long resident of São Tomé, walked around with his head down, shaking it from side to side, saying, *"O meu Deus! O meu Deus!"* What was happening to his island? Leo got a side job helping to assemble the prefab buildings.

Planes were parked nose to tail. Transavia had five DC-6s (one used for spare parts); Braathen had one DC-6; Fred Olsen had a C-46. Bob Hall's C-46 took up a place. ARCO had two DC-7s, including Lima, which was nearly ready to fly. There was the Canadian Super Connie and the two JCA C-97s. This airport used to handle one commercial flight a week, the mail plane from Luanda. Two more C-97s were waiting in Brazil until parking areas and new facilities were ready. Two more Super Constellations were expected. ARCO planned to bring down two more DC-7s from Europe, one with cargo doors. Captain Baekstrom would be returning.

4.

By the time we had finished unloading on the night of January 22, the first quarter moon had set, and we were surrounded by deep darkness. I flicked on my flashlight for a moment to position myself on the ladder as I descended to the ground. Shouts came from unseen soldiers in the night.

"Off de light!"

"Off de light!"

"Off de light!"

They enforced strict blackout conditions. No cooking fires lit the surrounding bush anymore.

At the bottom of the ladder I felt a presence slip up beside me. It was Reverend Aitken. I had expected to follow my usual routine, waiting for the second shuttle, but Aitken had another task for me. I followed him to the line of bush at the edge of the parking finger. As my eyes became thoroughly dark adapted, I could make out a parked van. Several Biafran men were standing about, silent and uneasy.

There were children in the van in the last stages of starvation: limp bones, distended bellies, skeletal faces, large eyes. The men removed them from the van and laid them on mats. I looked down at the children, unable to place that sight into any context I had ever known. I had seen pictures of the starving Biafran children, and I had seen the recovering children on São Tomé, but this was something beyond all else. Vacant eyes stared at a vacant sky. One boy mumbled something. A man said to me, "Do you know what he is saying?"

"No."

"He is saying, 'My father, why don't you speak to me? Don't you know me?'"

I went all hollow inside.

Uwa di egwu!

We carried them up the ladder one by one. They were so very light. Soldiers, grim and silent, permitted a small-small light as we lifted our delicate cargo into the plane. We folded blankets on the floor and placed the children on them. I sat beside them on the long ride back to São Tomé. Their eyes remained open, but they never uttered a sound. In turbulence, their light bodies rocked gently on the floor.

I carried one child down the ladder and handed him to a social worker from San Antonio. I rode my Honda back to the apartment and climbed the stairs to the second floor, more spent than usual, though not as late as usual. Because we flew at night to avoid the MiGs and we had to get out of Biafra before daylight, we never met the people who got the food. So our activity was more abstract than personal — until I lifted that small child and carried him up the ladder into the plane. As he was about to pass into eternity, he felt that no one knew who he was, not even God.

Falling asleep was difficult.

California Academy of Sciences Cultural Identity Graphic

CHAPTER 12

Igwe Bu Ike

Unity is Strength

Early Portugese navigators sailed out into the Atlantic Ocean, down the west coast of Africa, and around the Cape of Good Hope, exploring, establishing colonies and trade routes. When they crossed the equator heading south, they came upon a ruggedly beautiful volcanic island, an uninhabited paradise. They named it Saint Thomas — in their language, São Tomé. The smaller island of Principe lay just to the north, and the Portuguese claimed this two-island group as their possession. They established coastal plantations in the rich volcanic soil; the interior of the island was too wild for cultivation or habitation. For laborers to work their land, plantation owners snatched slaves from different parts of the African continent, wherever Portuguese ships sailed, such that the Africans of any one plantation were not related by custom or language to the Africans of neighboring plantations. They had no common heritage or identity.

Slavery ended, but bondage of a sort did not: former slaves continued to work the Portuguese plantations or as servants and laborers on the island. Some fished in the rich waters or farmed small plots. They remained poor.

Centuries passed. At the center of the world, São Tomé and Principe were virtually unknown to the world, like a lost continent, until an event of the sun brought them into the context of the universe. In 1915, Einstein published his General Theory of Relativity concerning spacetime and gravity. Nobody understood what he was talking about until 1919 when Sir Arthur Eddington, a British scientist, observed bending of starlight by the gravity of the sun during a total eclipse, which he measured from the island of Principe. This result made Einstein instantly famous all over the world. Because of General Relativity, we understand how the universe works and how space and time began in the Big Bang 13.8 billion years ago. Time is deep.

São Tomé and Principe slipped again into obscurity until the Biafran Airlift made it a kind of Grand Central Station, people pouring in from all over the world on ships and planes, from 1968 to

1970. With these new people arrived new ideas about social class, color, and equality. While the people of São Tomé were largely unnoticed by the Airlift population, the locals were paying attention. A few years after Biafra lost its bid for freedom, the people of São Tomé threw out the Portuguese and became an independent country of their own, although one with an undefined heritage.

In the early years of the 21st century, scientists at the California Academy of Scientists turned their attention to the islands in the Gulf of Guinea, including São Tomé and Principe. Because they were volcanic islands forever isolated from a mainland, and virtually unknown to science, they had the potential to yield discoveries comparable to those of Darwin's Galapagos Islands. The scientists were right. They have made many expeditions to São Tomé and Principe and published discoveries of plants and animals unknown to the rest of the world. Although it was a "lost continent" they found no dinosaurs.

But what the California Academy of Sciences did next is truly remarkable. They taught the people of São Tomé how special they are as inhabitants and custodians of a unique and beautiful place in the world. They created a motto and a symbol: "Only here on São Tomé and Principe." They created classroom materials for primary students with pictures and descriptions of the fascinating plants and creatures that most islanders had never known were there. They went into the schools and taught all this in the local version of the Portuguese language. The scientists gave them their own unique identity and heritage. From disparate groups of people, they created a unified culture. Is there any other instance in history when something like this has been done?

I worked most nights in Biafra, and when I came home, I usually slept into the afternoon. On Thursday, January 23, on the morning after we carried those children out of Biafra, the regular mail plane came in from Luanda. Some hours later there was a knock on my door.

It was Elner.

She had come on the mail flight. I had been expecting her on the Boeing, but she had bought a commercial ticket and flown from New York to Lisbon to Luanda to São Tomé. Someone at the airport had shown her where I lived and brought her loads.

POW! What a surprise! I think all I could do was squeak.

I brought her suitcases into the room; she had a lot of stuff. Of course, the room was a mess. I hadn't finished fixing it up. I'd worked my 15-hour schedule for the last four nights, according to our rotation. I had the 23rd and 24th off, but we did nothing about the mess — just enjoyed being together for two days.

When we went out, I took her to Café Yong and some of the nicer places to eat. I showed her the warehouses, the shops, the market, and, of course, the only reason for being there, the airport. Everywhere we went, I introduced her to many people, people who had heard so much about her and wondered if a real person would get off a plane someday. To the Portuguese, like Senhor Lopes, and my Cape Verde friends, Valerio and Oscara, I introduced my wife as, "*minha mulher.*"

Oscara had a wife, too, whom he called, with a big smile, "*me hooman.*" In the coming weeks, Elner insisted on teaching him to say, "my wife."

At the airport, on her first evening on São Tomé, I got Elner a copy of the flight schedule. It read:

DEPARTING TIMES 23-rd Jan. 1969. Thursday

STD Sao Tomé				ARR over UDB in Biafra
~~F O~~	~~FOP~~	~~C46~~	~~1620~~	1820
~~A R G O~~	~~BOW~~	~~D07~~	~~1630~~	1800
TSAVIA	TRB	DC6	1650	1830
..""" ..	TRD	="=	1710	1850
..""..	TRL	="=	1730	1910
..""..	TRZ	="=	1750	1930
BRÅTHEN	SUD	="=	1810	1950
CAN-RELIEF	NAJ	sCon	1830	2000
A R C O	BCW	DC7	2120	2250
F O	FOP	C46	2210	0010
TSAVIA	TRB	DC6	2220	2400
..""..	TRD	="=	2240	0020
..""..	TRL	="=	2300	0040
..""..	TRZ	="=	2320	0100
BRÅTHEN	SUD	="=	2340	0120
CAN-RELIEF	NAJ	sCON	2400	0130

All W.C.C.

observe: THIS SCHEDULE SHALL UNDER NO CIRCUMSTANCES BE EXPOSED
IN PUBLIC.

In all, eight planes were listed for each of two shuttles that night, including four from Transavia, one Braathen, and one Canairrelief, NAJ, making its first flight to Uli that night. It gave the scheduled time of departure from São Tomé and the time of arrival over the non-directional beacon in Biafra. All flights were for WCC.

Elner dubbed these schedules "TV Guide," which, back home, listed the television programs for the evening. On São Tomé there was no TV, the radio worked only sometimes and there were no magazines or newspapers. Other than old movies with poor sound quality and Portuguese subtitles, the only entertainment was watching planes landing and taking off. To follow the action, Elner needed a copy of "TV Guide." When everything was going well at Uli, the planes came and went on schedule, but when the activity deviated from the schedule, Elner and the other "airport widows" knew that something was going on. Back in our apartment, she would lie in bed counting the planes going over. After the last one she would listen for the sound of my motorcycle.

After two nights off, I worked the next four nights.

"I feel a lot better about David's job since I've been here," Elner said in a tape we made for my parents. "It's very hard but he seems to be able to stand up under it. It doesn't bother him as much as it hurts me to watch him go. He is going in to Biafra, but I've come to realize that a lot of other people are doing it, too, and they come back. He leaves about 4:30 in the evening and comes back about 5:00 in the morning, so tired he can hardly walk. And he smells like a fish. I've convinced him that it would be better for him to bathe before he goes to bed. I honestly feel that he could sleep better, and I know that I could."

I had the next Wednesday and Thursday off, and Pastor Mollerup excused me from duty on Friday so I could work on the apartment.

"This place is a stable," Elner said about our first home together. "When I first saw this place I didn't see how I was going to make it," she told my mother.

It wasn't the first time she had slept in a two-room house. "My mother's father was a sharecropper down in Arkansas. It was a long time ago, but I remember sleeping in their tenant's shack. It was two rooms. One room was very hot – the fireplace was in there and they cooked there — and the other one was very cold. I had to ask them, 'wasn't there any way you could equalize the heat?'

My grandfather raised his crop. In the beginning of the year, he went in and borrowed some money from the Man, and he got his seed and enough money for flour and molasses — molasses was a big thing — and meal and salt and fatback. He made a crop and everything he got went to pay the Man back."

The first thing we did for our apartment was to buy a refrigerator and a stove with two burners and a small oven, which ran on bottled gas. Before Elner got there, I had ordered a lot of stuff that was beginning to come in: a nice dresser, a kitchen table and chairs, cabinets and shelves. I had already bought all the paint and brushes and rollers. On Wednesday, I painted all day long — ceiling and walls and trim in the bedroom. The ceiling and walls were white. The trim on the base boards, around the doors, and on a border around the ceiling was bright baby blue enamel. It looked like the frosting on a cake or like peppermint candy. Elner called it the Candy House, or, in pidgin Portuguese, *Casa Candy*.

During the next two days we worked on the kitchen and the floors. The kitchen looked like something that had been cooked in for a long time, with residue on the walls and ceiling. The ceiling was a dirty green; I painted it bright white. The walls above the ceramic tile were dirty yellow; I painted them a soft, cheerful, clean yellow. The sink was made out of some kind of speckled concrete; I painted it emerald green.

We rubbed wax on the floors, then we went away for a couple of hours. We came back and polished them. In the coming week when I was back at work, Elner would wash the wooden doors and shutters. She would go to the market and buy some material for curtains, some lively African patterns that matched the colors of *Casa Candy*.

Along the street, our building adjoined others on either side; there were no driveways or alleys between them. The front door opened on a central courtyard with two floors of single rooms arranged around it. At the right rear corner, a concrete stairway of two flights at right angles led to the second floor. (When I came home from the airport, I walked my Honda through the front door and parked it under the stairs.) Our two rooms were along the back wall. From the top of the stairs, we turned left to enter our door. Each of our rooms had a window opening on a veranda overlooking the courtyard. We shared a washroom with the other patrons along the right wing, a small room past the head of the stairs, a very small room. "You have to sit on the toilet in order to take a shower." Elner did not like that.

After one week on the island Elner said:

There is no place in the world like São Tomé. I have been to a lot of West Africa. It's just unbelievable. I never thought it was like this when he was describing it. There is actually nothing here. I mean nothing. The people are not like Africans on the main land and therefore it's not as interesting. There are a lot of things the Portuguese have not done for comfort, which doesn't make any sense to me. I don't see why they don't have hot water. I mean, as big as this island is, and they're Portuguese — they're from Europe — surely they know about hot water baths. I don't understand why the food is so bad.

This is very different from the rest of West Africa in at least two respects to me: the people and the lack of conveniences. The language is a very difficult problem for me, because I'm very poor in languages. I never know what's going on. I just follow around behind him and he does everything. He buys everything and he tells people what I want. But fortunately, I have David, and that makes a big difference. And with the stove and fixing up our house, we can be comfortable. It's a lot better than being in New York without him.

It would not be long before Elner was making her own way, and her own waves, on the island. After I would come home at five in the morning, and bathe, and eat something, and go to bed, Elner would go out to the market as the African women were setting up their wares. She began to learn Portuguese words. *Petrolio* meant kerosene. Quantities were easy: kilograms and liters, which she knew from her degree in Biology. She got to know the African women, and they her. They helped her adjust to São Tomé. They watched how a black woman from far away conducted herself around white people, especially Portuguese, and they recognized possibilities.

On the tape we made for my parents, I said this to my mother:

In the process of deciding whether it would be better for me to come home or for Elner to come here, in order for us to be together, I realized that it would be best if she came here, because if I went home and tried to explain to her, as I really couldn't ever do on tapes, what it's like here, she would never understand it, as you will never, either. If she came here and saw what it was like for herself, then she could begin to comprehend and appreciate what the whole thing is all about. And this she has done in the week she has been here. She said that she never, ever, would have realized what it was like here, what I was doing, what it was all about — the whole feeling that you get being here and associated with the planes and food and Biafra. Since being here she feels much easier about me being here than she did back home. I was actually worried about her. From her letters and tapes, she seemed to be getting nervous and upset and in an extreme sort of state, as I know you are about me, and I hope that her example of coming here and not finding it so bad will cheer you up a little bit too.

Other than Elner and me, no people from the airlift lived in our boarding house. Reverend Aitken had stayed here on one trip out of Biafra, but all the others were Portuguese and seemed to be long-term residents. The couple living nearest us, across from the washroom, regarded us with reserved distaste. They ate all their meals out, and we sometimes saw them in the Café Yong. They would turn to look at us, but never greeted us.

Most of our meals we ate at Senhor Costa's Café Equador with the other UNICEF guys and Bob Hall. A week after Elner arrived, I liberated from warehouse K a large can of beef in a gravy sauce from Germany. I gave it to the cook at the café. I told her to slice some potatoes and onions and other goodies and dump them in the pot to cook with the meat and mix and mash it all together and grunge it all around with salt and pepper. It came out something like hash. It was wonderful. I ate so much I was unable to paint any more that night.

When the floors were polished and we had moved in and arranged all our furniture, Elner began to unpack. She emptied one suitcase onto the dresser. It was full of bottles and jars.

"What are those?" I asked.

"My products."

"What do they do?"

"They're for my hair and my skin — you know — beauty products."

"Oh." I grew up with a brother, not a sister, so I hadn't realized what it took to keep a woman beautiful.

"What's that jar for?" I asked.

"I rub it on my elbows."

"What would happen if you didn't?" I could tell she was starting to get mad, so I shut up.

That was adjusting to married life. There was no doubt that I was married when she presented me with her bills: Macy's, Sak's Fifth Avenue, B. Altman's and other elegant New York shops, and car insurance. I now owned another Volkswagen. We laughed. I no longer had a mechanic's job, but UNICEF had reinstated me, so I had a steady, if meager, income. We would get by.

"What would I do if there is an air raid on São Tomé?" she asked.

I laughed. I had never thought of that as a possibility. "There won't be any air raids here," I said.

"Why not?"

I had to search for a reason. If we could fly our rickety old planes to Biafra, Nigeria could fly its jets to Sao Tome. "Because Portugal is a NATO ally and NATO would get after Nigeria." That seemed plausible.

"But what should I do? In case of one, what should I do?"

"In case of a bomb attack, if you're in the house, stay there."

She laughed, derisively.

"Stay inside, not facing a window," I said.

"Oh, thanks. I already know that from school." In the United States, we had air raid drills at school during the cold war.

"Okay. If you're out in the street, lay down."

"Thank you. Very much."

"If the bombs fall, you will hear them. Just lay down. Because if you're running or standing upright, the chances of you getting hit are much greater. Lay down. If there is something for you to get behind, do it. If there is a strafing attack, run! Run for cover, fast!"

"What is that?"

"Strafing is when a plane is shooting machine gun bullets at you. If they are just dropping bombs, well, drop. Hit the ground."

"These things happen, you know."

"It's not going to happen on São Tomé. No."

"All right. If you say so"

"*No problema. Nsogbu adighi.*"

Sixty Americans were to accompany the four C-97s: air crew, mechanics, load-masters, and JCA officials. On this small island it would be an invasion, like Marines taking an atoll. The few of us Americans already there convinced Senhor Costa to expand his café to an American style nightclub for the entertainment of the crews. Construction work began at Costa's, paralleling the activity at the airport and many other sites around the island. When Elner and I finished our own apartment, we made Costa's night club our major project, together with Larry, Barry, and Leo. A Canadian among us offered to work as a bartender. Leo said he would be the bouncer. Larry secured a four-track stereo tape recorder and began collecting American music. Elner prepared a menu of items like hamburgers, spaghetti, chili, pancakes, and donuts. Her social status among the present Americans soared. She would do the cooking, although she insisted, "I can't cook." She designed an American-style ladies room for the nightclub. We named the club "The Beacon."

Senhor Lopes worked with Oscara to convert other dubious spaces that he owned into rooms for the Americans. Senhor Lopes and I took Elner to inspect them, to see if they met her standards for American habitation.

"Terrible," she said. "Cattle pens. I'd hate to live in there." She insisted that they separate the toilets from the showers.

A once quiet little town before the Biafran Airlift, São Tomé was absorbing some heavy changes. While I was away for fifteen hours a day, Elner worked at the Beacon, and she also did some work in the warehouses, and at the orphanage.

On the Thursday after Elner arrived and a week after I had helped evacuate the Biafran children, I took her to visit the orphanage at San Antonio. Most of the new kids could sit or stand up, eating their bread. One boy, still looking very weak, sat hunched on a mat with his legs crossed under him. His hands lay on his lap. No longer vacant, his eyes now followed me. No longer nameless, his identity I now know, something else I learned as a result of publishing *Far Away in the Sky*.

We discussed the children on the tape to my parents:

ELNER: They are damaged. I was really disturbed by what I saw. They are very well cared for. In fact they are probably getting better care than anyone else on the island. They have decent housing, as far as I'm concerned by American standards. It's decent, but I think I saw signs of things that cannot be recovered from. They don't look like children looked in Biafra before, to me. But they still act like Biafran children, different from the children we see on São Tomé.

ME: Much different.

ELNER: They come up and hold your hand. One little girl, of course, fell in love with David. She followed him around, and finally he had to take her up in his arms. When we left she said, "*Ka omesia.*" Goodbye. One little girl was rubbing her hand against my leg, a natural affection. I think it's important for them to have human beings to touch, because that's the way it is in Biafra.

ME: Yeah, there's an awful lot of physical contact among families, between the children, between the adults and children. There's a lot of natural warmth and affection.

ELNER: Yes. There are no orphan homes in Biafra.

ME: Right. There's no such thing. If someone is an orphan, he is just absorbed by the greater family, the extended family system. The children in this orphanage are not orphans. They have families back in Biafra. As long as they live, they will have family.

ELNER: Children are so valuable.

ME: Children are considered extremely important. None of them is ever left out, uncared for as an orphan. Right now, they're living a very dormitory type of existence, a little mass colony of children here. That sort of experience is not in the culture, not in the way they expect to be treated. Of course, you know, this is why they are starved for affection, why they run up to us when we come and grab our hands and want to climb on us. It's so extreme because they lack it. The nuns keep them clean and well-fed, but orderly, well regimented, so they don't have the contact they are used to having. Anyway, they are still alive. Not too many look as if they have suffered too much brain damage, but they are suffering right now some cultural damage, as Elner pointed out.

ELNER: But I think they have some very serious physical damage besides brain damage. David doesn't think so, but I do. If there is any doubt that what he is doing is important, seeing those children will remove it, because I think that this generation of Biafrans will be different from the previous ones. They have had enough deficiencies to be stunted mentally and physically. And this is unbelievable to anyone who has lived in the old Biafra. An Igbo child seen like this is really heartrending, because they are such energetic and aggressive people. This makes it worth David being here.

While we were at the orphanage, a nun told us a story about a boy who had since been repatriated to Biafra. He was about seven years old, one of the older ones. The children were thriving on their plentiful diet, but they did not like a spread that was put on their bread. The nuns said it was good for them and made them eat it. The boy organized and led the whole camp in a *hunger* strike to protest. Biafran children on a *hunger* strike! At a given signal from him, all the children put down their bread. Some of the newer, younger ones were very hesitant about taking food away from their own mouths, but they did it.

The nuns relented, and the children were no longer forced to eat the obnoxious substance – peanut butter.

And the children of Ocean Hill-Brownsville stormed police barricades to open their school.

Uwa di egwu. The world is deep.

Author and Portuguese Soldier Examine Bomb Damage

CHAPTER 13

Nsogbu Adighi

No Problem

A phase change occurs in nature when a substance transforms from a gaseous, nebulous state to a more ordered but fluid liquid state. Liquid evolves into a rigid solid. With the transition to a JCA operation, the Biafran Airlift was moving away from that former fluid, sometimes exasperating, endeavor to a larger, more controlled phase. Curiously, as I look back on it now, I feel more comfortable with that crazy "not-a-normal-island" period.

1

The two C-97s got off to a shaky start. In the first two weeks they flew very few missions. One C-97 went in to Biafra for the first time to try it out. He landed, but made only one shuttle that night. The next night, the two planes were added to the regular flight schedule. Nineteen flights landed in Biafra, a record at that time. This did not include the Americans, because they couldn't find Uli. The American military pilots had flown in Viet Nam and were used to radar and air traffic control. They had Strategic Air Command radios and lots of up-to-date military equipment, all of which was useless for a single non-directional beacon over a dark road in the African bush. When the captain of the Braathen plane returned to São Tomé, he sported a huge smile as he stood in the cockpit door and announced, "The Americans couldn't find the field!"

From then on the Americans found the field and slowly built up their experience, but they contributed relatively little to the tonnage of food delivered to Biafra, in spite of their large individual capacity. One or the other plane was usually grounded with mechanical problems. A C-97 on the first shuttle blew a tire at Uli, flew back to São Tomé, and did not fly a second shuttle. ARCO or Transavia crews would have changed the tire in time for a second shuttle. ARCO, Transavia, Fred Olsen, and Braathen were pushing up the nightly tonnage by flying steadily at maximum capacity and short turnaround times. In one seven day period, Bravo Charlie Whiskey made 21 flights, a record. On February 3, while Bravo Charlie Whiskey and one Transavia plane made three shuttles, one American plane landed in Biafra. Two C-97s took off on the first shuttle, but neither one landed at Uli. On the second shuttle, one C-97 lost thirty gallons of oil in one engine thirty seconds after take-off. It needed an engine change, but the mechanics didn't have the tools or the crane to do the work. That plane was permanently grounded, parked next to the hangar where Delta used to sit, to be used for spare parts for the other three. The European air crews and mechanics resented being upstaged by the North Americans, who weren't producing very much.

At 5:10 p.m. GMT on February 1, 1969, I was sitting in Bravo Charlie Whiskey on the runway on São Tomé. We were waiting for clearance to take off. One plane had already left on time at 4:30 with Larry on it. We were about to start engines for our turn when the tower got a telephone message from Biafra House to hold all flights until the Biafran Representative could get here with a special message. We got down from the plane. We learned that there might be some trouble in Biafra that night. The previous night, we heard, there had been some air raids on Nigerian occupied Port Harcourt and Enugu, by whom and with what we didn't know. It was feared that in retaliation for those raids Nigeria was going to try something. For some reason, maybe mechanical trouble, the intruder was not expected to fly that night. But Nigeria was expected to take extreme measures to stop the airlift. It would not be by ground fire, because that had not been effective. It was speculated that they might use one of their two Illyushin twin-jet fighter-bombers, adapted for night fighting, with radar. The Biafran Representative told us to expect anything and to avoid certain routes where the Nigerians might be waiting for us.

With that caution, we were cleared to fly normal operations that night. Larry's plane was already on the way — we hoped he had been briefed by radio. The pilots and crews had a conference out on the flight line. They worked out a strategy to fly high, descend rapidly, and get in as quickly as possible to avoid air action against us. Bravo Charlie Whiskey couldn't fly high because of the hole made by the wayward propeller. It was patched up, but we couldn't pressurize the plane, restricting it to a maximum altitude of 10,500 feet. We couldn't fly high, but we could fly fast. We would avoid the risky route and see what would happen.

"What would you do if an IL-28 got on your tail?" I asked the captain.

"Well," he said, "I'll tell you. Reduce power, dive, go into a full forty-five degree bank and lose him."

(A few months later a MiG got on the tail of a Red Cross DC-7 and shot it down.)

All the pilots seemed confident, but they were scared of the Nigerian jets. They were going to go ahead and fly anyway. As a member of the crew, I would go with them — just scared, not confident.

We crossed over the coast while it was still fairly light out. I was strapped into a spare seat in the john in the tail at the suggestion of the captain, in case he had to make any violent maneuvers. Catholic missionaries occupied the three other seats in the main cabin. A few minutes before, I'd had a discussion with the captain. Because I had been in the delta, we talked about elevations and the geography of the area, and the locations of possible enemy airfields within range of Uli, other than Port Harcourt, Benin City, or Calabar. Makurdi was to the North, where we thought the Illyushins were based. As yet nothing had happened. We were flying a different route and altitude than usual.

The pilot wanted to know about elevations and geography because, at some points, we were flying *very* low.

Larry remembers that "the MiGs scared the pilots the most. They tried to stay in the clouds or very low as they approached Biafra. On occasion they flew so low that you felt like you were in a boat skimming across the water, watching the porpoises jump below you."

Johnny Correa said that Nigerians had radar on Russian trawlers off the coast. At Uli, Johnny and his crew "put protective covers over the [runway] lights — could see the lights only if you were coming in on final at about 1000 feet —otherwise would only see a light here and there which would look like the bush."

I recorded our descent and landing at Uli. On the tape you can hear the voice of the copilot reading the air speed and altitude to the pilot while the pilot keeps his eyes peeled looking for the runway. The pilot's vision is their only radar. The copilot notes the deployment of the flaps and landing lights and changing the fuel to a rich mixture for greater power and control.

> We are now at 4000 feet over the field, descending on our approach. No enemy action so far…We are at 1000 feet on our final approach…Pilot is calling for runway lights…Runway lights straight ahead…Gear down…See the runway…Air Speed One Forty…Altitude 640 feet…Mixture to rich…Landing lights on… Full flaps…150 feet…Air speed 140, still…134, 300 feet…One three zero…Runway lights under us now…128…We're down!… runway lights have gone out…engines under reverse…turned out the landing lights…navigating by moonlight down this strip…all lights are out. No sign of enemy action yet. I see no anti-aircraft fire. We are going to taxi to our parking area. Out for now.

We unloaded the cargo of stockfish from three doors: the forward cockpit door, the main cabin door, and the rear emergency door. On my recording I sound out of breath. The activity was frantic. There are sounds of a scuffle. A Biafran voice says, "Get out, you idiot!"

I yell, "Stop it! Stop it!"

Biafran team leader: "How you disobey when I'm giving you orders?"

"You two move forward and bring this stuff to the door. Team leader, is anyone unloading from the front door?"

There are muffled voices and sounds of things scraping and bumping along the floor.

"Can you station some more back this way, so they can slide them? Come on! This plane wants to make three trips. Quickly! Quickly! Push that bale. Now grab the other one. Kick it out! Very good. It's working well. OK, very good. Keep going. Keep it moving."

On the recording, there is the roar of heavy engines from a plane taking off over us. It was the plane Larry had come on, and it was heading back to São Tomé for another load. It would try for three shuttles. Although we left late, this plane was fast enough to make three trips.

A European voice joins the frantic effort, probably the copilot: "Push it! Push it! Get behind it and push it! Look! Push, push, push!"

"It's easier to push it," I say.

"Get behind it and push it! Move it! Move it!" the copilot says.

Thump, bump, slide, slide.

"How much more we got up there?" I ask.

"We're halfway, but we're much too slow."

"Keep it moving," I say. "Step up here and push behind it. Push it down. OK, keep it moving…OK…Hey! You put that fish in your pocket and eat it later! Put it down. Put it in your pocket."

They were hard working Air Force fatigue workers, as hungry as everyone else.

Listen while I whisper into the microphone:

Now I'm lying alongside this strip on an air mattress. It's about eleven o'clock at night. Peaceful. The sound of crickets emphasizes the quiet, and moonlight softens the night.

A lone plane passes far overhead, unseen against the star field. It is not the intruder. Even the enemy is still tonight. It's one of ours or a French Red Cross plane from Libreville.

I'm waiting for the second shuttle. The first plane should be along in about thirty minutes. The wait is usually between one and three hours. I use the time to rest and to do some trading, but no more Indian hemp. I bring trade items in my bag, like cigarettes, razor blades, soap, and cloth. Batteries are in demand. Some of the deals are made in advance and I bring specific items: a Honda spark plug, a bicycle tire, or sanitary napkins for a man's wife. In return I get some drums, *ekwe*, and various other musical instruments. There are 45-rpm records of High Life music recorded before the war, like *Baby Pancake* by the Eastern Star Dance Band of Aba and *Nsogbu Ndi Nigeria* by Jonas Nwa Ukpo and His Group. I trade for craft items like woven baskets, carvings, and masks that we will use for decorations in the Beacon. And a basket of oranges. On São Tomé, a tropical island, we get a lot of fruits: bananas, paw-paw, mangoes, and pineapples — a great variety, but no oranges. Tonight I obtained a piece of Akwete cloth, which is woven in Biafra — very scarce now. Akwete has long since fallen to Nigeria, but the people from Akwete who used to weave this cloth now practice their art in the Aba sector.

Time passes; the full moon and the stars drift across the sky. That plane is now coming in to land. It will probably pass right over my head. I will try to identify it as it goes over. [The sound of strong, steady engines approaches and roars overhead, fading forward as it crosses the threshold]. It is Bravo Charlie Whiskey back on its second shuttle. That was good time. The breeze is blowing over me now. After the main gust, little wispies follow behind, whorls of turbulent air flow from propellers and wing tips. I feel them brushing my face. Since the plane landed at this end, it will park at the other end, and I will not be involved in unloading it. The quiet returns.

A profound peace settles over the moonlit scene, and me. Amazing to think that those iron bombs could violate this splendid night. No, not this night. The universe turns above me and the night slides by in silence as it should.

The next night, February 2, the intruder returned. We were on final over the field when we suddenly lost the beacon and didn't get runway lights when we expected them. We climbed out and returned to the holding pattern. The intruder dropped six bombs off our tail, but missed the runway again. We held for a while until he left – he had no more bombs – and then we landed. On our approach the next night, he dropped one bomb, saving the rest while he waited for us to try again. We held, then returned to São Tomé without landing.

"Genocide" was the Biafran code word for the intruder. Apparently, the intruder knew the code word for himself and all of our planes. That night of February 3, while we were all holding, he radioed the Canadian plane.

"HOTEL PAPPA ALPHA, this is GENOCIDE. I have fuel for fourteen hours holding. What are you going to do?"

Captain Patterson replied. "GENOCIDE, this is HOTEL PAPPA ALPHA. We're going to land."

He landed. Genocide dropped a bomb. Missed.

Unrelated to the bombing, the Canadian plane, whose real call letters were November Alpha Juliet, returned to São Tomé with a feathered prop, due to an over-speed propeller. The next morning the Canadian mechanics showed up to work on the engine, but the Portuguese officials would not let them on the flight line because the authorities had not yet issued their proper ID passes. They stood there at the fence with their fingers through the wire mesh and their noses up to the wire looking helplessly at their "blue canoe with the over-speed paddle." Once they got their passes and fixed the engine, Patterson had to fly the plane to Europe to have the landing gear x-rayed. It was out of service for a few more days.

2

By Sunday, February 9, NAJ was back in service. Although he had a permanent load-master on his crew, Patterson requested my help that night because they were trying for three shuttles. I was free to do so. As I was walking across the ramp toward the Connie, with the runway on my left, I saw Lima taking off, airborne for the first time since Baekstrom brought it in from Biafra. I watched it rise and fold its gear into the wings. Although battered, the DC-7 was still the sleekest looking plane in the airlift. The landing gear locked in place, and stayed there.

But Lima was not going back to Biafra; it was headed for Europe. Pastor Mollerup had ordered ARCO off the island to make room for all the North American planes that were to come. Transavia had to reduce its fleet to two aircraft. Braathen was gone. Bravo Charlie Whiskey was gone. Even with all the new construction, there wasn't enough space for the big JCA planes yet to come. Even though ARCO and Transavia had been the workhorses of the airlift all along, and even though they were making a record number of flights at this time, Nordchurchaid told them to leave. Baekstrom was gone; Tangen was gone; Delahunt and Nolan were gone; McCombie was killed. The new names for JCA were Glenn, Gossman, and Cutler. I didn't know them.

So I was free to fly with the Canadians.

We went in early and landed at 6:00 p.m. GMT, 7:00 p.m. Biafra time. It was still just a little bit light out. As we were taxiing to our parking slot, the load-master came over to where I was sitting on the right side of the aircraft. I was just finishing a delicious sandwich that Elner had prepared for me, pork shoulder with hot mustard on a bun.

"Well, I think I'll sit over here tonight," he said, "because this is where the bombs usually drop." I didn't understand that remark, because the bombs could fall anywhere. Maybe he was just trying to scare me. But sure enough, a bomb burst in a great flash just off to the right and a little behind the aircraft. We waited, holding our breaths, for the next explosion. "Genocide" usually drops two or three at a time. The Canadians, flying "Snoopy's Dog House," referred to "Genocide" as "The Bloody Red Baron."

"Damn it, drop the other shoe!" I said. But he didn't. At our parking place I pumped open the large hydraulic cargo door and I heard another bomb fall about 100 yards off the end of the runway. It seemed to be smaller than the usual bombs. The cargo master and I got the slide board out the door. Usually lorries and fatigue workers were right there waiting for us. This time they weren't, because bombs were falling and they were in the bunker. He and I started unloading the plane by ourselves. We continued working until the sacks of food piled up at the bottom of the slide board.

"I'll go down and unjam it," the cargo master said. After he cleared the slide board, I never saw him again that night. I worked alone for a long time. After a while, Reverend Aitken appeared out of the night, as he often did, and started helping me unload, just the two of us, working silently. I worked forward of the door and he worked rearward.

I heard the whoosh of a bomb falling. It sounded heavy, huge. From outside on the ground I could hear a bomb falling for a long way. Sometimes between shuttles, lying on my air mattress, I would listen to the intruder flying overhead and watch the AA going up around me, like a fireworks show. If a bomb fell I could tell if it was coming my way, and I would jump in a bunker. When it hit, the ground would shake and rumble. From inside the aircraft that night, by the time I heard it, I knew that the bomb was already close. By the gigantic shriek of it I knew that it was here RIGHT NOW. I dove for the floor between the sacks of food. As I was in mid-leap, I saw the flash out of the windows on the left side of the plane.

When I hit the floor I felt the concussion shake the aircraft. I jumped up and looked out the door. I saw a plume of smoke going straight up into the air, and sparks, and I heard the pitter-patter of stones and metal falling all around. The blast damaged the plane slightly.

Aitken and I continued unloading the plane, just the two of us in silence and lengthening time. Then a marshaller joined us. His job was to direct plane traffic on the ground with his long red flashlights, but he came up to help. Bombs fell all around us, one side and the other. Some I never heard coming, just saw the flash out the cargo door to the left. The first I knew of them was the explosion, flash, and shaking of the aircraft. If it's already gone off, I thought, don't worry about it. Just keep working. But in the back of my mind floated images of jagged pieces of metal ripping through my body. I kept working like crazy, sweating profusely, every muscle in my body aching. Aitken and the marshaller worked furiously. Four fatigue workers joined us. The usual complement is twelve or fifteen.

At one point, I saw Captain Patterson outside on the ramp hollering and bellowing for people to come out and unload his aircraft. A bomb was falling while he was standing there. He must have heard it coming for a long way. I heard it just before it blew up. Patterson stood there hollering the whole time, in mid-sentence when it detonated, not far from where he was standing. I felt the concussion. It gave me a violent headache.

"All right, that was the last one, number six!" Patterson yelled. "You can all come out and unload the goddamn aircraft!" More workers joined us, but two more bombs would fall before we finished unloading.

Eight was an unusual number of bombs. In addition to the six heavy bombs he carried on wing racks, Genocide must have had some smaller ones for throwing out the door. They fell one at a time, each from a separate bomb run, and all clustered around the end of the runway where our planes were parked, an unprecedented level of accuracy.

When we finished unloading, Reverend Aitken went with the marshaller to direct a plane just landing, the fourth one of the first shuttle. I brought in the slide board, secured the cargo door, descended the crew ladder, and went down into the bunker. There were so many hot, sweaty bodies in the bunker that there was only room for me by the door at the bottom of the stairs. That was fine with me – I feel claustrophobic in confined spaces. From my spot I could see a patch of sky at the top of the stairs, only slightly lighter than the tight darkness. The flash of bomb number nine lit up the mouth of the hole. I heard the concussion and felt the bunker shaking. I came out and saw that NAJ, which had been ready for immediate take off, was still on the ground. Patterson was waiting for the Transavia plane that just landed to clear the runway.

The marshaller was trying to direct the plane to a parking finger near us, but the pilot, Don Merriam, a determined man who made his own decisions, wanted to go to the One-Six end. Perhaps he knew that all the bombs this night had been clustered at Three-Four. As he was rolling, looking for a turn around, the bomb hit the center stripe of the runway, right behind his tail, seconds after he passed that spot. Merriam did a one-eighty and headed for the other end. But his plane was damaged. A bomb fragment had hit the left elevator, jamming it. After parking, while the plane was being unloaded, the crew worked on their aircraft. They banged at the jammed elevator and worked it loose. There was a hole as big as my fist in the carburetor air intake on engine number three. A big chunk was knocked out of one of the propellers. The fuel tank for engine number four was punctured and leaking. They drained it. Because of the valve system on the plane, fuel could not be cross-fed from one tank to another, so Merriam flew back on three engines.

Aitken saw the flash. He thought the bomb might have hit the runway. He took the marshaller's flashlights and sprinted down the center of the runway toward the impact. When Merriam pulled his wounded plane off the runway, Patterson prepared for take-off. He ran up his engines while the engineer checked the instruments. Aitken reached the crater. Patterson advanced the throttles and began his take-off run. Aitken turned and ran straight at the accelerating Super Constellation, waving the red tipped flashlights. The four 3250 horsepower engines roared on full take-off power. Aitken kept running right at it. Patterson saw the small waving lights dead ahead. He didn't know what to make of them, except that something was on the runway. He chopped the throttles.

"Reverse engines!" he ordered. He went to full power reverse and stood up on the brakes, blowing a tire, stopping before he hit Aitken, or the crater.

After I came out of the bunker, I heard the Connie begin its take-off run, then stop. Strange. I started down the runway and I met Aitken coming back.

"There's a hole in the runway," he said.

He and I set off down the runway together. Some of the flight crew from the three planes that had already landed followed us. Bits of pavement and rocks were spewed all over. Gashes radiated out from the crater where pieces of the bomb had pin-wheeled across the tarmac. It was three feet deep and five feet in diameter, centered on the white line painted on the runway. Patterson stood looking into the hole with a pensive look on his face. He said to me, while Reverend Aitken was talking to someone else a little distance away, "I could have taken off. I'd have been going fast enough by the time I got here that the nose wheel would have skipped over the hole." The main landing gear would have been beyond the diameter of the crater.

Patterson decided to take off, even with a blown tire and a short runway. He was 2400 feet from the near end with 5300 feet on the other side of the crater. Empty, he had enough room to take off. He maneuvered around the hole. I watched him go until he lifted off a mile away and rose past the church at Uli. Some of our other planes from the second shuttle landed later, dropping down right at the end of the runway, using full power reverse and serious braking. One plane couldn't land because of the short runway, probably the C-97.

Although it looked cavernous to me, the crater wasn't big enough to span the tarmac. It had probably been made by one of the smaller bombs of the night, a 100-pounder, a little leftover surprise from "Genocide." There was a lot of junk at the bottom of the hole, pieces of tortured, ragged black iron. I picked up three pieces, still hot, and put them in my bag. Others helped themselves to these grim souvenirs. Aitken did not. The largest piece I collected had probably been a tail fin, once straight, now twisted in a spiral, as if it had been molded around a hot whirlwind. The black iron was scored with brown striations. There were bits of brown dirt and red laterite clinging to it. Something inside had ripped a two-centimeter hole through it. I doubted that the skin of an airplane and a few sacks of food could have stopped something like that from hitting me. I felt a weird sense of exhilaration that I had not been hit that night. Nine bombs, and nobody had been hit.

All those bombs fell at the Three-Four end of the runway, where I routinely worked unloading relief planes. I never saw any of the arms planes at that end, although I worked all night. Those planes must have been unloaded at the One-Six end or elsewhere along the airstrip. Since the intruder knew the codes for our planes, he must have known which ones were our relief planes and where we parked. "Genocide" preferred to target us rather than the military. To starve civilians was a Nigerian military objective.

Four of our planes had landed on the first shuttle. Four were hit, but all four returned to São Tomé. Two of them were seriously damaged and could not fly a second shuttle. Not one person was hit.

BBC radio later reported that a bomb had destroyed one plane on the runway and another plane had crashed in a bomb crater. The crews were killed. Perhaps "Genocide" had exaggerated his report and the BBC accepted it without checking. Perhaps there is no excuse for false reporting. Like other BBC reports, it provoked a lot of laughter back on São Tomé when I told the crews that they were dead.

3

I went in later with Aitken and the 2 I C (Second In Command) of the air base to find the head of the Ministry of Works so his crews could repair the runway. When a smaller bomb had hit the runway in the past, Ministry of Works fixed it in hours. Now, not so. Before workers would go near a crater, bomb demolition experts from the Biafran Air Force (usually Johnny Correa) had to certify that the bomb had in fact gone off. They had filled a bomb hole back in November, and were rolling it, when the bomb detonated, destroying the roller and killing about eight people nearby. The 2 I C said he had been close to it but had not been injured. After about half an hour, the bomb demolition crew came out. Of course, they found nothing in the hole because I and others had removed all the pieces. We assured them there was no longer a bomb in there.

Ministry of Works kept a bulldozer, a roller, and lorries of sand and laterite standing by to patch holes, but no one was around to operate them. So Aiken and I and the 2 I C went looking for the boss. We went to his house. We found him at the same time that a car full of Air Police found him for the same reason. Both cars blasted horns outside his gate to wake the man up. A huge man with a booming voice and a sense of humor, the 2 I C stood at the gate, hollering for the man to come out.

"Ministry of Works is holding up the whole nation!" When the man finally came out dressed in his wrapper, 2 I C told him to get out there and get the equipment moving and patch the hole "or you're going to make a trip to Umuahia tomorrow." The man knew that a trip to Umuahia meant he would have to stand before Ojukwu and explain why he held up the whole nation.

We went back to the airstrip and dropped off the 2 I C. A Canadian missionary named Alex with the WCC reported to Aitken. He had been escorting a convoy of lorries from the first shuttle, four plane loads including those from Patterson's and Merriam's planes, back to central stores when they were attacked. Two armed soldiers in Biafran uniforms, one a lance corporal, and ten men in civilian clothes carrying machetes halted them. They attacked Alex, drove him to the ground and pinned him there, threatening his life. The men unloaded a couple of the lorries. They took fifteen bales of stockfish and head-loaded them off into the bush. At 250 stockfish per bale, they made off with at least 3750 fish. As they were doing this, Alex got up off the ground and watched them. While the soldiers watched the men carry their pilfered cargo, Alex went up to one of them and smacked him on the head with his flashlight. The soldier spun around and stuck his gun right in the missionary's face. Alex decided he meant business, so he backed off. When the men and stockfish disappeared into the bush, the soldiers approached the missionary again.

"*Fada*, you have cigarette for us?"

"Next, you'll be wanting my blessing," Alex replied.

He reported the incident to the 2 I C and Aitken. The 2 I C made arrangements for mobile police with automatic weapons to escort all future consignments of food transported from the airstrip to the stores. I went with Aitken and the 2 I C to escort the next convoy.

"I guarantee you," the 2 I C said, "that if any convoy is interrupted, THERE WILL BE AN EXCHANGE OF GUNFIRE!"

We were to meet our armed escort at a certain point across the airstrip as we were joining the main road. We were to call them when we got there, but the telephone was out. We waited for a while and then left without them. I was with Aitken and others in the lead car. We proceeded slowly through the bush, using only parking lights until we were well away from the airfield. We followed bush roads, dark bush on all sides interspersed with cassava plantations here and there. There were access roads and crossing pathways from which an ambush could come at any moment. To me, the prospect of "an exchange of gunfire" at close range was scarier than waiting for bombs to fall. I was in the back seat, and I picked out a spot on the floor to lay my body if bullets started flying.

But nothing more happened that night. When I landed at São Tomé, I noted that two more C-97s had arrived.

Looking back on that night from forty years into the future, I understand why I was unloading that plane during a bombing attack. But why did I accompany Reverend Aitken on an errand to fix the runway and on a mission to protect a convoy of food? When I was alone in the plane, heaving fifty-pound sacks of food on to the slide, I felt very much alone, cosmically alone. Then Aitken showed up out of the night, once again. We worked together wordlessly, a missionary and an atheist. For me at least, a bond formed. And for the rest of the night, we remained together until I flew back to São Tomé.

4

With our old planes gone and the new JCA planes carrying their own load-masters on the crew, UNICEF had little to do, once again. We continued flying for a couple more weeks. One night in the last week of February, I flew in with Transavia, unloaded that plane, waited nine hours in a cold rain for the next flight, unloaded it, and went home on it. It seemed pointless to continue offloading only one or two planes. I went back to working in the warehouses, helping with inventory. Elner was working there too, in the employ of *Das Diakonische Werk*. Since she couldn't pronounce that, she called it "Das Vitchawitch." They paid her $50 a week.

"The first day I went to work," Elner said, "I asked David what I should take. He said to take something to write with and something to write on. And take a bag so you can bring stuff home." In addition to her salary, *Das Diakonische Werk* gave her some "Nathan food" that would normally be given to missionaries and other relief workers. On our pantry shelves we had puddings, pancake mix, Campbell's soup, and Comstock Pumpkin Pie Filling. None of us knew how to make pie crust.

We both spent some time working at the Beacon. We put a flashing red sign above the front entrance saying, "Beacon." I found a rotating blue light that we mounted above the sign. A tin-knocker in the market fashioned some conical light fixtures to look like runway lights. Technically, they would be called taxiway lights, because they were blue — runway lights would be white. We ran these from the front door along both sides of the hallway to the open-air club in the back, a rectangular room with a bar at the far end. Two-thirds of the space was open to the sky. A roof slanted over the rest of it, covering the bar, stereo, and some of the tables. The stereo was mounted above the bar, and the speakers were mounted in recesses along the side walls. Four long neon lights — two red, two blue — created a nice effect, along with some potted palms.

Elner said, "We have our African masks from Biafra on the walls, which gives it a very different effect. Under one of the red lights is a very large one, and it's especially lovely to look at over the bar. A month ago when I first walked back there and saw that pile of rocks, I didn't believe there would ever be a club there."

The Grand Opening was Saturday, March 8. The new Americans and everybody else poured in. It was packed. People ate hamburgers, chicken, and roast suckling pig. They drank beer, wine, or whiskey. Lots of it. Me, too. In addition to the recorded music, we had a band.

It was just what we had planned — a place for flight crews to blow off tension from the dangers of the airlift. It was so successful that the Portuguese virtually shut us down.

Senhor Costa, the proprietor of the Beacon, was an African, and the Portuguese did not want all that business going his way instead of to the usual, more sedate places like the Café Yong, with Portuguese owners. The police charged Costa $50 for staying open after midnight. After midnight was when the flight crews came back from Biafra. Costa barely had $50 for operational expenses, and he had yet to make enough money to pay off his debts for building the place. The police would charge him $60 more for a permit to allow dancing on the premises.

How calmly Costa accepted this astounded me. To me it was gross injustice, but to him it was the way of life for an African living under the Portuguese. Was this a fight we could, or should, pick? I wanted to talk to the Governor. Or should we follow Costa's lead? Any repercussions would fall on him. Or I could be deported, like Tom Hebert. Back then the Portuguese controlled São Tomé with a rigid grip. A few years after Biafra lost its bid for independence, the Africans of São Tomé and Principe overthrew the Portuguese, not peacefully. A man named Costa became the first President. I don't know if that was our Senhor Costa, but I know that our Senhor Costa would have been free to manage his business on an equal footing.

To what extent the Biafran Airlift might have influenced the independence movement, I don't know, but today, this day, more than forty years later, if you look down in a satellite view of São Tomé, and if you zoom in on *Parque Popular* along *Avenida da Independensia,* you will see resting on the lawn, among the trees, the top of a large airplane.

The Beacon remained open, and people still came in to relax. Sometimes in the evening people would grab a guitar off the wall and have a lively jam session. But under the new restrictions, it was like the Portuguese had dropped a no-fun bomb on the place. Twisting the whole thing around another way, Biafrans from Biafra House could come to the Beacon to unwind. Although the airlift was about them, Biafrans were not welcome in the Portuguese establishments. They weren't excluded, but they weren't welcome, either, and Biafrans were seldom seen eating or drinking with the people of the airlift.

"It is dreary and lonesome," said Edmond Okun, speaking on my tape. He had been stationed at Biafra House for two months, and he was referring to São Tomé. He was having a beer at the Beacon. "It's not all that bad. We're making it fine," he said without enthusiasm. The families of the people at Biafra House were all back in the enclave.

"The Beacon is a welcome projecture. We are most welcome in here. We are black. It is good to spend an hour or two at the Beacon after a hectic day at the office." He laughed. "It makes all the difference."

"I spend half my day thinking of my wife," said Edmond.

"Where is your wife now?" I asked.

"She is at Umuahia," he said. "She works in a clerical office for the military government."

"Where are you originally from?"

"I am from Uyo. My wife is from Calabar." They were people from the Rivers area, not Igbos, and Nigeria had long since occupied their homes.

Oscara entered the Beacon and started a lively conversation in Broken English with the Biafrans. Oscara spent a lot of time with Elner and me — in the Beacon, at *Casa Candy,* and riding around São Tomé in our car. We became good friends. Elner continued her project of teaching Oscara to say, "my wife" instead of *"me hooman."*

"I succeeded, too," Elner said. "David indulges him in this, but with a little patience, you can teach him the right words."

"My hife," Oscara tried.

"No — my *wife*," said Elner.

"My life," said Oscara. Elner accepted this intermediate step for a couple of weeks. Then she persisted.

"My *wife!*" she said.

He eventually got it, but he used the word "wife" as a noun for every woman (*hooman*) that he saw.

"Another thing Oscara does," Elner said, "riding along in a car, he says, 'Stand up!' when he means, 'Stop, we are at the place.' But we are very grateful for Oscara's little attempts to speak English. There aren't many people we can communicate with. Most people speak only Portuguese."

Oscara and his brother Valerio felt comfortable enough with us to express their political views, deep anger, and resentment of the Portuguese. They skipped out of Cape Verde one step ahead of the law for speaking out or acting out. They knew that the Portuguese on São Tomé had been alerted, and the brothers were keeping quiet. But with us, they could let loose. If Costa felt the same way, he kept it tight.

By not hanging out with the top managers of the airlift, we developed a different perspective than the official views carried back to the rest of the world by newsmen and politicians, just as we did in our years with the Peace Corps. More interesting things were swirling in the undercurrents.

Other people who spoke English to us were the mercenaries. The mercenaries preferred the Hotel Salvador, the high ground. I took Elner up there to show her the first place I had come to on São Tomé, with its magnificent view of the northern part of the island — the town, the bays, the rain forest, and the airport. Most of the mercenaries had little to say. They sat quietly and drank and watched. They were from South Africa, Rhodesia, Germany, and Britain.

Johnny Correa, a Puerto Rican American from New York City, breezed in and out of the usual hangouts on São Tomé, always ebullient. Everyone knew him; everyone liked him. He had been an American soldier in the Korean War, and he started working with Biafra as a maintenance engineer from early June, 1967 and remained until the end of the war. His wife and daughter, Juanita, lived in New York City but came to visit Johnny in Biafra. He adopted a Biafran daughter named Buka, and Buka's brother, Kanjo, served as Johnny's house boy.

"I hate the word 'bastard,'" he says, "because I was an illegal child — my birth certificate had 'unknown' — my mother wouldn't put down the name of the father — rumors that he was a rich man, taking care of her — this was in Puerto Rico." He came to the U.S. at age six. His mother married a stepfather, then she died when he was nine. The stepfather put him in "an orphanage asylum in Staten Island" where he was the only Black and treated with great prejudice.

"I never trusted anyone who was white — I distrust them because they proved themselves over and over."

Taffy Williams, who looked something like Peter O'Toole from *Lawrence of Arabia*, boisterous and gregarious for a clandestine fighter, boasted of their exploits. He told of Steiner leading a few Biafran fighters through enemy lines to blow up planes in Enugu. He said that Biafrans were the best fighters in Africa. "With a company of men like that, we could make it all the way to the Mediterranean and no one could stop us." I thought, why the Mediterranean? Why not Port Harcourt? Or Opobo?

A ferocious white mercenary fighting in an African war, Williams did not intimidate Elner. No big white sheriff at home could do it, and that guy wouldn't either. In fact, she baited him, teasing him. Williams' fingers were stained yellow and brown from heavy smoking. Elner told him that he should stop smoking because it was bad for his health. He started laughing and nearly choked to death on a coughing fit. She offered to help him with his job.

"I don't know how to shoot," she said, "but I could go in after a battle and sweep up the bullets."

Taffy Williams talked of a code of honor and behavior among mercenaries. They respected their fellow fighters, and they respected the women of their fellows. So he said. But I was surprised when the South Africans and Rhodesians, the silent ones who acted only with their eyes, treated my wife with great deference — even though she was African American. I wonder, did they think I was a mercenary? I was not a war fighter, only a blockade-runner. Maybe they thought that was close enough.

5

In addition to doing warehouse inventory and working at the Beacon, I also worked at the airport. I checked passengers through on their way to Biafra: journalists, missionaries, JCA officials, and representatives of foreign governments, from British Lords to American congressmen. I made sure they had proper clearance.

I checked cargo manifests. When the planes were loaded, I was given the manifest. I got on the planes and verified the contents, the weight allowances, and the load balance. There were tinned meats, milk powder, corn meal, black-eyed beans, rice, stockfish, lots of salt, and Formula II, a blend of corn meal, soy, and powered milk. It was a good balance of protein and carbohydrates. There were medicines: vaccines, anti-tuberculosis medicine, bandages, and dressings. There was a large shipment, over several days, of Kaopectate for diarrhea. I typed up six copies of the manifests and signed them. I gave three copies to the pilot, who gave them to the WCC or Caritas representative at Uli. The pilot signed one copy and brought it back for me to file. JCA also had its own forms that had to be verified and signed by the cargo masters.

Larry also worked at both the airport and the warehouses. In a letter home he wrote:

> I am working nights now at the airport and sometimes days also since Barry is away on vacation. I am now waiting for the medicines to arrive. Barry was due back on today's plane but did not show. I am very tired and am ready for a break when he gets back. Have not been able to get to the beach or any other recreation. Am at the airport until 3:00 in the morning. It can be very interesting work, but the hours are long and often boring. If there is a full schedule of planes flying, it is ok. I am kind of the man on the spot to make manifests, advise, and translate. My Portuguese is not good but it is better than most of the foreigners.

For three days, March 10 through 12, I even worked as an aircraft mechanic again, on NAJ, helping the Canadians with 150-hour engine checks, lube and oil, and all the airframe systems.

The airlift had languished for most of February with ARCO and most of the other charters gone, but by the first week of March the pace picked up. Three C-97s flew regularly, and Nordchurchaid reversed itself and asked Transavia to bring back some more planes. Tony Jonsson, an Icelandic pilot famous for serving in the RAF during WWII, flying Spitfires and

Mustangs, flew a Transavia DC-6 for the duration of the Biafran Airlift. On the night of March 11-12, the airlift from São Tomé logged twenty-four arrivals in Biafra, a record, delivering 260 tons of food. Of the three C-97s, two made two shuttles each, and one made three shuttles, together delivering 100 tons.

Counting planes from São Tomé, Fernando Po, Libreville, Abidjan, and Lisbon, there were forty-four arrivals one night at Uli, making it the second busiest airport in Africa after Johannesburg. Remember, all those planes where swirling around in the dark with no navigation lights, no radar, and no air traffic control system. The pilots maintained their own separation by radio. Throughout the airlift, there never were any midair collisions, although planes had crashed on landing at Uli, including two Super Constellations, a DC-7, and a C-97. According to Johnny Correa, some Biafran military supply planes disappeared over the ocean.

All this air traffic was uninterrupted by the bomber. Where was he? Some speculation had it that he was air dropping food and ammo to Nigerian troops who were surrounded in Owerri. Nigeria had gotten into the airlift business, too. Maybe the MiG showed up instead of the bomber to keep pressure on the Biafran airlift.

With so many arrivals, offloading was once again becoming a bottleneck. Pilots and crews reported it in their daily logs as a major problem. So I flew again. I flew in a C-97 on or about March 14. Compared to a DC-7, the cargo hold was cavernous. You could drive a truck in the back of it. The back of the plane opened up and we sent cargo down aluminum rollers instead of slide boards, making it much faster. Fourteen tons could be unloaded faster from a C-97 than ten tons from a DC-7.

Unlike the cockpit of a DC-7, with the pilot and copilot pinched into a streamlined nose, the cockpit of a C-97 was an enormous dome. I had never imagined any cockpit so expansive. It seemed more like the bridge of a ship. Nine large windows wrapped around at eye level, two windows looked out at foot level on each side by the pilot and copilot, and six windows stretched overhead. From up in the air, it felt like the crew was floating in a bubble in the sky.

I can still see the layout of the cockpit in my mind. Picture the flight deck as an aluminum floor with a Plexiglas dome over it. Build a pedestal up from the deck toward the left front of the dome. Mount the captain's chair on it. Place a post with the control column in front of the pilot's chair. Repeat on the right side where the copilot sits. Between the two pilots build up a console of engine controls and behind that, put a seat for the flight engineer. To the right, place the radio operator/navigator. Behind him put a small seat for the cargo master. Overhead and all around them place hundreds of instruments. It was incredible.

I found a place to sit at the rear of the cockpit along the left side, with my bag on the floor between my feet. It felt like a clubhouse atmosphere, everyone relaxed and joking, very different from many flights I had had into Biafra. I observed all this as a stranger. I was the old kid on the block, and the block had changed. They talked and joked and never looked my way. Since the Beacon did not become the American hangout that we envisioned, I never did get to know the Americans.

Larry related that he never got to know the American crews either, even though he stayed with the airlift a year longer than I did. Sometime after I had left the island, he overheard one of the American mechanics brag, "We killed another nigger tonight." A Biafran fatigue worker, fleeing a falling bomb, ran into a turning propeller. Larry said the mechanics were from Alabama. It was only eight years after President Kennedy had ordered National Guard troops to protect the Freedom Riders in Birmingham and four years after the civil rights marches on Selma, Alabama.

When we came in for a landing, the view of the runway was wide, wide open before us as the huge plane dipped and side-slipped down through the inconstant air before contact. From a perspective outside the plane on the ground, imagine Grandmother Nzeribe watching a B-29 Superfortress descend out of the night and land on her Trunk "A" road.

That was my only flight in a C-97. Six months later, C-97 N52676 crashed on landing in Biafra, killing five crewmen. A missionary loading lorries at the airstrip saw the explosion and the charred bodies of the American crewmen scattered on the runway.

Bob Hall, who couldn't get a job with Nordchurchaid, and who was the only person losing money on the airlift, started flying cargo for the Biafran government.

Feral dogs ran the night. São Tomé presented a neat, tidy, lovely appearance, so well-ordered that it had the feel of a Disneyland construct. The airlift activity gave it an overlay of lively messiness — shipping in the harbor, trucks shuffling back and forth, aircraft in the skies, busy cafés in the evenings. But late, late at night the town fell quiet. When I returned from Biafra, the airport terminal was dark. A few Portuguese soldiers stood inconspicuous guard. I hung my bag over my shoulder and mounted my Honda for the ride to my apartment. There was no traffic along the road from the airport to the town, not even crabs crossing the road to the beach. The sea, to the left of the road, was calm. In town, the shops and cafés were shuttered. In the dimly lit streets, I was the only thing in motion, except for the feral dogs.

They were large dogs: tan, brown, dirty yellow, shorthaired, thin and strong; no lost lap dogs could survive in that society. They watched me go by. I watched them. Over time I began to recognize some individuals. One night, as I stopped my Honda in front of the apartment building, a yellowish dog stood nearby, watching me. He just watched me, — not with malice, but with curiosity. I slung my bag over the handlebars and hunkered down in a posture that I had used to greet my own dog back home. I made a few noises, just as I did with my own dog, and spoke in a low, calm voice. The dog came nearer. I held my hand out, palm up, below his jaw where he could see it clearly. I scratched his chin. We began to play. We played the way dogs play, pretending to fight. I held my hands out wide. When I moved my right hand toward him, he turned that way and then I poked him in the shoulder with my left. The play got spirited. It got aggressive. I was dead tired, as I was always after a long night in Biafra, but the dog wouldn't quit. The play was escalating, getting rough, beyond my expectation and my control. I edged toward the door of the building. I grabbed open the door, slid inside and slammed it, leaving my bag on the Honda.

Another night, as I neared home, a dog ran beside me. He swerved in front of me, as if he were playing chicken. I hit him, the front wheel of the Honda jamming him in the ribs. It knocked him down, but he jumped up and ran off. I flew over the handlebars, bounced, and skidded to a stop. I got to my feet, bruised, sore, and bleeding from a few scrapes. I picked up the Honda and inspected it. The left mirror was bent in. I straightened it out. Otherwise the bike seemed okay. I kick started it and drove the rest of the way home. Gingerly, I climbed the stairs to our apartment. I opened the door and turned on the light, waking Elner. I asked her to help me get my shirt off, because I was too sore. Half awake, she saw the torn clothes and the blood.

She was terrified. She thought a bomb had hit me. No. Only a dog.

Future Doctors, Educators, Lawyers, and Scientists

CHAPTER 14

Gini Bu Mmadu?

What Is Man?

Take up the White Man's burden –
Send forth the best ye breed –
Go bind your sons to exile
To serve your captive's need;
To wait in heavy harness
On fluttered folk and wild –
Your new caught sullen peoples,
Half devil and half child.

   - by Rudyard Kipling (1899)

You never win if you give up when things are easy.

Someone said that the airlift prolonged Biafra's agony by bringing false hope. Without food for their people, the leaders would have given up sooner. It sounds like a bad idea whose time had come — an idea that someone put forward and many others adopted without thought, a piece of facile wisdom. It only makes sense if you don't stop to think about it. In fact, if you accept the idea, you can stop thinking altogether — no need to consider the complexities.

The idea can be accepted by people with no personal, immediate concept of large-scale random killing. They have not seen gangs running through their neighborhoods, dragging people out on the street, and chopping them up. Biafran people saw the trains full of refugees pouring in from all over Nigeria. They accepted those refugees into their homes and villages. They heard their personal, immediate stories. Biafrans noticed how Nigeria strafed the people and bombed their markets and villages instead of military targets. They understood that Nigeria was deliberately starving them.

People who know they are facing genocide do not give up. Israelis say, "Never again." An old Igbo proverb says, "Only a tree stands still when it knows it's being cut down." If you keep starving people, they will continue to believe that you intend to annihilate them. But why didn't Biafra's leaders, especially Ojukwu, just stop the war to save the people? To suggest that Ojukwu could take the whole nation into and out of war at his bidding is a common notion of Western journalists and politicians whose own Western histories are dominated and determined by pharaohs, kings, presidents, czars, and generals — an Aristotelian concept of the wise and powerful leader. Other cultures need not follow that precept. In Igbo culture there is no strongman, no absolute ruler. Village chiefs hold their positions by merit, not by heredity, and not by conquest.

"Ojukwu," observed Johnny Correa, who spent a lot of personal time with him, was "a normal human being, not trying to be God or a dictator — he wasn't that fearsome...This war continued only because the people felt that there was no survival if they lost the war."

To add another layer of complexity, we can consider the inverse of the question asked above: Why didn't Gowon just stop the war to save the people? He could have put heat seeking missiles on his night flying MiGs. The rockets would have found us in the dark, flown right up the exhaust pipes on our engines, and blown us to bits. The airlift would have ended in one night. Why this didn't happen puzzled us. The ready availability of heat seeking missiles, air-to-air and surface-to-air, in today's international weapons market explains why there never will be another *civilian* humanitarian airlift.

Memories fade. Over historical time, without an anchor, the meaning of an event can drift and deform to fit the prevailing interpretation. Four decades after the Biafran war, the causes and events of that time are forgotten. What remains is an historical lesson: the idea that the Biafran Airlift was a mistake, a failure, that it caused many more deaths by prolonging the war, that "a quick death" would have been the more merciful solution. That doctrine is taught in universities to our future Foreign Service officers, and it has settled onto the library shelves in international aid books as a given, as accepted wisdom without challenge or thought. (*Does Foreign Aid Really Work*? by Roger C. Riddell, Oxford University Press, 2007).

Philip Gourevitch, in his article, "Alms Dealers" (*The New Yorker*, October 11, 2010) writes, "Had it not been for the West's charity, the Nigerian civil war surely would have ended much sooner. Against the lives that the airlifted aid saved must be weighed all those lives — tens of thousands, perhaps hundreds of thousands — that were lost to the extra year and a half of destruction." Furthermore, the humanitarians who delivered that aid should be held accountable for all the extra lives lost.

I have been told to my face that what I did in Africa, in the Peace Corps and in the airlift, was not only a waste of time but also morally wrong. "If you help people they will just become dependent."

Then we have this statement by the European scholar, Perouse de Montclos: "...we don't really know if Africans would be better with or without emergency aid." ("Humanitarian Aid and the Biafra War: Lessons

Not Learned," *Council for the Development of Social Research in Africa, Africa Development* Vol. XXXIV, No.1, 2009). This is hardly an advance in wisdom over the ancient cartographers who labeled the interior of the African continent as *terra incognita*. Beyond some vague characterizations of Africans, all rolled into one lump of mud, aid recipients are half-seen undifferentiated victims of charity. The fears and aspirations of widely disparate peoples are not known and not considered. Africans are not eligible to determine for themselves whether they should resist their own destruction or to accept aid.

In international politics, this doctrine impedes the impulse to intervene in humanitarian disasters like Rwanda or Darfur or Syria. The utility of humanitarian intervention is judged by its value to the intervener. This Biafra lesson explicitly condones massacres, acts of war, and mass starvation of a people by its government, as long as it is done quickly.

The children of Biafra who would have been allowed to die, whose deaths would have forced their country to surrender, have now grown up, and they detest that doctrine. Look at it from the other side of the issue. Instead of condemning humanitarian aid for keeping people alive too long, condemn that government which uses mass starvation to subdue its own people.

Ben Kiernan in his book, *Blood and Soil* (Yale University Press, 2007), a history of genocide, refers to Article 2 (c) of the 1948 United Nations Convention on the Prevention and Punishment of the Crime of Genocide. He writes on page fifteen:

> Since the Nazi Holocaust, the crime of "extermination" has been a crime against humanity, and its definition includes not only massacres but also the intentional infliction of conditions of life, *inter alia* the deprivation of access to food and medicine, calculated to bring about the destruction of part of a population.

In 1948, the Nazi genocide was still fresh and raw in world conscience, but another event happened that year. The Soviet Union blockaded Berlin, preventing food, fuel, and medicine from reaching the city. The Royal Air Force and the United States Air Force mounted an airlift involving over 200,000 flights in one year to supply food and coal to the people of Berlin, breaking the blockade. Perhaps that blockade and the airlift that defeated it had some influence on the writers of that Convention. Nations of the world could act to stop genocide.

Twenty years later, in 1968, in Biafra, the United Nations was not yet ready to act on the Convention, except to send six UNICEF volunteers to deal with it. Biafra was the first instance since Berlin in which the Convention could have been applied, but was not. Was it not applied because Biafra was in Africa? Was the United Nations at that time a European club? The Biafran Airlift was not a massive government effort, but a raggedy group of missionaries and civilians flying rickety old planes. No similar *civilian* operation was ever mounted before or since.

James Traub, on October 15, 2009, forty years after Biafra, wrote a review for the *New York Times* about another book on genocide, *Worse Than War* by Daniel Jonah Goldhagen. Traub wrote:

> In 2005, The United Nations General Assembly adopted the principle known as the responsibility to protect, which stipulates that states have an obligation to safeguard their people from mass atrocities, and that the international community must step in when states fail to act.

In 2011, the United Nations stepped in to safeguard the people of Libya from destruction by its leader, Col. Moammar Gaddafi. The UN used warplanes, not just humanitarian relief. It was a controversial intervention. Some would have preferred the Biafra solution — let Gaddafi impose a quick death on his population, returning Libya and, by example, the rest of the Middle East, to stability. Both concepts were applied in the Arab Spring when oppressed people sought their freedom — intervention in Libya and quick death in Syria and Bahrain. Death in Syria has not been quick.

The two ideas compete for the power of policy in world affairs: quick death or intervention. But the world is deep, too complex to be shackled by a single notion or two. A policy may be adumbrated by an ideal, but it must be fleshed out with the complexities inherent in each community of living people and the larger context in which its people thrive or die. Those people who are responsible for acting in world affairs, those who must choose to intervene or to ignore, bear a heavy responsibility to act on the unique conditions of each event, not on slogans.

Slogans muddied the response of world governments to the human catastrophe in Biafra: "One Nigeria." "Quick Death." "Food, Not Weapons." U.S. State Department officials believed that "Starving Children" was just a slogan invented by Biafran propaganda.

People of Biafra were grateful for the food relief provided by the airlift, but they were puzzled that the world would feed them, yet not help them prevent others from starving them. If they lost the war, they expected to be annihilated.

After the end of the war, there was no genocide, no more mass atrocities. Nigeria took up the task of healing, although slowly.

To prevent genocide requires worldwide condemnation, intervention, and a leadership that responds to international pressure. Without scrutiny a country can brutalize its own people with impunity. The Biafran Airlift provided intervention on a scale that thwarted the attempted starvation. But more than food traveled over that tenuous lifeline. Information did also. Journalists, dignitaries, and government officials from around the world brought intense scrutiny to the war and awareness to people who would never have known what went on in that corner of Africa.

After the war, some Nigerians wanted to continue the killing. They had weapons; the Biafran Army had collapsed; and the people were defenseless. It was a perfect opportunity. But the Nigerian leader, General Yakubu Gowon, insisted that the killing stop and that reconciliation begin. Gowon could have taken the position, as some leaders do, that Nigeria's civil war was an internal affair and nobody else's business. Instead, he listened to the pleadings of church and government officials and the opinion of people around the world.

Mrs. Murphy's can of beets did not end hunger in Biafra, and Gowon never saw all the random stuff in Warehouse K, but all those cans of food were the voice of people everywhere saying, "we want Biafrans to live." Gowon heard that.

Did white people seventy years after Kipling's poem, in 1969, think of Biafrans as "half devil and half child," as colonial captives, as a responsibility, a burden? I believe that some did, and I know that many did not.

The people of Biafra were not helpless primitives languishing in the jungle who depended on our mercy to exist. They were intelligent, resourceful, industrious, caring, humorous, and deeply thoughtful, as their language suggests. They still are. They represent some of the best of Man.

Another dimension, beyond security, for continuing the fight, was the concept of freedom to control one's own destiny — not just to avoid disaster, not just to provide a common defense, but to build a positive future. In the shrinking Biafran enclave was the highest concentration of Ph.Ds in all of Africa. Biafrans "know book," and that got them in trouble in other parts of Nigeria and was partly responsible for the killings. The motivation to learn and to grow into a modern society kept Biafra going.

That was also a motivation for their neighbors to keep them down.

Biafrans were building an intellectual identity, a sense of an original nation that grew out of their own identity and self-sufficiency, not a derivative European identity. Countering the effort to choke them into surrender, Biafrans formed their own unique institutions, like the Biafran Science Group and the Research and Production Group, to do things for themselves that were formerly done by others. They refined their own oil; they made consumer products like lipstick; they made their own weapons. They had the confidence to build their own two-stage ballistic missile.

Biafran intellectuals led by Chinua Achebe codified the principles of the new nation in a document called the Ahiara Declaration, which was delivered to the people in a speech by Ojukwu, who "had a gift for oratory," according to Achebe. He said in part:

> Our struggle is not mere resistance — that would be purely negative. It is a positive commitment to build a healthy, dynamic and progressive state, such as would be the pride of black men the world over...It was, and still is, a firm conviction that a modern Negro African government worth the trust placed in it by its people, must build a progressive state that ensures the reign of social and economic justice, and the rule of law.

The blockade of Biafra created the inertial confinement for a fusion of ability, but without victory, it amounted to only a glimmer in the potential for human achievement.

As long as there was a possibility of winning, Biafrans continued the fight. Until they just couldn't.

That war is long over. *It should remain finished.* It should never be fought again. The best of what was Biafra should be nourished within the best of what Nigeria can be.

I have said, and many others have said, that the sad fate of One Nigeria was locked into history by the British when they created their colony out of 256 different cultures. I am now willing to reconsider that piece of facile wisdom. Let's stop blaming Great Britain — think of how many tribes comprise *that* one country. Think of the United States of America — our people come from all over the world; we fought a savage civil war over slavery; and we are still squabbling with each other. China — we think of that big country as populated by only Chinese, but the Han Chinese of the East know little about the people who inhabit the far western provinces of China. In Italy, very few genetically Roman people remain. Northern and Southern Germans don't like each other. Think of France. Think of Spain. Think of Russia. Go on, keep thinking. Keep thinking that Nigeria, composed of many different people, can still be one country.

Think less about the animosity of the past, and think more about the astounding accomplishments of a small part of the population under great duress. All of us Peace Corps Volunteers who served in every region of Nigeria in the 1960s know of the talent and vitality that exists all over the country. Bring together the best of Nigeria and contribute to the best of Africa and the best of Man. I don't know if that will ultimately work out, but diversity can actually yield strength through a new fusion of ability. When you sit down to the table with your brothers, bring kola, not guns.

Author in 1969

CHAPTER 15

Onye Wetara Oji, Wetara Ndu

He Who Brings Kola, Brings Life

Long ago, Ghana was known as the Gold Coast because of the source of its economic value to European traders. Ivory Coast was named similarly. Nigeria was the Slave Coast. Slave raiders penetrated the rain forest for their contribution to a huge and long-lasting economic system. Ancestors of Biafran people were subject to that form of terrorism in their day. Anyone could be snatched at any time. Everywhere in the world and everywhere in time, security is a paramount concern. People need to feel safe. This is true in Paris and Brussels, in Boston and California, in Iraq and Syria. Can a prolonged exposure to treachery penetrate a culture such that a normally hospitable people can become suspicious during times of great stress? Offering kola is a symbolic way of saying, "You are safe here."

1

On my final trip to Biafra I was arrested as a Nigerian spy.

I had flown into Biafra, not on a relief flight, but with Bob Hall on his C-46, carrying Biafran cargo. Not that it makes any difference, but it was probably the Ides of March. On previous flights, Bob had carried boots and shoes, weapons, and food for the army. That night, I sat on sacks of hops intended for the brewery in Umuahia, where the German engineers had once made my barbecue spit for the Fourth of July parties. Biafra wanted to resume making Golden Guinea beer, trying to simulate normalcy, like making lipstick and other consumer goods, to bolster morale and a sense of self-sufficiency in the face of isolation, physically and psychologically, from the rest of the world.

They had already been bottling *kai-kai*, a gin distilled from palm wine. I copied the following label from a bottle I still have:

LIQUORE DE SURVIVALLE

Vee Brand
(A 'Research and Production' Product)

Made in Biafra   80 Proof Spirit

I flew with Bob for no good reason, just for the ride, just to be going to Biafra. With cargo masters assigned to most planes, I seldom flew anymore. When we landed, I got off and stood to one side to watch the unloading, expecting that we would soon get back on board and fly off to São Tomé. We were parked some distance from the relief planes, I noticed. It was a dark, still night. I could just make out the activity around the C-46 from a small light within the plane. I stood about fifty yards behind the tail and a little to the left side, so I was looking directly at the cargo door behind the wing.

Someone came up to me on my right side and greeted me.

"Are you Mr. Koren?" he said.

"Yes, I am." I was very surprised that someone would know me on a dark night in the middle of Biafra. He said he knew me because his sister had been one of my students at Ohuhu Community Grammar School.

While we were talking, I noticed that people were loading something into Bob's plane instead of unloading it. Two odd things were occurring at once: being greeted by name and seeing the unexpected loading. Men were handing crates up to the plane. Then a winch was rigged in the cargo door of the C-46 and a large cylinder was hoisted on a sling into the plane. It was not a sudden revelation, but a slowly forming realization that I was watching men load bombs into Bob's plane. Those were the dud Nigerian bombs that the Biafran Air Force had recovered and refurbished, stocking them until the day that they had a plane.

Then another man approached from my left. He was dressed in a military uniform.

"What are you doing here?" he asked, very politely.

I told him the simple but stupid truth — that I was a relief worker and that I had just come along for the ride.

"Come with me." he said.

That's when full comprehension hit me. I was witnessing a secret military operation, and I had no business being there. He continued to be polite, and I remained calm and also polite, hoping that my innocent intentions and goodwill toward Biafra would be apparent. That is the behavior I projected throughout my captivity. But at that moment, just as when I arrived in Lagos during the coup, I was unable to frame a sense of future.

I was taken to the base commander. Unlike the burly 2 I C, he looked trim in his Air Force uniform. He sat behind a desk in a small office. I was invited to sit in a chair on the opposite side of the desk. He asked me my name and what I was doing there. I told him my story with calm confidence, knowing it sounded lame.

"Empty your pockets and put everything on my desk."

I did. He examined my passport. He looked at my UNICEF identification. He checked my clearance from Mr. Osuji at Biafra House to work at Uli. And he looked at the contents of my wallet. There was a picture of Elner. There were some escudos, money from São Tomé, some American dollars, some Biafran money that I got from Mr. Yeager in Umuahia, and a One Pound Nigerian Note that the Japanese photographer had given me on São Tomé as a souvenir. Oops. I got a bad feeling when I saw him pull that out of my wallet.

So did he.

"Why do you have Nigerian money? Are you a Nigerian spy?"

"No. It's just a souvenir." I told him how I happened to have it. He interrogated me for many hours, for the rest of the night. I told him that I had served as a Peace Corps Volunteer at Ohuhu Community Grammar School at Amaogwugwu for three years, and because of that experience I had accepted an opportunity with UNICEF to help Biafra. Johnny Correa would tell me later that O.C.G.S. was no longer a school, but the headquarters of Biafran Military Intelligence. Oops. In addition to his job defending Uli, Johnny also served as a high level officer in Military Intelligence. Biafrans "are very suspicious people," he wrote. "Once they suspect you, they lose all faith in you — there is nothing you can do or say to make them feel that you are okay."

By morning I was very tired. The base commander's questioning was relentless, but throughout the interrogation I remained respectful. I answered everything honestly. I was not confrontational. I was not indignant. My interrogator was firm, but not belligerent. He never threatened me. He never touched me. And he never referred to what I had seen.

After the interrogation, in the morning light, I was led to a small room, my cell, furnished with a simple couch and some chairs. It would turn out to be a very interesting incarceration because that room was also used as the VIP waiting room for the Uli airport.

I had two armed guards outside the only door. They escorted me to the latrine and showed me the location of the nearest bunker. I curled up on the couch and slept. By the end of the first day, I had only one guard, armed with a rifle. I was allowed to sit on a bench out on the veranda. The guard sat there, too, looking calm, at ease, not the least bit mean or terrifying. I looked at his rifle, wondering what kind it was and where it may have come from. I remembered the BBC reporter giving all those details about the Biafran weapons I was supposedly hiding in the relief food.

So I just asked. "What kind of gun is that?" Here I am under armed guard and under suspicion of being a spy, and I ask a dumb question like that.

"Here," he said, holding the gun out for me to examine for myself.

"No thanks!" I put my hands behind my back and leaned away. I knew enough not be seen with a gun in my hand.

By the end of that day, I had no guards. It was evident that the gun was not loaded; all the ammunition was needed at the front.

I didn't run away and jump on a plane.

Meanwhile, back on São Tomé, Elner was frantic that I hadn't returned. It happened that Mrs. Effiong, the wife of Ojukwu's Second in Command, General Effiong, was on her way to Rome to pick up funds for the Diocese of Enugu. Instead, she stayed with Elner to comfort her until I returned.

"Mrs. Effiong stayed with me that time or I would have lost my mind," Elner said.

They prepared a bag with some of my clean clothes, including my African shirts, shaving kit and toothbrush, sandwiches, cigarettes, magazines that someone had brought down from Europe, and a couple of bottles of beer. They put it on one of our relief flights.

Reverend Aitken brought it to me the next day. As usual, he said little. The look on his face was disappointment, not sympathy. I had screwed up, and the burden of defending me would likely fall on him.

After reading the magazines, I had nothing to do. Usually, I had too much to do. The VIP lounge was undecorated, barren and uninteresting. I stared at the walls and tried to maintain a positive attitude, but captivity wore me down. Staring at the bush from the veranda gave me a little relief. At night I listened to the planes landing and taking off, knowing that's where I should be.

Visitors arrived, mostly journalists. I remember Graham Hovey, an editorialist for the *New York Times*. Avidly, he listened to my story of working with the airlift. I did not tell him, or anyone else, that I had seen bombs being loaded on Bob Hall's C-46. He wrote down my name, and offered to buy me lunch whenever I returned to New York. Eventually, he did that. Graham Hovey had written the editorials I had read in the *New York Times* urging Biafra to give up. Correspondents for *Time* and *Newsweek* came through. One of them commented derisively how Biafran immigration officials acted as if this airstrip were a real place in a real country — they stamped his passport with "Enugu International Airport."

"It's an airport in exile," I told him.

His eyes widened at that concept. "Do I have your permission to use that in my dispatch?"

"Yes." I don't know if he ever did.

One of the young Customs workers would sometimes sit with me and chat. He seemed very friendly. I wondered if I could gauge from his attitude how much trouble I was in. Probably not. If he was sizing me up for the commander, he had no better luck. I talked about my Peace Corps days, and he told me about his family.

On the fifth day, I gave him five shillings of the Biafran money that the Commander had returned to me. (He kept the Nigerian money). I asked the young man to buy some kola nuts, *oji*, and palm wine, *mmanya nkwu*. We invited a few others and sat outside in the warm African evening. We broke the kola according to custom and shared it. "*Onye wetara oji, wetara ndu*." He who brings kola, brings life. We got very friendly drinking the palm wine. I told them about the time that I had helped Reverend Aitken carry some wounded people from the village to the hospital at Awomama. I asked if anyone knew what became of the young woman and the boy. None did.

The next day someone came to tell me that the boy and the young woman were recovering well.

The commander called me to his office again on the eighth day. He told me that they weren't sure what they were going to do with me. They were thinking of sending me to Umuahia, which was at that time the seat of the Biafran government, a Capital in exile. The way he said it implied a threat, but I turned it around and said that I would love to go to Umuahia, that Dr. Okpara had insisted that I come to see him the next time I was there. Johnny told me later that they took spies and saboteurs to Umuahia to be shot. They took them to Military Intelligence Headquarters, my former school. They shot them by the garbage pit behind my house on the compound. Johnny lived in a house directly opposite mine across a driveway. Once, when his wife and daughter, Juanita, were visiting and they were just sitting down to dinner, he saw the people being shot and dumped into the pit.

They didn't send me to Umuahia.

The next afternoon, in full daylight, the Bofors guns began firing. I heard the scream of a bomb. From the Doppler shift, I knew it was coming toward me and I had no chance to reach the bunker. I looked around the room and found no cover. The best I could do was lie down on the cement floor and cover my head. My "cell" was a government building at the end of the runway and no doubt it was a choice military target. The intensity built to a scream much louder than anything I had heard before. I said, "I'm sorry, Mom." No child should precede its parent in death.

The scream passed right overhead, rooftop level, and continued away. It was not a bomb. It was a MiG. It had flown right down the center of the runway and released its bombs in the marketplace beyond.

2

Isolated, starved, massacred, bombed, and betrayed, Biafrans suffered also from paranoia. They worried about spies and saboteurs.

Just before Christmas in 1969, at a fundraising party for Biafra in New York City, I met Johnny Correa again. I was home from the airlift, working for The American Committee to Keep Biafra Alive. Johnny had been in Biafra at the time I was a prisoner, and he knew that I was there. Biafran Intelligence was ambivalent about what to do with me. If they shot me, the churches might stop the airlift. He suggested that they throw a grenade in the VIP room with me and tell the churches that a MiG had bombed it. He told me that to my face. And that is when he told me that he lived in a house at my school. I thought that was a very unlikely coincidence, so I quizzed him about it. He knew the place very well.

But Johnny also listened to me tell my story about working with the airlift and my experience as a suspected spy. He listened intently. I had told the story to other people who listened with interest and expressed a few "WOWs." But Johnny sat in a chair close to me and watched me with fixed interest, gravely, silently. Why the intensity?

He returned to Biafra just after Christmas, shortly before the war ended. He got out of Biafra for the last time on the last relief flight, under fire, with Captain Tony Jonsson and Father Cunningham. Back in New York he delivered a manila envelope to the place where I worked with instructions to give it to me, personally. There was no note. The envelope contained his story. He wanted me to have it. I'm looking at it now as I write this:

On December 3, Johnny got a telegram from his wife telling him to come home, because one of his children was sick. "The Air Force commander stopped me from going home until it was decided what to do with" two British mercenaries who were accused of being spies. Johnny was ordered to keep them at his place while Military Intelligence considered the "evidence" against them. The two mercenaries had not been informed that they were under suspicion. The Director of Military Intelligence "said they had to be careful about killing white men who had come to help them, because that would give the impression that once [you] had done what you could and were no longer useful, you would be bumped off."

The two men stayed with Johnny for nearly two weeks, drinking heavily and behaving with "bearishness and a sadistic nature." Kanjo was Johnny's house boy and the brother of his adopted Biafran daughter, Buka. One of the men "used to twist Kanjo's hand until it brought tears to his eyes — then he would slap him and say it would make a good soldier out of him." Johnny said, "If they had behaved nicely, I think they would be alive today."

The men were shot December 15th. "I didn't take pleasure in it, but I didn't want someone else doing it — then I regretted taking part because it was so gory." He shot one guy in the chest four times. Blood came out of his mouth when he tried to speak. Johnny left Biafra on December 16, and a few days later he was staring at me while he listened to my story.

This paragraph is Johnny Correa's moment in time, not mine. "I have nightmares about those two guys — if I see someone who looks like them, I go into a sort of trance — I recall the situation." Had Biafra decided to eliminate me, he would have been the one to do it. As he watched me tell my story, was he having a superposition of visions, seeing blood burbling up out of my mouth as I talked?

3

I was called before the Air Force commander again on March 25, nine months before that meeting in New York.

He said, "David, I am ordering you deported from Biafra. You must never return again." As he said it, he was trying to sound very stern, but his demeanor was that of a father chastising an impetuous young man.

Bombing delayed the relief flights that night. NAJ, the lead plane on the schedule, had to hold for an hour and 15 minutes. Eventually he landed, followed by the three C-97s. The first of four Transavia flights had to hold too long for his fuel load, and returned to São Tomé. The next three landed.

Around nine o'clock I was escorted out to a Transavia DC-6, Tango

Romeo Zulu. I asked my escort if I could do the job that I was supposed to be doing and help unload the plane. Very courteously, he said that I could. It was a load of salt.

The Captain of the plane was Tony Jonsson, known as "The Salt Guy," because he was the only pilot who would willingly carry salt. It took longer to unload the heavy sacks of salt, exposing the planes longer on the ground.

Back on São Tomé, I strode across the tarmac and into the brightly lit terminal. Elner ran up and hugged me. Others welcomed me back. It was a high moment. The head of airport security, a small Portuguese man in his flawless white uniform, grinned at me. He held his arms up in the air with two fingers of his right hand crossed over two fingers of his left. The gesture indicated jail bars. I nodded and smiled back at him. The ordeal was over.

4

The next day I went back to the airport. I looked at the flight schedule and flight reports from the night before, noting the delays due to bombing. Patterson reported light flak on his way in on the first shuttle. The second shuttle was uneventful, except that Waldorf, his copilot, made a bad landing. At 1:00 a.m., I called my parents on a radio-telephone patch. I felt the need to talk to them after feeling certain I was going to die in the MiG attack.

The C-97s had worldwide Strategic Air Command radios, a unique benefit on São Tomé. The grounded C-97, which was used for spare parts, still had a functioning radio. One of the young American radio operators was standing by that night ready to help anyone who wanted to call home. On the left side of the plane behind the cockpit and in front of engine number two, a door folded down from the lower cargo hold to the ground with a built in stairway. I climbed in there and up to the flight deck. The radio operator was alone in the cavernous, dimly lit cockpit. He spoke in a low, soft voice, as if we were in a cathedral.

"Where do you want the call to go?" he asked.

"Ithaca, New York."

"What number?"

He wrote down the number. Then he began the process. He gave his call sign and location and asked for anyone listening in the vicinity of Ithaca.

After about twenty minutes a ham radio operator in Utica, New York responded. He patched us into a phone line and made a collect call to my Dad, who was petrified when he answered the phone. He thought something had happened to me. Why else would he get a call from overseas? And he thought he was paying an enormous long distance charge. The radio call across the Atlantic was free. He was paying for the relatively short distance from Utica. I didn't mention my imprisonment, but I told them we would probably be coming home soon, because my UNICEF contract was up in April. I suppose Mom and Dad were glad to hear from me and know that I was all right, but they sounded very nervous. They had real difficulty with radio talk. After you speak you must say, "OVER," so the radio operator knows to switch from SEND to RECEIVE. It was a difficult conversation, but I enjoyed hearing their voices.

Since I was banished forever from Biafra and since my UNICEF contract would be fulfilled — for real this time — in a couple of weeks, it was time to go home. Actually, I had a couple of job offers if I stayed beyond the contract. A man named Dr. Pope wanted me to help him set up a media health service in Biafra. Don Merriam, the Transavia pilot, had transferred over to Canairrelief. After all, he was a Canadian. As Captain of NAJ, he approached me. He was tall, and he cocked his head slightly as he looked down and spoke to me.

"I would like you to fly with me as permanent cargo master on NAJ," he said.

That was a tempting offer. Everybody liked Don Merriam. He donated all of his flight pay to the orphanage. Six months before, or two weeks before, I might have accepted.

"Thank you, but I've been banned from returning to Biafra," I said.

"I don't think that'll be a problem. I can clear it with Biafra."

I considered it for a few minutes. I was sure that he could clear it.

"Sorry, I'm going to go home."

Merriam offered the job to Larry, who also declined, because he was preparing to marry the pretty young woman who had been teaching him Portuguese, and he wanted to remain on the island with her.

Three months after I returned to the States, while I was driving along a street in Syracuse, I heard on the car radio that NAJ had crashed on landing in Biafra. Merriam and all aboard were killed.

On Easter Sunday, April 6, Elner was mad at me, furious about something. I don't remember what it was, but I remember being puzzled by the intensity. She wouldn't speak to me. I left the apartment and went to the airport. I called home using the C-97 radio link. Since it was Easter, my aunt and uncle and cousins were all visiting my parents in Ithaca, all those who had helped collect the books for my library in Umuahia. I spoke briefly to them. They were all vastly intimidated by a radio call (OVER. Hello?...OVER) from across the world.

When I returned to the apartment, Elner was curled up on the bed, glaring at me malevolently.

"Would you like to talk to your mother?" I asked. "On the C-97 radio?"

Her expression changed instantly. The tight lips parted slightly. She made a small sound that might have been, "yes." Uncoiling, she got off the bed and followed me to the Honda. At the airport I spoke to the Portuguese security officer, requesting permission to take her out on the flight line to the plane. He agreed. I took her up through the open hatch and introduced her to the radio operator. Then I left.

Waiting at the airport lounge, I considered what I could have done wrong. What set her off was a minor thing, I was sure, but there was a much bigger thing behind it. A week and a half had elapsed since I had returned from captivity in Biafra, a time we had enjoyed together. We went to the Bay of the Seven Waves and played on the beach with no one else around. But when the crisis was over and we felt secure again, the repressed fear and anxiety began to rise. She must have felt that I had abandoned her and caused her unbearable suffering.

An hour later, she returned to the lounge and we were okay again.

Up until April 4, Good Friday, I worked at the airport typing manifests, and the following week I prepared to leave São Tomé. Elner accompanied me to the airport on some of those nights. While I worked, she talked to people on their way to Biafra, like Lloyd Garrison, a reporter for the *New York Times*.

At the end of March, a plane returned from Biafra bringing some children. I wanted Elner to experience what they were like just coming out of Biafra, before they went to the orphanage. She did not have a pass for the flight line, but the Portuguese security officer gave her permission to help us bring in the children. She brought one of them down the ladder.

"It was weird," she said. "The children were lifeless and weighed like paper, but they were so clean and well dressed." Remember, they were not orphans.

Imagine, imagine what their parents felt when they bathed them and dressed them in their best little clothes and sent them far away in the sky with strangers.

PART III

Author Flying Home

CHAPTER 16

Ije Oma

Safe Journey

Now we come to my trip home, the passage from my past life in Africa to my future back in America. As we flew away for our journey across the sea, the war continued and the Biafran Airlift carried on. My part was done. From high over the ocean, I could see far and wide, but I couldn't envision what was to come decades later when Biafra rose up into my life again so powerfully. It's a story that continues to gather meaning as it soars forward into history.

1

Bob Hall bought me lunch at the Beacon. I had a hamburger and a beer. "I think I owe you an explanation," he said with genuine contrition, I thought. "Being locked up like that can take all the piss and vinegar out of you."

"Yeah." My usual enthusiasm had pretty much all trickled away.

"I had no idea they were going to commandeer my plane that night. I had gone in there prepared to *sell* them my plane. We had talked about it and agreed on a price. As a condition, I insisted that they use a particular kind of oil. If they didn't, the engines would seize up and the plane would crash. They said they didn't have that kind of oil and they would take their chances. I wouldn't take responsibility for that, so I refused to sell the plane."

I ate my hamburger and listened.

"They were furious. They had a mission planned for that night, and they were going to fly it no matter what. They offered me a lot of money. I said I would do it just this once, but I wouldn't sell them the plane.

"We flew, and somewhere over the Mid-West the Air Force guys threw the bombs out the door. Back at Uli, it was starting to get light, and it was time to head back to São Tomé. I tried to get them to let you come with me. They refused. One reason may have been that they were so pissed off with me because I wouldn't sell them the plane. I'm sorry."

"Okay." I accepted the apology. I didn't understand why the specific kind of oil was a problem, but I knew that Biafra really wanted airplanes.

Bob had more to say.

"Later," he continued, "we heard that some people were killed in that raid, including a high ranking Nigerian officer. Art and the rest of my crew were scared shitless. They worried that it might come back on them. They packed up and went home. I had to pay them what I owed them.

"So I have a plane with no crew. I can't — won't — sell it to Biafra, and I can't fly it home. I can be my own mechanic, but I need a copilot. Would you help me fly the plane to the States in exchange for a free ride home?"

Whoa! What was that? Something more than an apology, I think, something desperate. He had no crew and probably not much money.

"If you'll fly as my copilot to Ft. Lauderdale, I'll pay for your commercial flight from there to your home," he said.

"Bob," I said, "I have always wanted to fly. I wanted to take lessons, but I could never afford them. I can't fly."

"*No problema.* I'll teach you to fly in the air."

"I'll have to talk it over with Elner." I said it to put him off until I could think of a way — or a reason — to decline.

Elner and I had been discussing how we would get home. There was the commercial route, which she had followed to get to São Tomé. UNICEF would pay for my airfare home, and I would pay for Elner. Or we could catch a Boeing back to Europe and get to New York on Icelandic Airways. NAJ was scheduled to fly to Los Angeles for maintenance on April 15. We could hitch a ride.

Elner was not helpful.

"If you want us to go home with Bob, that's fine with me," she said casually, as if she had unlimited confidence in my ability to fly a plane. Across the Atlantic Ocean. Or else she thought it would be the surest way to get me to go home, for real. After hours of further discussions with Bob, I agreed.

To fly was a dream too strong to deny.

While working with the big four-engine planes of the airlift, the DC-7s, DC-6s, Super Constellations, and C-97s, I regarded Fred Olsen's twin engine C-46 as a minor player. But it was not insignificant. It was steadfast, flying when other elements of the airlift faltered. With its wide body and powerful R2800 engines, it could carry six tons of cargo, compared to eight or nine tons for a DC-6. Parked next to its larger cousins, resting on its tail wheel — some pilots called it a "tail dragger," with a smirk — it looked small, but it was not a light aircraft. It stood almost 22 feet tall, and it was 76 feet long with a wingspan of 108 feet. The comfortable house I live in now is 44 feet long.

The inside of the old C-46 was filthy. I couldn't expect my wife to ride in that. I spent a day cleaning the interior. Then I dealt with the toilet. It was a ratty-looking bucket bolted to the deck just behind the bulkhead that separated the cockpit from the cargo hold, topped with an old wooden seat. I took the bucket out and disinfected it, scoured it. I stripped and sanded the toilet seat, and then I painted the whole thing a baby blue enamel with paint left over from decorating *Casa Candy*.

Bob regarded it without revealing his opinion.

He prepared for the flight by reinstalling his 1000-gallon transatlantic fuel tank. It was approximately ten feet long by four feet tall by 3½ feet wide, and stood on short legs bolted to the floor along the centerline of the deck in the cargo cabin, just aft of the toilet. Fully loaded with aviation gasoline, the tank weighed about three tons. The weight shifted the center of gravity of the aircraft rearward, but still over the broad wings. Bob connected the fuel line to the pumps and tank selector in the cockpit.

At 4:30 a.m. on April 13, 1969 Bob and I and Elner packed our loads into the plane and began preparing for takeoff. A Shell truck was fueling the tanks. A passenger showed up, a passenger Bob had not mentioned before. I knew the man. I had seen him come out of Biafra one night when I was working at the airport. What his real name was, I don't know, but people called him Johnny *Moluco Dentista*, the crazy dentist.

He was a small, poor, middle-aged, skinny, bald, Italian Jew with a little black bag full of dental instruments. He was an itinerant, meandering from place to place providing basic dental care to those who had none, strong enough within himself not to require payment or homage. He came out of Biafra, and he hitched a ride with Bob, headed for Brazil to work with Indian people up the Amazon. He rolled out a sleeping bag on the right side of the plane between the big fuel tank and the wall, and he made a little camp back in there, where he stayed until we reached Brazil. I never heard him say a word.

Bob had filed a flight plan from São Tomé to Robertsfield, Monrovia, Liberia, 1250 miles, where we would lay over before flying across the Atlantic to Natal, Brazil. If you look on the globe, or on *Google Earth*, you will see that the flight path from Monrovia to Natal is the shortest distance across the Atlantic Ocean, about 1900 miles. From Natal we would fly to Trinidad, 2200 miles, and from there to Ft. Lauderdale, 1600 miles. Altogether, it would be almost 7000 miles. Allowing for sleepovers at each stop, it should take about four days. Actually, it took us closer to two weeks.

At 5:20 a.m. we were ready to go. As copilot, it was my job to read the checklist to the pilot. Relevant excerpts:

ME:	De-icers.
BOB:	Don't need 'em.
ME:	Electric power supply.
BOB:	It's on.
ME:	Control blocks and ladder.
BOB:	Off, out and in.
ME:	External pre-flight.
BOB:	Completed.
ME:	Doors and hatches.
BOB:	Closed.
ME:	Emergency brake control.
BOB:	"Emergency brake control."…oh, yeah. It's there.
ME:	Tail wheel.
BOB:	Umm, locked.
ME:	Cross feed.
BOB:	Off.
ME:	Oil coolers.
BOB:	Cool.
ME:	Trim tabs.
BOB:	Let's see…this one's OK…this one's set. (The trim tabs are set to compensate for the propeller rotation during takeoff and for the cargo weight distribution).
ME:	Propellers.
BOB:	Two.
ME:	Throttles.
BOB:	OK.
ME:	Altimeters.
BOB:	About 30 feet. Note what you have over there. In the middle window.
ME:	In the middle window?
BOB:	Yeah. There. Set the altimeter.
ME:	Fuel oil quantity.
BOB:	Yeah, should be plenty there.
ME:	Warning light.

BOB:	Uh, let's see. (Sound of alarm bell). Okay.
ME:	Heaters.
BOB:	We don't have any.
ME:	Tank selectors.
BOB:	OK.
ME:	Booster pump pressure.
BOB:	OK.
ME:	Manifold pressure.
BOB:	Uh huh.
ME:	Okay, prepare for starting engines. Inverters.
BOB:	Off.
ME:	Fuel boost pump.
BOB:	OK, all good.
ME:	Props.
BOB:	Clear.
ME:	Two's clear. Turning two. 3…6…9…hit it. [I watch out the right side window as the electric motor turns the propeller. I count the prop blades going by a point. For a three-bladed propeller, the count of nine indicates three full turns. The engine coughs once, then keeps turning without effect].
	Oops.
BOB:	[Says nothing].
ME:	Come on! … [Turn, turn, turn]. Try one?
BOB:	Stop. Try one.
ME:	OK.
BOB:	Go ahead. One turning. 3…6…9
ME:	OK. [Engine starts].
BOB:	Now two.
ME:	Turn two. 3…6…9…hit it. [Engine starts].

Then Bob looked at me and said, "Go out and pull the chocks."

"Pull the chocks?" I said. That hadn't been discussed when we were listing my responsibilities in the week before departure. Chocks blocked the wheels and prevented the plane from rolling when you didn't want it to. They were in front of the tires and right behind the turning propellers. For as long as I had been working with the airlift, I had never seen a copilot get out of a plane and pull the chocks. Ground personnel did that. Besides, what was all that stuff in the checklist about doors and hatches being closed and the ladder stowed?

"If you don't do it, we aren't going anywhere," Bob said.

"But the props are turning." I remembered Hans sticking his head in a roaring DC- 7 engine.

"Stay away from the props."

"Okay."

I unbuckled my seat belt and eased myself out of the cockpit, through the bulkhead door and back through the cabin along the big fuel tank. The plane rocked gently as the engines idled. I opened the cargo door and secured the ladder. I approached the chocks from behind, walking upstream in the prop wash. A rope snaked out from each of the chocks. I pulled the ropes and the chocks came free easily enough. Back in the plane, I stowed the chocks and the ladder and secured the door, once again. Not only a copilot, I was also Bob's ground crew.

Bob taxied out to the One-One end of the runway, lined up facing the ocean to the East. He locked the toe brakes and advanced the throttles for the engine run-up as we studied the engine instruments. With the engines roaring, the plane rocked but didn't roll forward. Without chocks. Why didn't Bob set the brakes before we started the engines, after removing and stowing the chocks, as the checklist indicated? I think he just forgot.

The oil pressure, manifold pressure, and rpms were all nominal. Fuel flow from the tanks was good. Bob rechecked the trim and the altimeter setting. Since we were at the One-One end of the runway we were headed at 110 degrees (90 degrees would be due East), and we set the directional gyros to 110 as a starting reference.

Bob removed the handheld microphone from the radio, thumbed the switch and called the tower.

"São Tomé TOWER. This is C-FORTY SIX — NOVEMBER SIX NINER THREE FOUR SIX. Request permission for take-off."

Airport control towers all over the world use a specific language called Air English. It has set rules and forms, such as names for all the letters, including November for N. Here, the Air English names for radio sources, TOWER or PLANE, are given in capital letters. The name for the intended receiver is given first and the caller second.

It was early on a Sunday morning. No planes were lined up before us, no small fleet of battered old planes that would burn themselves out on this mission, never to fly anywhere else again. They were all back from Biafra, some with their engines ticking, cooling from the heat of flight, still for the moment. We were number one on the runway.

"NOVEMBER SIX NINER THREE FOUR SIX. São Tomé TOWER. You are cleared for take-off."

Not knowing how to fly, I had nothing to do on take-off. Bob told me to keep my eyes locked on the engine rpms.

He released the brakes and advanced the throttles to full take-off power. We rolled toward the ocean. The tail wheel lifted up and the plane leveled. The engine rpms held steady. At the proper ground speed, Bob pulled back on the yoke and the C-46 Commando rose smoothly into the air. The landing gear rotated forward, up into the wheel wells at the rear of the engine nacelles.

We were airborne.

And almost immediately something went wrong. The sound of the right engine changed — a different tone but still steady. The plane banked to the right, curving toward the ocean. Not knowing anything else to do, I watched the engine rpms for all I was worth. Both instruments remained steady and equal. I called that out to Bob over the roar of the engines. His right hand jabbed out to the instrument panel near my left leg. He raised a small lever and snapped a lock over it. The plane leveled out as the right engine dug in.

The propeller pitch control had been set properly for take-off, angling the prop to bite more strongly into the air for greater power, like low gear. But with the vibration of takeoff, the pitch control lock had flipped open, and the lever slid down, allowing the prop to assume an angle more suited to speed than power. Although the rpms were the same, the right engine was not pulling as hard as the left.

Within seconds Bob had deduced the problem and solved it. It was good to have a skilled, experienced, intelligent pilot. It would have been useful to have a skilled, experienced, intelligent copilot as well. As we came about to a northwesterly heading and climbed out over the Isle of Goats to our cruising altitude, my eyes kept flicking back to that white-painted pitch control lock. Of all the functioning parts on that complex aircraft, that one little lock very nearly killed us, as soon as we started out, with 7000 miles to go.

The island of São Tomé receded behind us, fading away in distance and time. In 2012, after the publication of *Far Away*, I could look down on the island from a satellite image. I could see the hulks of two Super Constellations abandoned at the airport. A ground view showed that one of them had been converted into a café. Through the faded paint one could just make out the name CANAIRRELIEF; this plane had been a replacement for Don Merriam's plane, NAJ, which had crashed in Biafra. The other hulk was a Grey Ghost.

I talked to the last pilot of that ghost. Many people contacted me after the book came out and shared their stories. One contact led to a long phone conversation with Ed, one of the pilots who flew Bob's C-46 from Florida to São Tomé. He informed me that he had also been working for Biafra as a Grey Ghost pilot. He had been captain of that Super Connie when it was hit by a bomb one night. It lost an engine in the attack. Ed flew it out of Biafra as daylight was approaching. He flew right over the tree tops on three engines with the throttles at the fire wall. His engineer screamed at him that he was going to burn the engines up. He had no choice. If the MiGs found them in daylight, they'd be dead anyway. Once out over the ocean, he climbed to altitude and slowed down. The plane never flew again. It is no longer on satellite imagery of São Tomé.

A fully functioning C-46 had a performance ceiling of 27,000 feet, but not Bob's plane. The cabin leaked air, so it could not be pressurized. We carried no oxygen, and we had no cabin heaters. We flew no higher than ten thousand feet, where the air was thin but still dense enough that we could suck enough oxygen out of it to stay awake. The plane also lacked an auto pilot. Bob had to teach me to fly right away so that he could take a nap.

He showed me how to take hold of the yoke with both hands straight out in front of my shoulders and with my arms bent slightly at the elbows. I placed my feet on the rudder pedals, resting lightly. My first lesson was to maintain straight and level flight, against the mischief of air currents outside. It was a bright, sunny day, and the sky was steady. My hands were at the ten o'clock and two o'clock positions on the wheel, with the top section of the wheel removed to allow unimpeded vision of the instrument panel. The wheel was mounted on the steering column. I already knew how the controls were supposed to work; I needed to learn the physical pressure I would need to apply to make the plane go where I wanted. If I pushed on the yoke, the column tilted forward causing a cable linkage to fold down the elevator flap on the tail. The air stream pushed on that flap, making the tail go up and the nose go down. Likewise, pulling back on the yoke made the nose go up. The rudder pedals worked on the vertical part of the tail, swinging the tail left or right. Turning the steering wheel made the wings bank left or right. A smooth turn required a coordinated movement with the rudder and yoke.

The flight instruments told me how I was doing. The artificial horizon showed me if the wings were level and if the nose of the plane pitched up or down relative to the horizon. Other instruments told me the airspeed, altitude, and rate-of-climb. The magnetic compass sat on top of the instrument panel. Magnetic North could vary by several degrees from true North, so we used the directional gyro for a more reliable heading. A silhouette of a plane pointed to our heading. If I wanted to fly due West, I kept the nose of the little plane on 270 degrees. Identical sets of flight instruments were arranged in front of each pilot.

One set of engine instruments in the middle of the panel was visible to both pilots, and gave the performance of the engines, such as rpms, oil pressure, and manifold pressure.

Bob had me note the readings of all of the flight instruments, including the heading, then try each of the flight controls, very gently. Turn and bank to the left, then very gently return to straight and level on the original heading. Returning was harder because of the tendency to over compensate and go too far to the right. The resistance of the rudder pedals was harder than I imagined it would be.

Practice. Practice. Practice. Get the feel of the controls. Small, smooth movements. Steady. Steady. Steady.

Bob watched, giving simple commands. He seemed satisfied, even a little surprised, at how I was doing. While I held the plane steady, he turned his attention to navigation. With the headset over his ears, he tilted his head back, looking at a radio receiver overhead. Using a small knob, he set the frequency he wanted. He turned a crank to adjust the direction of the antenna on top of the plane, finding the strongest signal for that frequency. From his charts he knew the source of the signal, which could be an AM or FM commercial radio station near our destination. AM (amplitude modulation) stations were better, because they maintained a steady frequency, whereas FM stations modulated their frequency to reproduce the sound of voice or music. From the direction of the strongest signal, Bob determined the heading we needed to fly. He called that out to me, and I nudged the plane onto that course on the directional gyro.

Bob took back the controls, and we flew on.

About four hours into the flight, I saw a coastline below, out the lower right windows, down by my foot. We were flying parallel to the coast, and from ten thousand feet I could see a clear line of surf where the waves broke on the shore. From the charts and our intended course, I identified it as Ghana, with Ivory Coast up ahead.

Bob indicated that he wanted me to take the controls. When I was set, he told me to monitor the engine instruments every few minutes; that is, actively look at each gauge. Maintain straight and level flight and the current gyro heading. Scan the sky outside the windows. Stay alert. Then he put his head back on his chair and went to sleep. I glanced over my left shoulder at Elner on the bench behind me. She was stretched out on the bench sleeping, using her winter coat for a blanket. At ten thousand feet with no cabin heater, it was chilly in the cockpit. Johnny *Moluco Dentista* kept out of sight in his warren behind the big fuel tank.

I monitored the engine instruments. Everything was nominal. The engines droned on. I maintained our heading. From time to time, I looked out my lower side windows at the coast stretching below me as far as I could see. It was beautiful, a sight you can see only from an airplane. Bob and Elner slept. I was *flying*!

Without warning, the steady drone of the engines quit as both engines died. The plane nosed over. The long broad wings on the C-46 kept the airplane in a long glide, instead of dropping like an aluminum rock. I still had my hands on the wheel, but I was looking out the cockpit window at sea, not sky.

Bob snapped awake. He threw a lever on the floor by the right side of his seat and hit the starter buttons. The propellers were still turning, wind milling. After an unknown number of heartbeats, the engines re-ignited. Bob grabbed the yoke and pulled back sharply on the control column, bringing the nose of the plane back up. He advanced the throttles and we climbed back up to 10,000 feet.

"Some contamination went through the fuel line," he explained, "causing the engines to die of fuel starvation. Some bit of nastiness or corruption. I switched to the feed from the transatlantic tank and they restarted." Less than a minute had passed. Elner looked out the window dreamily for a few minutes, then went back to sleep. The air was thin up there. Bob, our well-trained, experienced pilot, resumed his nap.

After six hours and fifteen minutes of flying time, we landed at Robertsfield, one wheel screeching on the pavement a fraction of a second before the other — two distinct screeches.

"Excellent landing," Elner said on the tape, bright and cheerful. "It was a smooth flight."

I looked at her and chose not to spoil her mood. But what was she doing? The landing was safe, but not exactly excellent. She had been dazed through the second emergency, and she probably thought that the steep right bank on takeoff was part of the pattern. *That's just what planes do.* The leg from São Tomé to Robertsfield was not a smooth flight. Maybe she was trying to convince herself that what we were doing was perfectly normal.

We parked the plane and checked in at Customs and Immigration. There were three doors, marked *Residents*, *Visitors*, and *Crew*. It gave me a small thrill to go through the *Crew* door.

Liberia was a country established by former slaves returning from America to Africa. The airport had a distinctly American feel to it. Faded American money was the currency. In the cafeteria, we ordered pancakes, fried eggs, and mountains of bacon — all we could eat.

Bob offered this wisdom: "Do you know how to tell when you've had too much to eat?" This was a new kind of problem to contemplate.

"How?"

"Eat till it hurts, then stop after the next full plate." He demonstrated. He was tall, muscular and trim, but he could eat a lot.

"I want to leave here at midnight," he said, "so we have to get some sleep, but before that we have some work to do. The engines always leak oil. We have to find the leaks and fix them."

We went out into the hot afternoon sun. I took off my shirt in the African heat. We got out the tools and ladder and opened the engine cowlings. Engine number one looked pretty good, but we found leaks in engine two. I had my armpits in an engine once more, and it felt familiar in there. The R2800 engines were similar to the DC-7 engines, only smaller. There were eighteen cylinders arranged in two banks around the propeller shaft. We tightened up what we could, closed the cowlings, and hoped for the best. While airport personnel fueled the plane, Bob and I poured five gallons of oil into the reservoir on top of the right wing.

We had rooms at the airport hotel. We needed to get some rest, but I had difficulty falling asleep, anticipating our transatlantic crossing. By 11:30 Bob was checking the latest weather reports along our route. He was satisfied that we could go. He filed his flight plan. We took off at 12:15 a.m. on April 14.

3

It was a clear, moonless night. The thin crescent third quarter moon would not rise until near morning, off our tail to the East. The cockpit was illuminated with dim red light to preserve our night vision. The navigation lights outlined the wing and the turning blur of the propeller outside my window, the only sense of motion. Over the black ocean below, there was no reference point to show that we weren't just hanging in a starry sky. In my mind I knew that we were moving, but with no input from my senses to confirm it, I was free to imagine that we were suspended motionless in infinite night. Far ahead I could just make out the curvature of the earth as the star-filled horizon touched the dark ocean.

Bob flew while I nodded off into a nap. Elner slept on the bench behind me.

Planes had nicknames, especially warplanes. A P-51 was called a *Mustang*. A B-17 was a *Flying Fortress*, a B-29 a *Superfortress*. A C-46 was a *Commando*, presumably because of its wartime mission to deliver paratroopers to drop zones behind enemy lines. In Bob's plane, there were two large cargo doors in the plane's waist behind the wings. We used only the left side door; I never saw the right door open. Sixty men would jump out of those doors into the fight below. I wondered about the history of this particular aircraft. What kind of action had it seen? What lives had streamed through it? It was my age or older, built by Curtis in Buffalo, New York, perhaps as early as 1938. There was a dent near the leading edge of the right wing that I could see from my window. It was about two or three inches deep with the radius of a basketball. What was the story behind that dent? I never asked, and I would never know this plane's history, except for the slice of it that intersected my history. (Later I traced its future history using its registration number, N-69346, as it passed ownership through several individuals to a murky end somewhere in the jungles of Columbia.)

Near dawn the moon rose behind us and cast a silvery glow on a few puffy clouds scattered out ahead of us. Dawn smoothed the silver into pink, giving depth to the sky and a renewed sense of motion, slow dreamlike motion. We pressed on monotonously. I watched the propeller turning, turning, turning, hour after hour, flawlessly, the steady reliability mocking the worn blue paint on the cowling and the big dent in the wing. A glance at the engine instruments confirmed that the rpms were steady and the oil pressure was holding. We were on course for Natal, Brazil at 10,000 feet.

Receding behind me, for the third time, was Africa. Once more, I expected never to see it again. I had spent a significant part of my young, impressionable years there and accumulated some powerful memories. I had no specific plans for the future — perhaps finish my degree in broadcasting and find a job. Move forward. Press on. After experiencing the children of Ocean Hill-Brownsville and Biafra, Elner and I wanted to have children of our own and raise a family.

More puffy clouds had appeared by the time I took the controls again. Up ahead, I could see one on our flight path.

"What should I do?" I asked Bob.

"If the cloud is small enough, go around it and return to the heading. If it's too big, just go right through."

Unable to pressurize the cabin, we couldn't fly over the clouds.

From far out in front of a cloud, I would begin a gentle turn and bank to the right or left and then bring the plane back on course as we passed the cloud. It was fun. Although I was merely steering, I felt as if I were really flying an airplane. Purposely, I cut fairly close to the clouds. They were beautiful, big cottony mountains, white and gray, with plenty of depth and structure. Banking left and right around the clouds, I flew slalom across the sky.

Then we came to one I couldn't go around, big and gray. I looked at Bob. He nodded. With some problems in life, you have to fly right at them. There is a clear delineation between open sky and cloud. We jabbed into the cloud at two hundred miles per hour. The old Commando bucked in the turbulence and rain slammed into the windshield. I held on to the yoke and worked to keep the plane straight and level. With no visible reference outside the window, I kept my eyes on the artificial horizon and the directional gyro. Bob watched me, his hands folded loosely in his lap, and let me keep the controls. We couldn't pressurize the cabin because it leaked air. For the same reason, it leaked water. Rain ran down the inside of the windshield on the right and also on my side window, soaking the charts in a side pocket, and soaking me. We had no cabin heater. At 10,000 feet, soaking wet, I felt the coldest I had ever been in my life. Shivering and chattering, I held on grimly, flying the airplane.

We flew out the other side of the cloud into sunshine. Bob took the controls. Elner got a towel and a dry shirt out of our luggage. I wiped off my head, chest and arms and put on the clean shirt. I was still shivering, soaked down to my underwear. Elner draped her winter coat over my shoulders; it was much too small to go all the way around me. I continued to shiver for about an hour, until I became merely cold.

After about ten hours of flight we approached the East Coast of South America. Bob got out his charts for Natal, Brazil — those were still dry — and studied the approach patterns. He set his radio for the frequency of the tower at Natal. As copilot it should have been my duty to operate the radio while Bob flew the plane through letdown and landing. But I couldn't do that. Bob had to do both. His ancient headset had only earphones and not a built-in microphone. He had to detach the handheld mic from its mount on the instrument panel and hold it up to his mouth with his right hand while he thumbed the switch to talk. He held on to the yoke with his left hand. When the tower answered, he dropped the mic in his lap while he adjusted the trim and the air speed, then snatched the mic again to reply.

NATAL TOWER, this is C-FORTY-SIX COMMANDO NOVEMBER SIX NINER THREE FOUR SIX calling inbound on flight plan from Robertsfield, Monrovia, Liberia. Request landing instructions. Over.

No reply. We maintained our heading and altitude. The engines droned on. Elner was awake and alert now. There was no sign of Johnny *Moluco Dentista.*

NATAL TOWER, this is C-FORTY-SIX COMMANDO NOVEMBER SIX NINER THREE FOUR SIX calling inbound on flight plan from Robertsfield, Monrovia, Liberia. Request landing instructions. Over.

C-FORTY-SIX COMMANDO NOVEMBER SIX NINER THREE

FOUR SIX. This is NATAL TOWER. Stand by One. (*Wait small.* The Brazilian radio operator in the tower spoke Portuguese-accented Air English).

NATAL TOWER. COMMANDO THREE FOUR SIX. Roger One.

We waited.

COMMANDO THREE FOUR SIX. NATAL TOWER. Permission to land denied. This is a military airfield. You must divert to a civilian location.

NATAL TOWER. COMMANDO THREE FOUR SIX. Say again.

With the mic in his lap, Bob said to me, "I don't have charts for anywhere else. When I came through here in December, it was a civilian airfield."

COMMANDO THREE FOUR SIX. Permission to land denied. You must divert.

NATAL TOWER. Negative. We are on a flight plan from Robertsfield, Liberia. We have just crossed the ocean. We are low on fuel. Request landing instructions.

COMMANDO THREE FOUR SIX. Stand by.

NATAL TOWER. Roger.

Again we waited.

COMMANDO THREE FOUR SIX. What is your ETA?

NATAL TOWER. Uh,...ETA next hour plus twenty minutes.

COMMANDO THREE FOUR SIX. Winds are calm. Ceiling is unlimited. You are cleared for straight approach on runway Three Zero.

I read him the landing checklist and lowered the flaps on his call — quarter flaps, then full flaps. He lowered the landing gear.

The sky was clear, calm, and sunny on our final approach. As he lined up on the runway, coming straight in off the ocean, Bob worked the yoke and rudder pedals, looking jerky, harried, and nervous. We touched down too hard and bounced up in the air, still flying. We settled down and bounced again, then again. Finally the wheels stayed on the ground and we had landed for real. The flight time from Africa to South America had been ten and a half hours.

We taxied to our parking space and went through the shutdown checklist. When we opened the door and deployed the ladder, two Brazilian officers aggressively charged into the plane spraying something from cans all over us and all around the cabin and cockpit. I don't know what it was, but I was pretty sure it wasn't good for us to breathe. As a gesture, it wasn't the same as putting a floral wreath around our necks and welcoming us to Brazil.

At Customs, the Immigration officer looked at Johnny *Moluco Dentista's* papers and waved him through. We never saw him again. But Bob and I and Elner were in trouble. First of all, in the four months since

Bob had flown through here on his way to São Tomé, the Brazilian Air Force had taken over this field as a training base and diverted all civilian traffic to another airport along the coast. Bob didn't have updated charts. The tower permitted us to land there only because Bob convinced them that we didn't have enough fuel to divert after a long flight.

Secondly, when they examined our papers, they discovered that we didn't have a licensed copilot. Just as the Portuguese were in São Tomé, these Brazilians were very strict about regulations. Remember that our DC-7, Tango Alpha Bravo, was not permitted to take off for Addis Ababa as Bravo Charlie Whiskey without explicit personal authorization from the Governor.

Bob said to me, "Don't you have any kind of official looking ID that we can show them and claim it's a pilot's license?"

I had the flight line pass issued to me by *SERVICO DA AERONAUTICAL CIVIL, AERODROME Da S. TOME*, identifying me as an *AJUDANTE de MECANICO*. I showed it. Bob told them that, as a mechanic, I was qualified to fly the plane. They didn't accept that, of course. We were not allowed to leave the airport. In fact, we were confined to the airplane.

4

Day after day we sat in the plane in the heat. We slept on the floor of the cabin, using the clothes from our luggage as bedding and pillows. Bob slept closest to the tail where the ceiling sloped down over him.

"Every morning when I woke up," Elner said, "I would look over and see Bob staring at the ceiling. He would reach up and pull off some of the peeling paint." The original olive-drab-colored Army paint was in fact peeling all over the interior of the cabin. The ribbing of the hull was visible.

From my familiar right seat in the cockpit, I watched out the window as Brazilian Air Force B-26 bombers practiced touch and go landings and simulated bombing runs. We bought food from an Army PX on the base. I got a bad case of diarrhea. About twenty yards from the plane was a drab metal building with a door leading to a toilet. A friendly, funny, young Brazilian Army doctor took care of me. "*Comer peixe cozido e arroz,*" he said. "Eat boiled fish and rice."

Since we had more time to talk to Bob than ever before, we learned a few things. Our problem wasn't so much that we didn't have a copilot, as that we didn't have a pilot. When Bob flew for Air America in Laos, he flew as a copilot in a C-47, a similar but smaller plane than a C-46. He had a pilot's license, but he was "checked out" in a C-47, not a C-46, which was more difficult to fly. That is why he had needed a crew to fly his plane to Biafra. Furthermore, as I learned much later, he never intended to hire his plane out to the Nordchurchaid airlift; he had intended to sell it to Biafra from the start. He made up that dumb story about not selling the plane to Biafra because of the wrong oil. Biafra had sent two of its Grey Ghost pilots, Art and Ed — both Americans — to Ft. Lauderdale to help Bob fly the C-46 across the Atlantic. The pilots taught Bob to fly the plane in the air, and let him try a couple of landings. When Bob refused to sell the plane, and he wouldn't pay the pilots, they resumed flying for Biafra. Bob was stranded.

So what made him think he could fly a quasi-derelict old aircraft across the ocean with only me as a copilot? Desperation, perhaps, or maybe just the Air America bravado.

R.P. Baronti, a friend of mine who, as a U.S. Army spotter pilot, was shot down twice in Viet Nam, characterized the Air America guys. "They would drink all night and fly all day. No rules. They were flying way above their abilities, full of piss and vinegar. They would land in places where no one would think a plane could go."

We made the headlines of a local newspaper. On the front page was a picture of our plane with the caption: *"Um aviao clandestino de Biafra."*

After about a week we were allowed to leave the base and take a bus into town. Brazil was having a financial crisis of hyperinflation. A very inexpensive bus fare required a whole fist full of paper money so tattered and worn that you could determine the denomination only by the faded colors of the notes. Natal jutted into the Atlantic Ocean at the eastern most pimple of land in Brazil, suffering a semi-desert climate — arid, dusty, dirty, and impoverished — unlike the great cities to the South, São Paolo and Rio de Janeiro. Elner and I found what looked like a decent little café, similar to ones in São Tomé. As we ate with one hand, we constantly waved the other over our food to keep the flies away. When we stopped eating, with food still on our plates, the waiter asked if he could give our leftovers to that boy waiting outside. An ocean away from Biafra, we were still feeding hungry children. Elner herself, small to begin with, kept getting thinner and thinner.

I asked her how she was holding up, living in an airplane.

"I'd rather sleep in a hollow log and drink muddy water," she said, quoting an old saying.

"You look like a refugee from Dachau," Bob told her.

The Brazilians agreed to release Bob and his plane when he agreed to hire a licensed pilot to fly out of there. He paid for his Grey Ghost pilot, Art, to fly down from Ft. Lauderdale, Florida, and paid him to fly the plane back home. Bob would return home from the world's most lucrative aviation job with less money than when he started.

The night before we left, a mysterious benefactor paid for Elner and me to spend the night at a luxurious beachfront hotel. A hotel van picked us up at the airport. We had a third floor room with a balcony overlooking a swimming pool surrounded by palm trees. Beyond the pool stretched a broad white sand beach and a calm blue ocean. Elner stood on the balcony, looking out to sea.

"There is not a pain in my body," she said.

We may have been the only guests. The pool and the beach were deserted. A solitary maid was the only person we saw in the corridors. In those hard economic times, our room cost 42,500 cruzeiros, about $10.50.

Our flight from Natal to Trinidad was a bit longer than the Atlantic crossing. Art was in a more relaxed and congenial mood than I had ever seen him in São Tomé. He sat in the left seat and Bob sat in the right. I sat on the bench with Elner. As we neared Trinidad, Art turned to speak to me.

"You might as well do the letdown," he said. "You earned it."

Bob also turned in his seat to look at me, waiting for my reply. They must have discussed it and decided to offer me this "reward." Letdown was the segment of the flight when the pilot lets the plane down from its cruising altitude by a controlled descent preparatory to entering the landing pattern. Until then, my primary job was to maintain straight and level flight.

"Okay," I said.

Bob got up out of the right seat and made room in the small cockpit for me to take his place. I slid into the familiar seat. Sure, I wanted to do the letdown, but the second part of what Art said intrigued me: "You earned it." What did he mean by that? I felt that I hadn't been much help. During take-off, landing, and emergency I had been useless. But I got a strong impression from them that they appreciated me and were including me in the fraternity of aviators. It was the same feeling I got after Leo and I returned from our stranding in Biafra and after Tangen's flight in Alpha Delta with the bad feather pump. I felt a quiet elation.

Next to my left elbow was a metal wheel, like a steering wheel, about twelve inches in diameter, aligned vertically and parallel to my leg. It controlled the trim tab on the horizontal stabilizer at the tail. To lose altitude I could push forward on the yoke and hold it there while the plane descended. Better, I could adjust the trim tab, a small flap on the stabilizer that would nudge the plane's nose down and hold it in that position. As I slowly rotated the wheel, I watched the rate-of-descent indicator, until the plane maintained a smooth, gentle descent path. I let go of the trim wheel, and with my hands and feet on the flight controls, I kept the wings level and maintained the compass heading. Art watched me with approval, making small comments from time to time. After about ten minutes, at the desired altitude, I adjusted the trim tab to bring the plane back to level flight. Art took the controls, and I relinquished my seat to Bob.

Wow! Outwardly humble, and acutely aware of my ignorance of flying, inwardly I felt I could fly to the moon!

When we landed in Trinidad we went straight to a hotel to catch some sleep before the last leg to Ft. Lauderdale. In Ft. Lauderdale, Bob bought Elner and me plane tickets to Boston where my brother was keeping Elner's (our) green Volkswagen. That was the bargain, and even though he had to hire Art for the last part of the trip, Bob honored the bargain, losing money once again.

Before we left, Bob offered me a job, or a career, sort of. He said we could open a speed shop in Dayton, Ohio, near Wright-Patterson Air Force Base, where we would sell and service racing vehicles, like planes and motorcycles and boats. Well, thanks, but no thanks.

Elner and I boarded a DC-9 for our flight to Boston, my first flight in a modern comfortable aircraft for a long time.

Three years later we had a baby boy, David Dickson Koren, followed by Emeka Mark Koren eighteen months later. We raised two fine young men.

PART IV

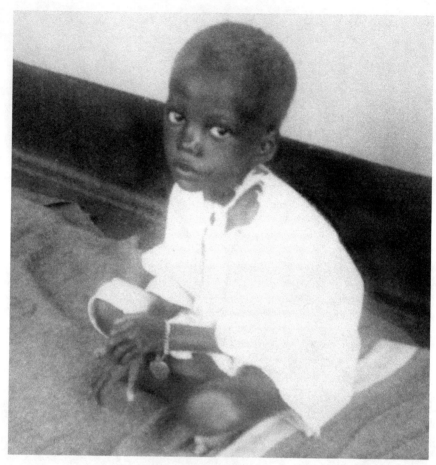

Etim Udo Akpan 1969

CHAPTER 17

Uwa Di Egwu
The World Is Deep

Biafra was the node of a significant event in human history, a strange attractor that curved people's life trails around it. Two parts make the event significant: the extraordinary efforts of those to keep others alive and the efforts of the survivors to do extraordinary things with their lives.

Of the different kinds of people who flocked to the airlift, whatever they loved about flying, whatever they loved about fighting, whatever they loved about faith, and whatever they loved about life, their paths crossed in a filigree of human motivational trajectories called Biafra.

Several years after the war, I gave a talk to a group of college students in Buffalo, New York. These were all students from the region formerly known as Biafra. I told them my stories, and I showed them my pictures. I concluded with an observation. Many Americans believe that most relief aid never gets to those who need it, that it is diverted by corruption. One young man from the back of the room stood up.

"When we were children," he said, "we heard your planes going over at night. We never knew who you were, but we got the food. Every person in this room is alive today because of what you did." Then they stood up and gave me a prolonged ovation.

Uwa di egwu.

On February 10, 2013 I received an email from Ndaeyo Uko, the journalist who was researching the Biafran Airlift, using *Far Away in the Sky* as a reference. He had found the names of the children we evacuated from Uli on the night of January 22, 1969. The boy who said to me, "My father, why don't you speak to me? Don't you know me?" was a seven-year-old Efik child from a village near Ikot Ekpene, named Etim Udo Akpan. He is not lost in history.

Survive and Excel

CHAPTER 18

Amandigbo

Igbo Village Square

1

Biafra's starving children claimed our attention in the late 1960s, along with the Vietnam War, Israel's Six Day War, the presidential election of Richard Nixon, and the Apollo 11 Moon landing. People donated food and money to a church-sponsored airlift to alleviate the starvation. In 1970 the Nigeria-Biafra war ended; Biafra ceased to exist; and the starving Biafran children fell away from our attention. What happened to all those children after they dropped out of the news? Did they remain alive, but destitute, dependent?

After I talked to that group of college students in Buffalo, Biafra essentially dropped out of my life until I read Adichie's *Half of a Yellow Sun*. Then the memories came back explosively, and I wrote my book.

Far Away in the Sky first appeared in March of 2012. Soon after that, I got a call from Dr. Ejikeme Obasi, a physician with a practice in Chicago. He had been one of those children in Biafra, 10 years old in 1968, who lived because of the relief food we brought on the airlift. Dr. Obasi invited me to Chicago for a conference of Igbo people called *Amandigbo* in July 2012. *Amandigbo* means an Igbo village square, an open meeting for all the people, similar to a New England style town hall. The conference was organized as an intergenerational dialogue by the college-age children of the original Biafra survivors, because those students knew very little about Biafra or their Igbo culture. Most had never been to Africa, and they could not speak the Igbo language.

The keynote speaker was Chimamanda Adichie, and so I got to meet her. Austin Okigbo, a professor of ethnomusicology and African Studies at the University of Colorado at Boulder, spoke. As a result of meeting him, I gave Dr. Okigbo my tape of the Biafran children on São Tomé. As a speaker and a symposium panelist, I talked about Igbo culture before and during the war, a time and place lost to many people at the conference.

The students were more than mildly curious about their heritage — they demanded answers from their parents.

"Why didn't you teach us Igbo? Who are we? Are we just American kids? Or is there something about our Igbo heritage that defines us? What culture do we look to for guidance in our interpersonal relationships? American culture is so diverse; where do we fit in?"

The parents — children of that terrible war — survived and grew up. Defeated and deprived of opportunity in their once vibrant homeland, they emigrated to the United States, Canada, Britain, and even to China, wherever there was a university and economic opportunity. Through education, determination, and skills honed in the fight for survival, they prospered. They became doctors, scientists, educators, engineers, and enterprising business owners. The second Igbo diaspora had spread around the world. The parents had not wanted to tell their painful stories to their children. They had not taught them Igbo because they wanted their kids to assimilate in their new homes and not remain as distinct and vulnerable as Igbos had been in the first diaspora in Nigeria. As most immigrants to the United States have done, they wanted their children to look to the future. At *Amandigbo*, at a time safely in the future, the parents were ready to talk.

Though the parents had not specifically taught their children about the nastiness that had driven them from their homeland, they did insist on teaching them the qualities that they themselves had required to survive and thrive: excel in their education and work hard in everything they did, including sports. That has paid dividends. Igbo names are appearing across our culture in college and professional sports, as movie actors, and as influential doctors, like Dr. Bennet Omalu, the doctor in the movie, "Concussion," who demonstrated the dangers of contact sports. James Ihedigbo, whose parents had been teenagers in Biafra; as a big, powerful linebacker with the Baltimore Ravens, he became a Super Bowl champion. Agusta Uwamanya-Nna and Harold Ekeh, American high school students descended from Biafran survivors, were each accepted into all 8 Ivy League schools.

At the conclusion of *Amandigbo*, there was a large picnic in one of Chicago's parks, the annual IGBO FEST, attended by 10,000 Igbos, mostly from the Midwestern United States and Canada: parents, students, and children. Surprised at the large number, I asked Dr. Obasi how many Igbos there were in the United States. He guessed about a million. There is currently a very large migration of Igbos and other Nigerians coming to the United States and Canada.

Regarding an earlier migration, there is a place on the outer banks of Georgia, on St. Simons Island at the mouth of Dunbar Creek, called Igbo Landing. In May 1803 a group of Igbo captives was brought to that place to work in slavery. Because they came from across the sea, the plantation-raised slaves called them "saltwater Negroes." Rather than submit to slavery, those Igbos turned around and walked back into the waters of Dunbar Creek, bound by their heavy chains, and drowned.

Those who still argue that Biafra should have surrendered early do not understand the culture of a people who refuse to submit easily. That character has come forward more than two hundred years to the people now coming to these shores by their own choice, for freedom and opportunity. The world is deep. Time is deep.

At the conclusion of my own talk at *Amandigbo*, Dr. Obasi and others came forward to present me with a plaque inscribed, "To David L. Koren, *Nwannedinamba*, By Igbo League Inc. On Behalf of the Biafran Genocide Survivors." They gave me the high honor of an Igbo name, *Nwannedinamba*, Brother from a Far Away Land.

Because we flew at night to avoid the Nigerian MiGs, those of us who delivered the food never met those who received it. I was the first person that those former Biafrans had ever met who had flown on the airlift. Grown men and women, professionals, openly wept and hugged me and shook my hand. They had been the starving children of Biafra. Every sack of food we shoved out the doors of those planes gave people a chance to live. They turned that chance into meaningful and prosperous lives for themselves and for their own future generations.

I accept the award on behalf of all the others, living and dead, who contributed to the Biafran Airlift. Others flew the planes. Others organized the effort. Others led the praying. Others donated. Others died. I recorded what I saw and heard, and then I wrote about it. I told the story of a brave and intelligent people, a story that may have otherwise slipped away into the gloom of history.

2

The fourth time I went to Africa, October 1999, I went to see my son, Emeka, who was a Peace Corps Volunteer in Guinea, near the headwaters of the Niger River.

Reverend William Aitken (far right) with his son Rob

AFTERWORD

Reverend William McCrae Aitken died in the late 1990s, quietly, unheralded, as he had been in life. Rob Aitken, his son, contacted me last summer thanking me for dedicating my book to his father. He sent a picture taken outside the Presbyterian secondary school in Abakaliki where Aitken had been the headmaster before the war. In addition to being a minister and a teacher, he was an engineer by training. Reverend Aitken returned to Scotland around Easter 1969.

Barry Bianchi died of AIDS in 1995. Leo Anderson has passed away. Larry Kurtz and Tom Herbert are still alive, and I thank them for their contribution to this narrative. I don't know what became of Johnny Correa. I never met Johnny's daughters, Juanita and Buka, but we have passed through the same space — Ohuhu Community Grammar School — at different times. If you are reading this, I greet you.

Bob Hall sold his C-46 after he returned to the United States. Sometime later, flying a different plane, he made a bad landing on a small field somewhere in Florida. The plane nosed over, exploded, and killed him.

Godzeal Umezurike called me in the summer of 2015. He was one of my students at Ohuhu Community Grammar School. I listed the names of all my students in the appendix of this book, and so far Godzeal is the only one who has contacted me. He fears that most of the others have not survived. Godzeal was a skinny little boy when he came to O.C.G.S., the first in his family to go to school. He is now an IT specialist living in Toronto, Canada. Of his four children, one is a doctor, one a dentist, and one is a pharmacist. Education has expanded in his family like cosmic inflation.

I have heard from others who were children at the time of the airlift, or whose parents were. It is very gratifying.

The Last Plane Out

Uli, Airstrip Annabelle, was already abandoned. Uga, the secret military airfield, was opened for one last incoming plane. Because of bad crosswinds and a rough surface, it was difficult to land the four engine transport planes. Johnny broke into a shack to start the generator for the runway lights. Then he headed for the runway.

Here is Johnny Correa's account, lightly edited.

> We got there in time to find the lights on and the plane had landed already — it was a DC-6 from São Tomé. The pilot was Captain Jonsson who had been a relief pilot since the beginning of the airlift. He had once landed at Uga and gotten a flat tire. The air force commander's brother was saying over the telephone to the generator room to turn the lights off, and not to turn them on again.
>
> We went to the end of the runway. The plane kept two motors on, so there was a strong wind toward us. The captain opened the door and started throwing down stockfish bales, him and Father Cunningham. There were only about 25 bales.
>
> "Who is down there?" asked Captain Jonsson.
>
> "Me, the air force commander." They were yelling at each other in the prop wind. It was 5 minutes before the Captain decided to let the ladder down.
>
> When the ladder came down the air force commander sent up the navy commander with his wife, kids, and house girl; then the commander's brother-in-law's wife. Then the fatigue men started climbing up in the aircraft — about 34 in the plane. Finally the air force commander blocked the ladder.
>
> "We will do it orderly!" he said. "Everyone line up!"
>
> I was on the end of the ladder and Ngozi was ahead of me — fatigue men were between her and me and trying to climb over her. One had stepped on my hand and I had to release the ladder and drop to the ground — I dropped my suitcase, used it to stand on. The commander said to Ngozi that she couldn't get on.

"No, commander," I said. "I am trying to put her on."

"She has no permission."

"Neither have any of those fatigue men in the plane," I said. "Let her go!"

"No!"

"She is not moving from there. If you want to stop everyone, okay."

The commander let her pass through. When he did that, one huge fatigue man stepped on my suitcase, grabbed the ladder over my back, stepped on my shoulders, my back, my head, and stepped around the commander, pushing him aside and went in. So I finally got on the ladder and told the commander to go in. Then I went in. Men were still coming in. There were about 15 or 20 at the bottom of the ladder, and pushing to get in. Father Cunningham started to go down.

"There is room for everybody!" he yelled.

As he got on the ladder I heard "put, put, put," machine gun fire from off to the front and right, 50 yards away — very slow. The bullets were hitting the plane — he had over 30 holes in the plane.

"Come up!" I yelled to Cunningham. ""We're being fired on!" We pulled him up. I told Captain Jonsson to leave. He was standing behind us. He understood. He decided to go.

There were still men down there. There were two women on the ladder, the ADC's sisters. The plane started up and made a fast turn. The ladder slid out from under the plane and they fell down. Captain Jonsson put his motors on full power, heading toward the firing, then turned onto the runway and took off. While he was taking off we were closing the door — we never closed it properly, the bell kept on ringing. The cockpit window had bullet holes in it, and Jonsson's hand was cut from glass.

The last boy who came in got a bullet in his wrist. Everyone was told to lay down. I wasn't scared. I had gone past worrying. I went around checking people for wounds. We bandaged the boy and stopped the blood.

When we landed at São Tomé, newspaper reporters came on the plane and took pictures. About 2 a.m. Father Cunningham got a telephone call from the Governor telling him he had no right to bring military people to São Tomé and to get them the hell out of there. At 9 in the morning we were put into taxis, told to shut up, and put on one of the church's DC-4s. We were taken to Libreville.

My students, among the first Biarans, 1965, 1966.
Some did not make it through the war.

APPENDIX

Abalubu, Abel
Abijah, Okon
Abraham, Chukudi
Abraham, Levi
Adiele, Chinyere
Adiele, Onwudiegwu
Adiseyen, Anthony
Aguocha, Chikwere
Aguocha, Ikedichi
Aguocha, Okechuku
Aguocha, Onyenucheya
Agwu, Victoria
Ajoku, Rose
Akpukpo, Okezie
Akubueze, Onyesom
Alaukwu, Ikechi
Alozie, Festus
Amazu, Edmond
Anowi, Faustina
Arinze, Christian
Azinkpali, Margaret
Azuike, Gregory
Azuike, Mark
Bassey, Nnennaya
Chigbu, Comfort
Chigewe, Emmanuel
Chilaka, Augustine
Chinke, Nnennaya
Chukura, Josephine
Chukwu, Christian
Chukwu, Christiana
Dappa, Ibiene
Duribe, Nonjerem
Ebere, Uchechi
Ebigbo, Michael
Effah, Emilia
Effiong, Etuk
Egbukichi, Esther
Egele, Esther

Egwu, Onyekwere
Egwuonwu, Innocent
Ejionye, Agbai
Eke, Ukaegbu
Ekedebe, Jemimah
Ekeh, Patricia
Ekeh, Regina
Ekekezie, Patrick
Ekeleme, Love
Ekpo, Chilaka
Ekpo, Nwachuku
Ekpo, Young
Ekwuribe, Best
Ekwuruibe, Young
Elendu, Patience
Emejuaiwe, Uzoji
Emeruche, Cecilia
Emezie, Augustina
Emuwa, Akuegbu
Enelamal, Chidinma
Enelemah, Otuomasirichi
Enwere, Chukunedum
Evoh, Eziukwu
Evoh, Okebugwu
Eze, Oluchi
Ezechuku, Mercy
Ezeka, Onyebuchi
Ezeoma, Comfort
Ezeoma, Victoria
Fubara, Kariye
Gikunoo, Dorothy
Gobo, Hannah
Ibebunjo, Ndubuisi
Ifenkwe, Sunday
Igbokwe, Akobundu
Igbokwe, Godfrey
Igbokwe, R.
Iguwe, Chukwubueze
Igweonu, Patience

Ihekwoeme, Roseline
Iheomamere, Ngozi
Iheuwa, Chinenye
Ihueze, Uchegbu
Ikeajah, Abraham
Ikeji, Ahamefula
Ikeji, Mgbonye
Ikeji, Sunday
Ikeogu, Josephine
Ikonne, Elizabeth
Ikwuagwu, Ngozi
Imoh, Ibekwe
Isiocha, Enyinnaya
Isiuwa, Charles
Iweham, Patricia
Iwuoha, Joel
Izuagha, Ndukwe
James, Chukuemeka
Joseph, Nkemakolam
Kalu, Charity
Kalu, Christiana
Kalu, Nwankwo Titus
Kalu, Ucha
Khoko, Raymond
Maduako, Udodirim
Madukwe, Okereke
Madumere, Rufus
Marcus, Ngozi
Mba, Idika
Mba, Isaac
Mbakwe, Otuodirimadu
Mbonu, Ndubueze
Meniru, Paul
Meregini, Lovinah
Ndukwe, Monday
Ninimah, Gladstone
Nmesirionye, Okezie
Nnakwe, Obiageri
Nwabua, Augustine

Nwachuku, Comfort
Nwachuku, Ogechuku
Nwaeke, Charles
Nwaeke, Christian
Nwaeke, Emmanuel
Nwagboso, Cecilia
Nwanganga, Isaiah
Nwankwo, Charity
Nwankwo, Faith
Nweke, Christian
Nwobiara, Solomon
Nwoji, Iroechendu
Nwoke, Maduforo
Nwokocha, Ejike
Nwokocha, Uche
Nwokorie, Ihuoma
Nwokoye, Edmund
Nwosu, Diamond
Nwosu, Dickson
Nwosu, Florence
Nwosu, Nkechinyere
Nwosu, Peace
Nwosu, Vincent
Nwuba, Matthew
Obanye, Philomena
Obilo, Onyema
Ochu, Ugwunwa
Odiri, Rosaline
Odu, Catherine
Ogbonna, Michael
Ogbonnaya, Anna
Ogbuagu, Comfort
Ogbuehi, Chinyere
Ogbuehi, Elizabeth
Ogbuehi, Nnennaya
Ogbuihi, Anthony
Ohaeri, Christopher
Ohalem, Eunice
Ojukwu, Edna

Okara, Charity
Okechuku, Ezigbo
Okeiyi, Chioma
Okengwu, Rose
Okenkpu, Catherine
Okenyi, Gabriel
Okereke, Christiana
Okereke, Sunday
Okezie, Akpukpah
Okezie, Chijiago
Okonkwo, Christian
Okoronkwo, Dorothy
Okoye, Nwabuogo
Okugo, David
Okuku, Hannah
Olinga, Gregory
Omekara, Uzoamaka
Omeoga, Chioma
Onukawa, Hope
Onukwubiri, Nkechinyere
Onuoha, Rhoda
Onwudinjo, Bartholomew
Onwuegbu, Chidiebere
Onwumere, Mercy
Onyebuchi, Dick
Onyema, Chibuogwu
Onyema, Chinyereze
Onyema, Jonathan
Onyema, Nkechinyere
Onyemaneme, Samuel
Onyemechi, Margaret
Onyenkamara, Godwin
Onyenweama, Smart
Onyirimba, Salome
Opara, Cletus
Orumbie, Darlington
Osuji, Cordelia
Osuoha, Innocent
Owanta, Caroline

Ubabuike, Okechuku
Ubadineke, Udah
Ubah, Martin
Ubani, Chimaraoke
Uchegbu, Ihueze
Uchendu, Comfort
Uchendu, Monday
Udensi, Ikea
Udensi, Jane
Udenze, Eberechi
Udenzi, Achama
Udo, Njoku Kalu
Ugochuku, Julius
Uguru, Igwe
Ugwuibe, Grace
Ukandu, Uchechuku
Ukaogo, Oriaku
Ukoha, Ojiabo
Umezurike, Godzeal
Utaegbulem, Sunday
Uzoji, Emejuaiwe

THE PEACE CORPS

Mammy Wagon — Ije Oma

Wilbur O. Nsofor,
Principal O.C.G.S.

Okon Nkanta Abijah, Student
Senior Prefect O.C.G.S.

Koren's House at O.C.G.S. 1964

Koren's & Holt's House 1966

Shower

Ric Holt & David Koren
(Photo by Marie Holt)

Jim Bartley, David Koren, Bill Elliot, July 3, 1965

O.C.G.S. Classroom Building

Painting the Library

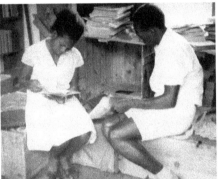

*Patience Igweonu
and Matthew Nwuba, Librarians*

Umuahia Public Library

Coffin Carpenter

Solar Eclipse

Ric Holt In His Lab

O.C.G.S. Students

David Koren & Okpara
July 3, 1965

Dr. Okpara & Wife at the send-off —
Enyimba Enyi

Speaking at the Send-off, 1966

November 7, 1966 Send-off

Enugu Market Before the War

Doris Palace Hotel

Palm Wine Tapper

Soldier on Guard at Enugu Airport, December 1966

THE BIAFRAN AIRLIFT

ID Card

David Koren, 1968

DC-7 Bravo Charlie Whiskey

David Koren & Leo Anderson with DC-7 Mechanics

DC-7 Ground Crew

*Portuguese Soldier Views
Shrapnel Holes in Lima*

Tearing Down a Junk Engine for Parts

Joint Church Aid C-97

Canairrelief CF-NAJ

*Bob Hall, Leo Anderson (front),
Larry Kurtz (rear), Barry Bianchi*

Barry with Broken Feet

D E P A R T I N G   T I M E S   23-rd Jan. 1969.   Thursday

STD Sao Tomé				ARR over NDB in Biafra
F O	POP	C46	1620	1820
A R C O	BCW	DC7	1630	1800
TSAVIA	TRB	DC6	1650	1830
-"-	TRD	-"-	1710	1850
-"-	TRL	-"-	1730	1910
-"-	TRZ	-"-	1750	1930
BRÅTHEN	SUD	-"-	1810	1950
CAN-RELIEF	NAJ	sCon	1830	2000
A R C O	BCW	DC7	2120	2250
F O	POP	C46	2210	0010
TSAVIA	TRB	DC6	2220	2400
-"-	TRD	-"-	2240	0020
-"-	TRL	-"-	2300	0040
-"-	TRZ	-"-	2320	0100
BRÅTHEN	SUD	-"-	2340	0120
CAN-RELIEF	NAJ	sCON	2400	0130

All   W.C.C.

s observe: THIS SCHEDULE SHALL UNDER NO CIRCUMSTANCES BE EXPOSED
IN PUBLIC.

Flight Schedule January 23, 1969

Koren & Recovering Child   *Road on São Tomé, 1969*

COMPANY	REG.	CREW	ETD TMS / ETA ULI NDB		ATD TMS/ATA TMS	PAYLOAD
CAN-REL	NAJ	Patterson	1630	1815	Rice	15000
J C A	915	Glenn	1645	1830	Beans, formula 2	14074
J C A	676	Gossman	1700	1845	Beans, Formula 2	14074
J C A	679	Cutler	1715	1900	Beans, formula 2	14074
TSAVIA	TRE	Polly	1745 1	1930	(No landing, holding,bomber)	
TSAVIA	TRD	Roocroft	1800	1945	Meat, Nathan food	9385
TSAVIA	TRZ	Jonsson	1815	2000	Salt	8500
TSAVIA	TRB	Evensen	1830	2015	Meat	7800
CAN-REL	NAJ	Patterson	2115	2300	Rice	15850
J C A	915	Glenn	2130	2315	Blackeye beans	14074
J C A	676	Gossman	2145	2330	Blackeye beans	14074
J C A	679	Cutler	2200	2345	Beans, formula 2	14074
TSAVIA	TRE	Polly	2230	0015	Medicine, meat	9540
TSAVIA	TRD	Roocroft	2245	0030	Milk powder	10100
TSAVIA	TRZ	Jonsson	2300	0045	Salt	9200
CAN-REL	NAJ	Patterson	0200	0345 TRB	Milk powder	8510
J C A	915	Glenn	0200	0345		
J C A	676	Gossman	0200	0345	(No 3rd shuttle, delayed	
J C A	679	Cutler	0200	0345	holding for bomber)	
			Proposed schedule March 26, 1969			
CAN-REL	NAJ		1630	1815		
J C A	679		1645	1830		
J C A	676		1700	1845		
J C A	915		1715	1900		

All W.C.C₂

Pls. adhere to T/O times on first shuttle.
Pls. observe: THIS SCHEDULE SHALL UNDER NO CIRCUMSTANCES BE EXPOSED IN PUBLIC.
Atencao : ESTE HORARIO NAO DEVE SER EXPOSTO EM PUBLICO.

E. Erla
C.o.Flt.Ops.

Distribution:	Nordchurchaid	10	Servico Aer.	1	Government	1
	CARITAS	1	STA	1	Police	2
	D.D.W.	1	Castela	1	Customs	2
	J C A	5	Elias	1	Airport	1
	CAN-REL	2	Health	1	Shell	1
	TSAVIA	5				

Flight Schedule March 25, 1969

Biafran Money

*Commando
346 on São
Tomé*

Bob Hall Navigating C-46

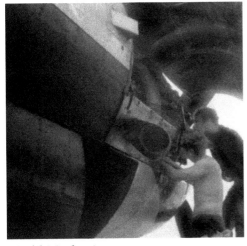

C-46 Mechanic

Baia Café

Edwardo, Warehouse Manager

Beacon Club

Pequeno Boeing

The church at Uli visible from the plane on aproach to the runway.
Drawing by Tony Palermo

PORTUGAL
PROVÍNCIA DE S. TOMÉ E PRÍNCIPE
COMISSÃO DE EVACUAÇÃO, TRATAMENTO E RECUPERAÇÃO DE CRIANÇAS VÍTIMAS DA GUERRA
(Committee of childrens)

FICHA DE IDENTIFICAÇÃO
(Identification Card)

DATA DA EVACUAÇÃO 5 / 10 /19.68 N.º DE IDENTIHCAÇÃO 122
(Date of arrival)   (Identification Number)
NOME NNADIKWE Abigail
(Name)
FIUAÇÃO NNADIKWE Lazarus
(Parents)   Cordelia
IDADE 3 anos   SEXO F.   GRUPO VI
(Age)   (Sex)   (Group)
NATURALIDADE Obodo - ANAINO
(Place of origin)

OUTROS ELEMENTOS DE IDENTIFICAÇÃO
(Further to identification)

Nome do Aut. Ad. e sua residência - Boniface Igbokwe -
Umuofor Amaimo - OWERRI.

O PRESIDENTE DA COMISSÃO
(President of Committee)
O REPRESENTANTE DA CARITAS INTERNACIONAL
(The International Caritas Representative)
O REPRESENTANTE DA DIAKONISCHE WERK
(The Diakonische Werk Representative)

Abigail, rescued child, São Tomé

James Ihedigbo, Superbowl Champ

345

Author and Dr. Ejikeme Obasi 2012

ACKNOWLEDGEMENTS

Ndaeyo Uko, whose probing questions encouraged me to dig deeper into my story. He is writing the full history of the Biafran Airlift, soon to be published.

Larry Kurtz, who lived the same story.

Tom Hebert, for sharing his story.

Johnny Correa, a strange brother, with a parallel, inverted, story.

My family, especially Jill, Emeka, and David, for their strenuous encouragement.

My wife, Kay, with love, for her forbearance.

Bob Kalan, for his delicate technical help with the tapes and many wonderful discussions about aviation.

R.P. Baronti, for his priceless observations about flying.

Kimberly Norris, for her graphic design and layout of the manuscript for publishing.

Julie Stockman, my editor.

Carolyn Schultz, my photo editor.

Dr. Ejikeme Obasi, my Igbo editor, a Biafran child, and a person who had an enormous influence on this book. My gratitude is boundless.

The California Academy of Sciences. In the early part of this century, the scientists made several excursions to the volcanic islands of the Gulf of Guinea, especially São Tomé and Principe. Because of their physical isolation from the continent of Africa, the islands, like the Galapagos Islands, evolved their own unique flora and fauna. Unlike the Galapagos, these islands had remained virtually unknown and unstudied. The scientists gave to the world a trove of new creatures and flowers, but they also gave to the citizens of São Tomé and Principe a sense of their own unique identity on earth, apart from their stolen histories of slavery-time.

In the beginning was the Word,

And the Word was Song.

As the bird sang to its mate

The adam learned to sing to his eve,

And they became one.

Then the Song became Story,

And the Story became Us.

DLK

Author Then and Now

ABOUT THE AUTHOR

David Koren lives on a mini farm in the Pennsylvania countryside with his wife, Kay, and their two tractors. He has enjoyed careers in teaching, rehabilitation counseling, laser physics, amateur astronomy, and now book writing. Beautiful in aspect and spirit, Kay abides all the puddles he gets himself into.

CPSIA information can be obtained
at www.ICGtesting.com
Printed in the USA
FSHW021602240821
84274FS